W9-AMP-051

THE PUBLIC LIBRARY IN
NON–TRADITIONAL EDUCATION

THE PUBLIC LIBRARY
IN
NON-TRADITIONAL EDUCATION

by

Jean S. Brooks and David L. Reich

An ETC Publication

1974

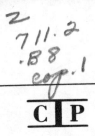

C | **P**

Library of Congress Cataloging in Publication Data

Brooks, Jean S.   1914 -
   The public library in non-traditional education.

   1. Libraries and adult education — Case studies. 2. Independent study — Case studies. 3. Dallas Public Library.
4. Dallas. Southern Methodist University. I. Reich, David
L., 1930 -   joint author. II. Title.

Z7111.2.B8   025.5'4   73-21903

ISBN 0-88280-008-6

Copyright © 1974 by ETC PUBLICATIONS
18512 Pierce Terrace
Homewood, Illinois   60430

Printed in the United States of America

Table of Contents

Foreword

1   A Concept 1

2   The Dallas Public Library's
    Independent Study Project 15

3   The Independent Student 39

4   The Library 69

5   The Librarian 95

6   The Tools 115

7   Academia 133

8   The Future 149

    Addendum 167

      The Proposal 168

      ISP Evaluative Processes 187

ISP Brochure 188

ISP Telephone Questionnaire 201

ISP Television Script 203

ISP Newspaper Advertisement 205

Newspaper Articles 206

A Guide on How to Study Independently....211

Afro-American History
Study Guide and Reading List 223

ISP Monthly Statistics 241

Index...............................242

Foreword

What adults learn today or fail to learn today can determine their tomorrows. In this day and time few would question this thesis. Instead, the dilemma facing many adults is not, "Should I learn?" but, rather, "Can I still learn and if so how do I go about learning what it is I need most?" A public library, whose services are available to all, can offer an individual such an opportunity to learn and to continue learning so that he can best meet, according to his individual abilities and personal judgments, the responsibilities of his own daily life and his hoped-for promises of tomorrow.

There should be little new or revolutionary in this philosophy. Generations of people in the United States have expanded their intellectual horizons and extended their social and economic potentials through the resources of an institution often unknown and seldom equalled in other countries, the free public library. However, the public library's history of adult education endeavors is as varied as the years in which these endeavors were effected: the 1920's, characterized by basic adult education offerings for immigrants who came to these shores; the 1930's, filled with self-education endeavors designed to fight the depression years; the war years of the 40's, dominated by a continuing educational renewal made mandatory both on the war front and the home front; the decades of 50's and 60's molded by requirements that education move closer to systems of precise and explicit information. Now the 70's are making new demands, demands brought about by changing lifestyles. For many persons in today's world, the personal

pressures, working habits, living standards, and leisure requirements of daily living have become increasingly complex; and with
such complexities can come a plethora of educational inadequacies.
An urban administrator, in reply to the question, "What are we
educating for?" said:

> Twenty, fifteen, five, even one year ago, I would have
> answered this query with a great deal more confidence
> than I possess in the spring of 1971 as we plunge deeper
> into what Peter Drucker has aptly termed the Age of Dis-
> continuity... much of what I learned at the collegiate and
> graduate levels and during a quarter century of public
> service is as naught when facing the problems and issues
> of today — to say nothing of the near future.

Adult educators and librarians responsible for services to adults
who do not set goals and make plans in a spirit of such change have
little hope of serving as contributing factors in the life of a pulsating
community.

For these reasons, it seemed appropriate that the Dallas Public
Library should enter into a study of one public library's role in the
rising forces concerning independent study. Such is described by
Jean Brooks and David Reich in their book, *The Public Library in
Non-Traditional Education*. Mrs. Brooks, a member of this
Library's Community Education team before appointment as the
Independent Study Project Director, was and is singularly suited
for this leadership role. She is imaginative, tenacious, and
experimental while being dedicated to the principle of educational
opportunities for all. David Reich's experiences as a teacher and
community college and public librarian provided a unique blend of
educational discipline necessary to the development of this project.
To me, a longtime adult services librarian, the promise of the
project lay in a broadened exploration into the role of the public
library and into stronger cooperative progress between the library
and educational institutions leading to academic achievement.

And so the study was undertaken by the staffs of the Dallas
Public Library and Southern Methodist University in a spirit of
involvement and inquiry. Presented here is a straightforward
account of these findings, findings which cannot be characterized

as quick and easy solutions to a pressing, timely topic but findings which offer some answers but more questions and possibilities for future investigations. It is hoped that this study will encourage additional research in order to achieve what is so badly needed in this age of educational change: effective ways to encourage learning so that any individual with desire to do so may find his chance to gain that unique potential of which he is most capable.

Mrs. Lillian M. Bradshaw
Director of Public Libraries
City of Dallas

Acknowledgements

The authors wish to express gratitude to:

The Dallas Public Library System which opened itself to a critical study of a service;

Southern Methodist University faculty members who prepared study Guides/Reading Lists and gave of their time to tutor and council the independent students;

All the librarians from the five participating Branch Libraries who so honestly evaluated their reactions to a "new" service and worked and learned with ISP: Miss Linda Allmand, Chief of Branch Services; Mrs. Cordie Hines, Assistant Chief of Branch Services; Mrs. Mary Lee Barbosa, Head, Oak Lawn Branch; Ms. Carolyn Bean, Miss Jane Bell, Mrs. Barbara Bender, Head, New Branch Office; Mrs. Sherilyn Bird, Conrad Burdge, Head, Hampton-Illinois Branch; Charles Durgen, Miss Judy Fouts, Mrs Andrea Harris, Ms. Carolyn Householder, Mrs. Ruby Hunter, Miss Carole Johnson, Mrs. Donna Johnson, Head, Crossroads Community Learning Center; Mrs. Gwen Oliver, Ben Rodriquez, Mrs. Ann Ross, Frank Schepis, Head, Audelia Road Branch; Miss Lee Shuey, Ms. Karen Smith, Mrs. Oraida Starr, Edward Voorhees, Head, Preston Royal Branch; and Miss Virginia Yang.

Members of the ISP Advisory Committee who, while they sometimes classified themselves as "paper tigers," served as a continuing source of encouragement and expertise: Mrs. Margaret Warren, Chairman, Community Education Coordinator, Dallas Public Library; David L. Reich, former Deputy Director, Dallas

xi

Public Library; Ervin Eatenson, Adult Coordinator, Dallas Public Library; Dr. Fred W. Bryson, Dean School of Continuing Education, Southern Methodist University; and Dr. James Early, Associate Dean of Faculties, School of Humanities and the Sciences, Southern Methodist University.

A National Interest Council which in living up to its title contributed much to the directions taken by ISP: Robert J. Kingston, National Endowment for the Humanities; Dr. Fred C. Cole, Council on Library Resources; Jose A. Toro, College Entrance Examination Board; Dr. Eileen P. Kuhns, American Association of Community and Junior Colleges; Gerald M. Born, American Library Association; Edward F. Sintz, Miami-Dade Public Library; James J. Mitchell, St. Louis Public Library; and Miss Margaret E. Queen, San Diego Public Library [representing the Serra Regional Library System].

The Project Evaluator, Dr. Betty J. Maynard, and the Project Public Relations Officer, Mrs. Jean Carpenter who helped keep ISP "alive and well";

The Volunteers — RSVP participants, independent students, and others who helped plan and lead GED help sessions, prepare the GED study packet, tutor and serve as telephone questioners for the Project Evaluator: Steve Crane, Miss Margaret Hayden, Mrs. Ruth Howell, Perry Marrs, and Mrs. Maybelle Smith.

The authors also wish to acknowledge the following for their support of, belief in, and enthusiasm for the Dallas Public Library's Independent Study Project: Mrs. Charity Herring, formerly of the Dallas Public Library, who helped launch the Project; Dr. Louis Shores, Dean Emeritus, School of Library Science, Florida State University, who recognized the Project in terms of his own "library college" concept; and Jack N. Arbolino, Executive Director, Council on College Level Examinations, CEEB, whose support of the Project was both intellectual and financial.

And, most importantly, to the three "experts," each of whom served for a time as assistants to the Project Director, under the title of Project Secretary: Mrs. Linda Glass, Mrs. Kathy Vittetoe, and Mrs. Sandra Starr (who typed the manuscript of this book).

Chapter 1

A Concept

While traditional educational institutions have long been cognizant of the many diverse ways in which adults learn, perhaps the public library has been that institution which has been most practically concerned with the experiential learning the individual student brings to those study tasks he sets for himself. The library has always served as a resource center for non-traditional or extracurricular study. It has been the place in which experiential learning serves as the input enabling librarian and student to arrive at an assessment of the base-line from which the librarian will aid the particular student in starting his personal learning project. Enlarging upon this basic fact, it has been recognized that the total span of an individual's life contains many learning situations within which the process of learning takes place. Allen Tough notes,

> Almost everyone undertakes at least one or two major learning efforts a year, and some individuals undertake as many as 15 or 20. The median is eight learning projects a year, involving eight distinct areas of knowledge and skill.[1]

[1]Allen Tough, *The Adult's Learning Projects: A Fresh Approach to Theory and Practice in Adult Learning*, Research in Education Series No. 1 (Toronto, Ontario: The Ontario Institute for Studies in Education, 1971), p. 1.

1

THE PUBLIC LIBRARY IN NON-TRADITIONAL EDUCATION

These situations and processes of learning are variously named as observing, conversing, experiencing, sensing, attending the school of hard knocks, learning through trial and error, on-the-job training, or formal education. The learning which takes place may be under circumstances which are not always purposefully planned by the learner. Often when habitual performance or study is undertaken for the specific purpose of learning, the learning process may become dull, distasteful, an unwelcome task. Many times the very act of being in a learning situation is neither recognized at the time nor readily recalled at a later date. But, when there is a pleasureable learning experience, it is more likely to be repeated or continued. Conceivably the public library, in its role as an institution which places no demands upon its users, could serve as the agency which could best create for the learner a positive learning experience he could take pleasure in repeating.

Most adults in today's world have probably been through many learning experiences planned and unplanned, recognized and unrecognized. That adult in the community who is no longer affiliated with a formal educational institution still continues to learn from the world about him. He may learn from his community at large, from libraries, museums, zoos, newspapers, magazines, radio, television, or by observing and conversing with his fellow man. He may learn alone, within his immediate family, on his job, or in a social group, but he continues learning whether he is consciously studying to learn or not. He continues to store facts of knowledge within his mind, and as his experiential knowledge grows his behavior is subject to changes of which he may be totally unconscious. G. Lester Anderson and J. Arthur Gates state,

> Through the process of learning, men acquire new ways of behaving or performing in order that they can make better adjustment to the demands of life.[2]

If that learning experience can be made pleasureable, or the response in meeting life demands is gratifying, and the learner can be made conscious of the growth and change which he is

---

[2]Theodore L. Harris and Wilson E. Schwahn, *Selected Readings on the Learning Process* (New York: Oxford University Press, 1961), p. 5.

undergoing, repeated learning responses could be encouraged. Quite conceivably then the public library could be the primary free public agency which could contribute positively to this learning environment.

In the course of normal living parents learn some basics of human growth and development as they raise their families. Cooks learn elements of chemistry, gardeners become amateur biologists or botanists, and housewives become decorative artists. Readers, whether of fiction or non-fiction books, may be well informed historians or literary classicists, and readers of periodicals and newspapers political analysts. On the job, the learner may have performed tasks in accounting, business management, or marketing, and report writing has probably increased his expertise in composition and grammar. Television, traveling, visits to local museums, and cultural events have enriched his knowledge of the humanities and of his neighborhood. If he is particularly observant, he may have been taught much about the sociological relationships of man. He has been learning along the fringes of the broad disciplines which make up formal educational curricula in the colleges and universities today. At the same time he may be experiencing informational needs which do not appear to be met within his present learning experiences. He may experience needs to learn which he does not know how to fulfill. Some individuals within our society have so little of this needed informational input that to all intents and purposes their learning projects are almost nil except what they may be gleaning from television or through encounters with their counterparts in society.

A large portion of the excitement of learning comes with recognition of the many ways in which all the seemingly unrelated pieces of information one has stored relate to each other. The consciousness of what we did not even know we knew and had learned and the growing ability to relate that knowledge to a plan or body of formal knowledge should continue to be as exciting as the first recognition of the relationship of numbers to addition and subtraction or the magic of transforming letters into words, sentences, and stories. The understanding of what one has already learned should lead to an understanding of how learning is accomplished. It is no mystery; learning is an integral part of our daily lives, natural, and wholly absorbing, a form of intellectual osmosis. Studying to learn without pressure, accepting the fact that what we like to do also teaches us, can and should free the mind for more pleasureable learning experiences.

The public library has always functioned as a learning resource center for the traditional student and as such has always had the potential for serving as a "peoples' university." The learning resources within these library storehouses of knowledge and the ideas of man contained therein are nibbled at in sporadic bits and pieces by the various publics the libraries serve. The library user is often not fully aware of the carefully organized and broad range of knowledge available for his use even though he may make use of library resources with some degree of sophistication. Conceivably, if an individual fully recognized his learning experiences as they occurred, he might begin to relate and inter-relate separate learning episodes to each other and to the world of learning at large. A principle of the Cognitive Theory of learning is that there should be an organization from "simplified wholes to more complex wholes."[3] For the adult individual outside of a formal structured learning experience, this cycle or pattern of knowledge is rarely defined nor related to the process of his learning as a total experience. But, within his immediate neighborhood is a resource center — the public libarary — with unparalleled expertise to help him organize his personal knowledge.

The concept of the Dallas Public Library Independent Study Project was that the library, functioning as a viable learning resource center, could be an active agent in orienting the unaffiliated adult student to the process of learning, helping him to recognize how his jig-saw pieces of experiential, often short-termed, and seemingly unrelated learning episodes fitted into an organized whole. Five branch libraries were chosen as sites to study the role of the public library and its effectiveness to serve as a catalyst to release learning from its restrictions of curriculum, resources, and time sets. It was conceived that free and unstructured learning could fall into a natural order of knowledge, that higher education could be relevant to individual needs and to man's life. Learning for the pleasure and excitement it offers could be realized once the

---

[3]Ernest R. Hilgard and Gordon H. Bower, *Theories of Learning* (3rd ed.; New York: Appleton, 1961), p. 563.

4

A CONCEPT

process was freed from what some view as its mysterious and awesome intellectual cloak, and resources within the library could be more widely and constructively utilized as the individual's familiarity with patterns of knowledge grew. Those community resources, mentioned earlier in this chapter, such as museums, educational television, and music and theater presentations, could be made recognizable as "options" for learning open to those who would avail themselves of such opportunities. The librarian could lead or guide the learner into independent functioning within the library by bringing him to a recognition of the never-ending nature of learning. Simultaneously, the adult learner could be guided to recognition of the multi-faceted and multi-dimensional aspects of learning which he could independently pursue.

Tough states,

> The adult's highly deliberate efforts to learn provide an excellent starting point for developing better competence and help in adult learning.[4]

When the individual is motivated to knowingly *try* for accomplishment, Tough suggests, he will more readily accept opportunities and help in developing competency.[5] The Independent Study Project (ISP) concept was that at this motivated stage any aids to learning which the library could offer would now be acceptable to the user. Perhaps it was in this conceptual area that the Project became involved with varying definitions of "independent vs. dependent" and "unstructured vs. structured" learning and/or study. John Coyne and Tom Hebert claim,

> Through Independent Study you can get around going to college. You don't have to go to college to learn, to study, to prepare yourself for some future. One of the elite educations available today is the *non-institutional* education. The message here is that you can organize your own education on your own terms.[6]

---

[4]Allen Tough, *The Adult's Learning Projects*, p. 12.

[5]*Ibid.*

[6]John Coyne and Tom Hebert, *This Way Out: A Guide to Alternatives to Traditional College Education in the United States, Europe and the Third World* (New York: Dutton, 1972), p. 8.

ISP at no time conceived of either usurping the role of the formal educational institution or of circumventing it. The offering of resources and information on educational alternatives open to would-be learners was merely an extension of the traditional role of the library in its function as a source of material expressive of all available information and viewpoints on a subject. It was also surmised that some of the users who would be interested in independent study might need introduction to the concept. This meant that for a time they would have some "dependence" upon the library for some guidance. Since the library conceived of this new learning program as a possible introduction to further formal education for some of the less assured students, there was more of a sense of drawing persons into the educational stream rather than educating them on how to circumvent it. There was also a recognition within the concept of ISP that as the present reality dictated, the student could learn to study on his own, he could organize his personal goals, but he would also have to be cognizant of terms, as Coyne and Hebert express it, other than his own which might influence realization of his goals. Consequently, within the independent, unstructured Project there existed those realistic dependencies and structures within which the student had to operate once he translated his new learning into practical use. Hopefully, at the same time, the Project would also alert these new learners to the possibilities of educational change for which they might work in the future.

One of the motivating forces, or "carrots," seen as a library role, was the ability to help the individual recognize those areas of his interest or responsibility which had resulted in experiential learning. These interest-motivated learning episodes are demonstrated to the librarian daily when library patrons pursue hobbies, borrow car repair manuals and cookbooks, or add new titles or authors to a growing list of books on history or some other subject of personal interest. The professional expertise of the librarian is suited to guiding the enrichment of such motivated study with resource materials, and the primary role of the librarian in Reader's Services has always been to help the library user locate those materials which will enable him to extend his learning experience. This type of learning search has usually been considered an extra-curricular or non-structured educational pursuit.

A CONCEPT

It appeared very simple to move one step to the same type of help for the library learner who wished to pursue structured curricula materials in an unstructured manner. The role of the librarian would now be as the helper who would advise this non-traditional, independent, free student upon resource materials for studies for college credit or for personal enrichment. The librarian could function free of set curriculum restrictions and, therefore, could more readily recommend variations of reading materials at differing levels of difficulty leading to a good general background knowledge of subject areas.

The mature adult who might take advantage of this new educational opportunity would be expected to have been out of school for some years, been engaged in other activities, some of which would have produced for him meaningful learning experiences. With minimal preparation and study, this new student could learn to study on his own either for personal enjoyment or to prepare himself to take College-Level Examination Program (CLEP) tests covering subject areas paralleling course offerings of the first two years of college. With acceptable scores on these tests, the adult in the community who so desired could receive credit for as much as two years of college credit. Those libraries engaged in the study would become the centers for learning, and the librarians would create the desired environment for a pleasurable and meaningful learning experience. It was not expected that the student would need much more help than the usual type of reader's services normally offered by the library. No book purchases were planned unless dictated by great demand by numbers of students, and it was expected that, with the help of the librarian, present library resources would be used to their fullest to augment the student's beginning knowledge.

The student would be encouraged to study for a general background knowledge even though he might be preparing for a a CLEP or other test. The total learning opportunity was to be completely without structure: no enrollments, no time limits, no classes, no assignments. Every effort would be made to keep the study area broad to encourage the student's leeway to follow his interests, and no pressure would be exerted upon the learner. For those independent students who chose to use their knowledge towards goals of academic credit or a degree, the libraries would be prepared to furnish college and university bulletins and CLEP informational materials, all designed to assist the student in functioning independently in choosing his steps to his goal. In his article on "Trends in Learning and Education," Passow states a case for school/library coordination which speaks to the type of higher education coordination conceived for the Independent Study Project.

> . . . insofar as education is concerned, schools and community libraries are, or should be, partners in a joint venture. The community library does not exist simply to provide supplementary services. Both the community library and the schools are educative institutions and must strive constantly to find ways of working together for the benefit of the children, youth, and adults of our society. In the quest for providing quality of educational opportunity, libraries and schools have joint responsibilities.[7]

Liaison between the libraries engaged in the Independent Study Project and the academic community would be an important aspect of the study if the student was to acquire any degree of "independence." In the area of "special aids" it was envisioned that reliance of the library upon the area colleges and universities would be heavy. While the student would be working on his own, it was considered important that the library have in hand a new type of "aid" or resource from which the user could choose to guide his learning while still maintaining a degree of independence from curricula.

Study Guides accompanied by suggested readings were conceptualized as the ideal tools to guide the independent student to that area of subject discipline he chose and to the librarian for reader's service aid. No attempt would be made to lead the individual student to study for the sake of a particular test. The guides — and the librarian — would stress learning, *not* preparation for a test, in order that, within this continually

---

[7]A. Harry Passow, "Trends in Learning and Education Affecting Community Library Services," Guy Garrison, ed., *Total Community Library Service* (Chicago: American Library Association, 1973), p. 14, [response to J. Lloyd Trump].

motivating learning project, a body of knowledge would be gained which would insure competence for any type of test. Since testing is merely a device to ascertain the extent of an individual's knowledge, the knowledge itself should be the goal. Under this concept, the guide and the reading could not be narrowed to a set curriculum. Thus historical novels, fictionalized biographies, travel books, many types of reading matter could be utilized. The Study Guide was to suggest only the framework of a discipline, and from this framework the student could build his broader knowledge, drawing always upon those inputs of experiential learning he had brought to his study. The list of readings were "suggestions" to lead the student into making his personal choices, eventually independently of any aids as his interest in the subject grew. A book from the Reading List, another recommended by the librarian, or one he chose from the shelf for himself, would fill in the shape of the knowledge which he would choose to acquire.

The learning responsibility lay totally with the student, whether his end goal be an examination leading to academic credit or learning for its own sake. The aids, personnel, and materials were to serve as guidance and evaluation steps for continuing motivation of the individual student. Freedom from all restraints of the structured classroom would keynote a totally unstructured learning experience which would be relaxed and meaningful. Accompanied by careful library guidance, the achievement of a good, strong, general background in a chosen subject area could be accomplished. The end goal, the purpose, might conceivably be the student's ability to pass a test, but in the conceptual sense this ability would merely be a spin-off benefit of the learning situation. If the student studied, organized, and understood the subject matter, the primary goal of the concept would have been achieved. Expecting that with growing understanding would also go growing interest in learning for its own sake, thorough knowledge gained gained would imply a total learning process reached.

As the librarian and the independent student worked together toward the student's accumulation of knowledge, an atmosphere, or learning environment, would be created within the library. The student could become cognizant of the many helps to learning which are integral parts of the library, such as catalogs, classification systems, and reference and bibliographic aids. The student thereby would become increasingly independent in the use of library materials and facilities, and, as his dependence upon the librarian lessened, the librarian's role would be directed by the student's needs. In turn, studying for learning could become a pleasureable habit with the student which would prepare and inform him for the transition to the traditional educational classroom should he elect that as a goal.

It was to be expected that the rapport which could be established between librarian and independent student would result in a meaningful learning and motivating environment. It was not expected that the role of the librarian would change greatly from that which he has always assumed, but the close relationship with the student learner could allow for greater knowledge on the part of the librarian as to the background goals, aspirations, and needs of each individual served. While this relationship to the user would not constitute "counseling" in the formal sense, it would certainly entail elements of input on possible steps to take for realization of desired goals expressed. In much the same manner in which the librarian recommended, or presented for choice, materials in the library, educational options available for student choice could be mentioned. The atmosphere created within the library would be one of ease, mutual exchange of ideas, and information. The library could be an open learning center where the student would be free to drop in at will to choose materials, ask questions, or probe ideas. In the natural course of events the librarian, therefore, could be expected to be the helper, the individual upon whom the independent student relied for his needs in independent study materials. The library would become the study center, with services available as the student's needs were voiced, and where services were convenient for his time commitments. In this free atmosphere, away from any sense of classroom pressures, competition of a group, a closely defined curriculum, and the "busy work" of timed assignments, the freedom of true learning could be achieved. In this totally free and unstructured environment, learning could become personal, familiar, and pleasureable. The student could attain that freedom of truly independent learning as he desired, following his interest where it led, pausing to explore in greater depth at will.

It was also anticipated that, in some instances, perhaps added subject expertise would be required by students; for that need, academic tutoring would be included as an additional resource. Meaningful learning most certainly would reach its ultimate level when the personal help of members of the academic community was available. The challenge of idea exchange away from the formal classroom situation could do much to free the student from any vestige of institutional structure. Both Tough[8] and Coyne[9] note that the student who directs his own learning program requires helpers, and both authors indicate choices of friends, family, librarians, and educators, to mention a few, and these authors indicate that these helps may be on a one-to-one or a group basis. Coyne and Hebert believe that although they are on the "same continuum," tutoring and independent study differ since they view independent study as "casting loose from much supervision." They also agree once the student is on his way the difference dissipates.[10] The ISP concept was that the group or individual helper is an added resource to independent learning which the student might choose to utilize. The tutoring was not to be more than an extension of the framework of guidance into a subject area offered in the Study Guide. Those students who found themselves having difficulty moving into independent study ran the risk of becoming frustrated beyond motivational margins, but with group discussion, or one-to-one idea exchanges with a member of the academic community, they could be helped to start their learning program. These tutoring aids would be offered on the request of the independent student. In most instances it was expected they would occur in group sessions. The format would be largely question and answer. It would be directed to the needs expressed by those students in attendance. The atmosphere was to be completely informal, one in which the student and the faculty member could establish a rapport which would create an enthusiasm within the student to probe into the subject area being discussed. From his depth of knowledge, the faculty member could impart to the student his personal excitement and interest in his subject. He could demonstrate its relationship to other disciplines and could illustrate its relevancy to the student's life. For the student, these

---

[8]Allen Tough, *The Adult's Learning Projects*, p. 78.

[9]John Coyne and Tom Hebert, *This Way Out*, pp. 16-25.

[10]John Coyne and Tom Hebert, *This Way Out*, p. 25.

sessions would also offer an opportunity to relate personally to the academic community thus dispelling some of its awesome quality. The student would begin to realize that his learning would require questioning and understanding on his part in order that it became more than mere rote memorization. The student would be expected to leave a help session eager to find out for himself what this particular subject area had to offer him.

No clear profile of the anticipated student was conceived other than that he would be from the adult population, that he would be eager for learning, and that possible pressures of time, family responsibilities, lack of funds, and accessibility had prevented his attendance on a campus. The personal privacy of this student was in no way to be invaded; so any evaluation model would depend totally upon the librarian/student relationship for information on the student himself. Neither was there any anticipation of the number of persons who might avail themselves of this educational opportunity; so there were no goals set for the study in the context of measurement by numbers. Rather, the concept was to study the quality of service the libraries were prepared to offer this independent student. This study was expected to provide some answers for the library and academic communities as to possible future roles for libraries in independent study. At the time the study was being explored, there was also the beginning of a movement toward the "University Without Walls." Thus knowledge of the library's effectiveness to operate as the resource center for the new educational options was most timely.

As the Independent Study Project concept developed in action, and as knowledge of the student and his needs grew, it became evident that the role of the public library could not be as simplistically defined as originally conceived. While libraries have always functioned as learning centers and librarians have always functioned as helpers for independent learners, the area of responsibility for this new student encompassed the learning function itself. It required a greater degree of personal involvement on the part of the librarian than that to which he was accustomed. The library and the librarian were confronted with a degree of commitment for which in many instances they were not prepared. If, as Allie Beth Martin suggests, "We must . . . plan now for

A CONCEPT

accommodation to continuous change[11]"; as the independent student grows and changes in learning, so must the library profession meet his growth with change, some of which might challenge concepts of the profession's traditional roles. If, however, the library is to play an active role in learning which means growth and change for the user, it follows that the library profession too must grow and change to meet the challenge of its users' learning needs.

BIBLIOGRAPHY

Coyne, John and Tom Hebert. *This Way Out: A Guide to Alternatives to Traditional College Education in the United States, Europe, and the Third World.* New York: Dutton, 1972.

Harris, Theodore L. and Wilson E. Schwahn. *Selected Readings on the Learning Process.* New York: Oxford University Press, 1961.

Hilgard, Ernest R. and Gordon H. Bower. *Theories of Learning.* 3rd ed. New York: Appleton, 1961.

Martin, Allie Beth. *A Strategy for Public Library Change: Proposed Public Library Goals Feasibility Study.* Chicago: American Library Association, Public Library Association, 1972.

Passow, A. Harry. "Trends in Learning and Education Affecting Community Library Services," *Total Community Library Service.* Chicago: American Library Association, 1973. (response to J. Lloyd Trump.)

Tough, Allen. *The Adult's Learning Projects: A Fresh Approach to Theory and Practice in Adult Learning,* Research in Education Series No. 1, Toronto, Ontario: The Ontario Institute for Studies in Education, 1971.

---

[11]Allie Beth Martin, Project Coordinator, *A Strategy for Public Library Change: Proposed Public Library Goals Feasibility Study* (Chicago: American Library Association, Public Library Association, 1972), p. 1.

Chapter 2

♫♫♫ ♫♫♫♫♫♫♫♫ ♫♫♫♫♫ ♫♫

The Dallas Public Library's Independent Study Project

On February 2, 1970, Mrs. Lillian Bradshaw, Director of the Dallas Public Library, addressed an interoffice memorandum to four members of her administrative staff. That memorandum announced a planned visit to the Library by Dr. Fred Cole, President of the Council on Library Resources (CLR); Foster Mohrhardt, Council on Library Resources; Louis Hausman, National Endowment for the Humanities (NEH); and Jose A. Toro, then Assistant Director, College-Level Examination Program of the College Entrance Examination Board (CEEB). The purpose of this visit, according to the Library Director's memorandum, was stated in a letter from Mr. Toro and in a proposal drafted by Mr. Toro, both of which were among the attachments to the memo. As Mrs. Bradshaw expressed her view of the meeting:

> It is my understanding that the group is seeking frank, honest advice and guidance on whether public libraries can be effectively utilized as agents in this program [that described in Mr. Toro's drafted proposal]. Mr. Mohrhardt explained that the reputation of DPL as an innovative

system with a reputation for an open mind on new ideas caused them to seek our advice.[1]

The message from Mrs. Bradshaw included a request for reactions to the drafted proposal from each of the four staff officers.

That memorandum from Lillian Bradshaw initiated the involvement of the Dallas Public Library (DPL) in what was eventually to be known as the Independent Study Project. Aside from a telephone call from the CLR in January 1970, a letter from Jose Toro also in January 1970, a conversation with Foster Mohrhardt at the Midwinter Meeting of the American Library Association in January followed by a letter from him concerning hotel reservations for the February 13 meeting, the Director was preparing to host a meeting for the purpose of exploring something about which she and her staff knew little: CLEP and how the public library might become an agent to serve those preparing for CLEP examinations.

The recipients of Mrs. Bradshaw's memorandum were Mrs. Margaret Warren, Community Education Coordinator; Mrs. Mildred Williams, Personnel Officer; Mr. Richard Waters, then Chief of Branch Services; and Mr. David Reich, Deputy Director and Associate Director for Public Services. The responses varied in degree of enthusiasm, caution, and concern, but all were hopeful that the Dallas Public Library would live up to the Council on Library Resources' opinion of it as an innovative system. Most of the caution and concern had to do with the proposal drafted and provided by Mr. Toro of CEEB, and questions and disagreements were directed specifically to elements of that proposal.

Mr. Toro's proposal, titled "The Library as a Counseling and Independent Study Center for Achieving a Two-Year College Education," introduced the Dallas Public Library staff to the relatively new (at that time) College Board's College-Level Examination Program and its intent ". . . to help the many adults involved in independent study gain recognition for the work they have done."[2] Independent students' needs outside the intent of the

---

[1]Unpublished memorandum dated February 2, 1970, from Mrs. Lillian M. Bradshaw to Mrs. Margaret Warren, Mrs. Mildred Williams, Mr. Richard Waters, Mr. David Reich, Subject: Attached Package (14 items).

[2]Unpublished proposal dated October 15, 1969, by Jose A. Toro, p. 1.

testing program were identified by the proposal's author, and the observation that independent students use libraries led to the suggestion that libraries could be the agency which could provide the services directed to meet the pre-testing needs. Mr. Toro listed advice, guidance, and counseling as ". . . services [which] would help adult students determine what and how they should study in order to reach their objectives [CLEP examinations]."[3] Since, according to the drafted proposal, libraries have traditionally provided reader's advisory service, that service could now be "expanded to include advisory or counseling service . . . "[4] It was also suggested that libraries could offer workshops of a group counseling nature, during which CLEP examination scores could be explained and credit by examination information would be dispensed. The preclusion of the author was that existing library staff and facilities could accommodate such an expanded service. He suggested, further, that some libraries might be interested in providing more services to the independent students but that more services might, he thought, " . . . require the entire attention of a part- or full-time staff member."[5]

Significant for both the reaction of DPL staff to Mr. Toro's proposal and the eventual proposal drafted by DPL staff are the following closing lines of the Toro proposal:

> . . . guidance and counseling services, then is clearly within the domain of the public libraries and may be nothing more than a part of the evolutionary process through which libraries will go. If this view is correct, the profession should be encouraged and helped to advance its movement into the area discussed here.[6]

The use of the words "guidance and counseling" was somewhat disturbing to the library staff who read the proposal. While, it was agreed, reader's guidance has always been within the training and

[3]*Ibid.*

[4]*Ibid.*, p. 2.

[5]*Ibid.*, p. 4.

[6]*Ibid.*, p. 5.

expertise of the professional librarian, the sort of "guidance" Mr. Toro's proposal alluded to was not quite what the staff felt librarians had chosen or been trained to do. Counseling, particularly, was questioned as an activity belonging to another profession. The reaction from Richard Waters stated the concern:

> I couldn't accept any librarian doing it, even one who had gone through a quick course provided by CEEB. (Quick course defined as a one or two day institute.)[7]

Mr. Waters did concede, however: "I would want librarians (M.L.S.) [rather than nonprofessionals on the library staff] to be the Counselor(s), but only after a two-four week training class."[8] He noted, too, that the counselor would have to be full-time. The Deputy Director, in his reactions, expressed the belief that "any academic *counseling* should be done only by professional counselors."[9] He did feel, though, that librarians could provide "academic advising," which he defined as "helping students arrange class schedules, choose courses to fit a program, etc."[10]

Two of the staff reactions included questions concerning the advisability of the Library's entering into such a program of service involving CLEP because of the existence of a multi-campus community junior college in Dallas. On the one hand the question was, would the Dallas County Community College District (DCCCD) think that the Library was getting into its business of offering the first two years of higher education. On the other the question was, with the community college easily available and accessible, would there be citizens who would not take advantage of the college who would, instead, be attracted to CLEP via the public library. In addition to the DCCCD were other institutions of higher education in the Dallas area which, besides offering inexpensive community service courses, continually work at attracting beginning students. The Library did have to consider carefully its

---

[7]Unpublished memorandum dated 2-4-70 from Richard Waters.

[8]*Ibid.*

[9]Unpublished memorandum dated January 15, 1970, from David L. Reich.

[10]Reich, *loc. cit.*

good relationship with those institutions and assure itself that, if it entered such a program as the drafted proposal suggested, it would not be thought of locally of having entered into competition for beginning college students.

One aspect of Dallas Public Librarianship which was recognized and noted as evidenced by staff responses was that additional staff would be required to handle any added responsibility, even if the new services were viewed as expansions of existing services. The librarians at DPL already were handling more than they were comfortable with, and trends noted in Dallas suggested no lessening of demands for public library services the citizens had learned to appreciate and to demand. No one believed that existing staff could assume (nor were trained to provide) "guidance" and "counseling" services.

With the reactions from the four staff members, Mrs. Bradshaw and Mr. Reich met on February 13, 1970, with the visitors from the Council on Library Resources, the College Entrance Examination Board, and the National Endowment for the Humanities. The staff concerns and questions were presented, ideas exchanged, and the meeting ended with two conclusions:

1. The Dallas Public Library would continue to consider the idea of proposing a project along the lines suggested by Mr. Toro's proposal and discussed during the meeting.
2. There existed a real likelihood that funding would be forthcoming if a project acceptable to the funding agencies represented at the meeting were proposed.

Following the February meeting and consequent conversations with staff, the Director appointed a staff committee consisting of the Deputy Director, Mr. Reich; the Personnel Officer, Mrs. Williams; and the Community Education Coordinator, Mrs. Warren, to develop a proposal. Drawing on all that had been gathered up to then and on her own insights into the Dallas Public Library and public libraries in general, Mrs. Bradshaw had written what she called a "rough draft" and which she titled "A Proposal Designed to Measure the Effectiveness of the Public Library As an Independent Study Center for Achieving a Two-Year College

19

Education." The initial "rough draft" was only a few pages long, and eventually it went through many changes before the final draft. However, the concept and much of the wording expressing the concept and the objectives developed by Mrs. Bradshaw remained constant.

"Rough Draft #2," completed in late March 1970, brought changes to the title: "Investigate the Effectiveness of the Public Library As a Center for Independent Study Toward Achieving a Two-Years College Education." The change in wording from "Measure the Effectiveness" to "Investigate the Effectiveness" resulted, it was felt, in a more realistic approach for the library to take. It was in writing this draft, too, that the decision was made to restrict the proposed project to the Dallas Public Library system, using the entire system for the base of the study, and designating five of the system's branch libraries as model public libraries to actually offer the services of the project. The branches would be selected to provide model libraries serving different socioeconomic communities including lower middle, middle middle, upper middle, high stratifications, and one inner city community of a socio-economically-culturally-ethnically mixed population.

Draft #3 was retyped in mid April 1970. It differed from Draft #2 only in refinements, such as expanding the role of the library as a center to include not only information about CLEP but information concerning the participation of area colleges and universities in CLEP. It should be noted that, during the months of drafting and redrafting, the staff serving on the proposal committee were continuing to ask themselves some of the questions that had come up at the time of the initial reacting to Mr. Toro's proposal. Among those were whether or not there were colleges and universities in the Dallas area that accepted CLEP examinations for credit. The Library had already decided that it would not initiate a program to encourage citizens to study independently toward seeking academic recognition via CLEP if there were no institutions in the area where the citizens could obtain that recognition. During that same time the CEEB's regional office in Austin was working with Dallas area colleges and universities to sell them on the idea of CLEP and to encourage them to develop programs of granting credit by examination via CLEP. It became known to the Library that the possibility of a project involving CLEP by the Dallas Public Library was being told to the colleges and universities visited by the CEEB representative.

While it was rather flattering to the Library, it must be admitted, the staff was not at all comfortable with the Library's being used to help sell a product, CLEP, even as well-meaning and legitimate as CLEP seemed to be. And, it was "seemed to be" at that time, for the philosophy of the College-Level Examination Program was still not fully understood by the Library staff. It was, however, taking shape in the minds of the proposal writers and in the wording of the proposal itself. That CLEP was not in competition with the local colleges and universities was soon recognized, and the opportunity CLEP offered those who were not, for whatever reason, enrolled in a formal program of higher education became more and more attractive as something of value the Library could — and probably should — bring to the attention of the adults in the community and, even more, assist them in independent learning that could lead to college credit.

Between Draft #3 and Draft #4 came one direct result of the College Board's using the possible Dallas Public Library project to encourage the local academic institutions. In June 1970 the Deputy Director received a telephone call from Southern Methodist University (SMU) reporting the University's knowledge of the Library's interest in a project involving CLEP and interest in participating with the Library in the project. The Library had always hoped for the support of the local colleges and universities in the project that was being designed, but it had not thought in terms of direct participation in the project. This new aspect of the participation of SMU provided the opportunity for the project to include some academic services the Library staff had been reluctant to presume could be handled by professional librarians, particularly busy librarians as those on the DPL staff were. Those academic services now worked into the proposal included:

1. Study guides and reading lists prepared by members of the SMU faculty.
2. Members of SMU's academic community to serve as tutors.

The study guides were to cover the subject areas included in the College-Level Examination Program and were to be made available at the five branch Libraries selected to serve as model public libraries in the project. Listed simply as an element of the project development, there was no real definition of "study guides"; the members of the committee, however, visualized the study guides as not course syllabi or outlines but introductions to the study of subjects. The reading lists were included under project development as annotated reading lists of non-textbook materials, obviously to support and accompany the study guides.

The tutors conceived at this point in the development of the proposal were to be faculty or graduate students who would provide guidance to the people in the program. Tutorial services were to be scheduled on a regular basis at the five branch libraries. The word "counseling" was not included in the listing of tutors and tutorial service, but "guidance" had made its way into the draft. It seemed to the DPL staff committee members that the participation of SMU did provide for more appropriate resource persons to offer guidance to the potential CLEP-takers.

In addition to SMU's providing faculty to prepare study guides and reading lists and acting as tutors, the involvement of the university in the project — in this draft proposal stage — suggested that SMU could and should be added to the proposed membership of the project's Advisory Committee. The Advisory Committee to the project had been conceived several drafts back. These and other refinements resulted in Drafts #6 and #7.

At the time the Library was advised of SMU's interest in the proposed project, the proposal committee members had been giving no little thought to the sort of person who might be considered for the Project Director. It had been pretty well decided that the Project should be directed by a person from the field of education rather than from librarianship. That decision was not a comfortable one for the committee, however, because it was suspected that the concept of unstructured, non-traditional learning assistance and encouragement in a public library (which was developing along with the drafting of the proposal) was more easily explainable and more appropriately within the understanding of a librarian experienced in adult services than to, say, a retired college instructor or high school teacher.[11] Now,

---

[11] It must be admitted even here that this was a not altogether accurate presumption on the part of the committee members, because, as it became evident later, librarians, who

though, with SMU's participation, the Project would have the academic aspects of the effort covered by the university, and the committee changed its thinking about the Project Director; it was then agreed that a librarian should be considered to serve in that capacity.12 This was done. Charity Herring, of the Dallas Public Library was selected. Four months later, after getting the Project off to a good initial start, Jean S. Brooks, who had been serving as Institutional Services Librarian for the Dallas Public Library, became Project Director. In addition to being a librarian, in prior years Mrs. Brooks had been a teacher.

During this phase of redrafting the proposal, the Library was in frequent communication with Jose Toro of CEEB. Mr. Toro's encouragement was appreciated, and it included some meaningful suggestions that were incorporated in Draft #7. It was here that the SMU-provided tutors took on the role of acting as seminar and workshop planners and leaders as well as tutors. Mr. Toro's original drafted proposal, it will be remembered, suggested workshops; the workshops suggested by Mr. Toro for the DPL proposed Project were quite different, however. These were to cover such areas as methods of effective independent study, the study of specific subjects, and reading effectively. This, it appeared to the committee, was a particularly significant addition to the proposed Project, a bringing together of the adults attracted to the Project and college instructors *in the library.*

It was also in this draft of the proposal that another role for SMU appeared, that is, an ongoing evaluation of the Project. Another addition to the project development was the requirement for professional public relations services to provide publicity for the project and promotional attention to the Project. Two other elements were worked into the development, these involving CEEB: (1) training for the Project Director, the librarians, and the faculty, and (2) the printing of the reading lists and study guides. Of course, the College Board was to provide CLEP materials and appropriate

---

themselves were products of traditional, structured educational experiences, found it most difficult to grasp — and, perhaps even to support — the notion of this type of non-traditional education.

12It was at this point in the proposal drafting that the possibility of *a project* began to seem more like the probability for *the Project*, thus the capitalization.

CLEP publicity materials for use by the Library and the local news media.

Another well received suggestion from Mr. Toro was that the Project include provisions for a body of library and higher education experts from around the country, who would observe and review the Project in terms of whatever implications it might have for other public libraries. Thus was added to the project development the National Interest Council. It was described as a seven-member body to be appointed by the Project's Advisory Committee; it would include representatives from the American Library Association, the Council on Library Resources, the College Entrance Examination Board, and representatives from other public library systems in the country. It was to meet semiannually during the two years' period of the Project to hear reports from the Project Evaluator and the Project Director. The National Interest Council, too, found its way into Draft #7.

The establishment of a College Information Center at each of the five branch libraries in the Project was listed for the first time in Draft #7 also. Based on a similar center in one branch of the Library at the time, the College Information Center was considered a particularly interesting element of the services being designed. Providing an audiovisual presentation of information about local colleges and universities, it was proposed that the adult entering the Project could have individual access to information about a college's entrance requirements, curricula, examination programs, etc.[13]

Draft #7, it is clear, was the most significant of all the drafts of the proposal. It incorporated refinements to the roles of both the Library and Southern Methodist University and suggestions made by Mr. Toro. To the members of the proposal committee, the Project was now beginning to be seen as a sophisticated, evaluative pilot program that could realistically attempt to demonstrate if providing assistance services to independent students is "clearly within the domain of the public libraries."[14]

---

[13]The disappointing lack of success of the College Information Centers is discussed in Chapter Three.

[14]Toro, p. 5.

Drafts #8 and #9 contained only minor refinements in wording and particular development of the Project's proposed budget. Draft #10 was the final draft, that which was submitted to the Council on Library Resources. The proposed budget totaled $109,029 for the Project period of two years. During the entire period of proposal drafting the Library, as a department of the City of Dallas, had been meeting frequently with a representative of the City Manager's Office to discuss the City's attitude toward grants and manner of handling grants. In a March 12, 1970, memorandum from Mildred Williams, the Library's Personnel Officer, to the Director, for example, the manner in which the City handles the hiring of employees whose salaries would be paid by grant funds was considered:

> A resolution would have to be prepared for the City Council to accept the grant. Council would accept the grant, specifying that personnel would be paid out of the fund.

> Personnel would be processed the same as other city employees and would receive the same coverage and benefits, and would be a part of our regular payroll.[15]

Other matters relating to the City's manner of handling grants were discussed, such as the requirement of the City to expect grant funds to purchase furniture and equipment for any new personnel provided by the grant, and such considerations were worked into the proposed budget.

The proposal that was eventually sent in January, 1971, to the Council on Library Resources and which, subsequently, was forwarded by the CLR to the National Endowment for the Humanities, was thirteen pages long (including the budget). The final paper was considerably longer, more involved, more encompassing, and more sophisticated than the first "rough draft" written by Mrs. Bradshaw twelve months earlier. Nonetheless, the "Problem" (introduction) as Mrs. Bradshaw saw it and the objectives and the basic elements of the "Project Development" as

---

[15]Unpublished memorandum dated March 12, 1970, from Mrs. Mildred Williams to Mrs. Lillian M. Bradshaw, Subject: Personnel Employed under a Private Foundation Grant.

Mrs. Bradshaw created them were the same. It is appropriate here to quote from the final proposal, even though the entire proposal is included as an addendum:

It would seem that, to most successfully utilize this [College-Level] Examination Program, appropriate information and advice about the Program and appropriate study guides, reading lists, and tutorial services should be provided in a setting conducive to independent study. Since many persons directed to independent study use public libraries and since public libraries have traditionally worked in the areas of self-education and continuing education, often in cooperation with other educational institutions, it follows that a public library, with an institution of higher education cooperating and participating, could be an effective agent in providing informational and advisory services to these adults, said services designed to encourage independent study toward achieving a two-years college education.[16]

Expressing the purpose of the proposal quite directly are the following, the final words of the proposal's introduction:

This proposal seeks to investigate the role and the effectiveness of one public library system, the Dallas Public Library, with the cooperation and participation of an institution of higher education, Southern Methodist University, in assisting adults pursuing self-education directed to academic recognition in area colleges and universities and information about those and other colleges and universities.[17]

[16]Dallas Public Library, City of Dallas, Texas, "A Proposal Designed to Investigate the Effectiveness of the Public Library As a Center For Independent Study Toward Achieving a Two-Years College Education" (proposal submitted to Council on Library Resources, Washington, D.C., January, 1971), pp. 1-2.

[17]*Ibid.*, p. 3.

It is also worth calling attention here to the first element listed under "Project Development" in the proposal: "This project will be directed exclusively to the adult reader."[18]

What needs to be pointed to as especially significant to the Dallas Public Library's Independent Study Project as it developed out of the proposal are several quite clearly stated intentions of the proposed project. In the first quote from the proposal, above, reference is made to the College-Level Examination Program and to proposed services that should encourage independent study toward *achieving a two-year college education* (via CLEP was understood.) In the second quote above, reference is made to the role of the public library which would assist adults in preparing for *academic recognition* (via CLEP was here understood, also.) In the third quote, it is emphasized that the service proposed is for *adults*. None of these should be surprising. It was, after all, an introduction to CLEP and the idea of a public library assisting people preparing for CLEP examinations that had stimulated the development of the DPL's proposal for a project. In other words, the Project, as originally conceived and as developed through ten drafts, was tied quite frankly and understandably to serving adults preparing for CLEP examinations.

That, of course, is not at all the limit to which the Dallas Public Library staff considered its efforts to assist independent students should or would be restricted. It was understood that the Library, as a public library, really did not have to be concerned with more than helping people learn via the library — staff talked a great deal about "turning people on to learning" during the two years of the Project. If any of those who took advantage of the assistance the Project could offer should go beyond that beginning to the point of taking CLEP examinations (or any other examinations) and actually gaining academic credit, that would make the Library's efforts to help even more meaningful for some. At the same time, those who learned for their own satisfaction, which might not include seeking credit by examination, would also be success stories for the Project. An understanding of these points was important to the Library staff as it struggled to see that the Library's role, if it were to be an effective one, was to help people learn enough (or well

18*Ibid.*, p. 4.

enough) to pass CLEP examinations, but not necessarily to help people get college credit. The aspect — and prospect — of gaining college credit through CLEP was, however, recognized as the drawing card of the Project. It is to the credit of the Independent Study Project staff and the librarians serving the independent student that the Project developed within, around, and beyond this drawing card during the two years of its existence, as other chapters in this book will indicate.

Since the public library is a *service* institution, and since the proposed Project was designed to provide service to "adults pursuing self-education," it is not surprising that the Project's objectives, except for one concerning the determination of the success of the Project and one concerning providing guidance to other libraries in the area of serving independent students, all begin with the infinitive *to serve:*

1. To serve as an information center for the examinations program of the College-Level Examination Program (CLEP) and of the participation of area colleges and universities.

2. To serve as a distribution center for materials relative to the College-Level Examination Program (CLEP).

3. To serve as a College Information Center by providing, for individual inquiry, multi-media presentations of information about area colleges and universities.

4. To serve as an advisory center to the adult interested in self-education by providing professional assistance in the selection of materials designed to further his goals in seeking academic recognition, by providing professionally prepared study guides and reading lists, and by making available tutorial services.

5. To serve as an educational resource in the motivation of business and industry to encourage employees toward independent study.

6. To determine, through ongoing evaluation of the project, the appropriateness and the effectiveness of the public library in this educational arena.

    7. To provide information on and guidance to the entire
public library field in this new area of educational
involvement.[19]

To meet those objectives the Library proposed the various
elements discussed above and the following personnel:

1. Project Director
2. Project Secretary
3. Consultant (part-time) for public relations
4. Professional librarians and supportive staffs of the
   five branch libraries selected to serve as model public
   libraries.

In addition, CEEB staff would be required to train the Project
Director and orient the librarians and SMU faculty who were to be
involved in the Project. SMU was to locate appropriate faculty
members to prepare the study guides and reading lists, perform the
ongoing evaluation, provide tutoring services, and conduct
workshops.

With a calendar and period for the project (two years) suggested
and with a budget of $109,029 proposed to support the objectives,
project development, personnel, and calendar, the proposal (Draft
#10) that was submitted to the Council on Library Resources in
January 1971 was thought by the DPL staff to be realistic enough to
be worthy of consideration. The Library began to hear expressions
of positive reactions from those in the three agencies who had first
brought the notion to Dallas in January 1970. The most critical
reaction (though not negatively critical) came from the NEH, who,
it was learned, would serve as the primary funding agency, if
funding were granted. The National Endowment for the
Humanities sent the Library its guidelines — somewhat after the
fact, it was noted, for the Library had submitted its proposal to the
CLR, not to the NEH — and these generated considerable
correspondence and conversations between DPL and NEH.

Matters which had to be resolved included certain items covered
in the budget. For example, NEH reported that it does not normally

---

[19]*Ibid.*, p. 4.

fund the purchase of equipment such as office furniture, and, unless there was a written policy establishing the basis for travel reimbursement, which could be submitted to the Endowment for consideration, travel should be computed on a per diem basis. Moreover, requested travel must be specific as to the person to travel, purpose, destination, period of travel, and mode of travel. The need for office furniture was easily explained as a City of Dallas requirement (mentioned above); the travel required more effort since it was necessary to project for two years. Both were done to the satisfaction of NEH, nonetheless, and the proposal's budget revised accordingly. Eventually the NEH requested that the Library round off the budget to $100,000 and break it down to $50,000 each year. This was done, primarily by reducing the amount of funds suggested for workshops and tutoring services.

At this time, the National Endowment for the Humanities also expressed its desire to be represented on the proposed Project's National Interest Council. The Library was pleased to add the NEH. Its exclusion from the membership of the National Interest Council in the first place was due to the DPL's unclear understanding of the role the NEH would eventually play in supporting the Project. The inclusion now of NEH on the Council's membership did not, however, change the travel budget proposed for bringing the Council to Dallas for its semi-annual meetings. NEH, as the principal funder, could not travel on its own granted funds, it was explained, so its representative would travel to the meetings on NEH's own operative funds.

These changes in the budget and in the composition of the membership of the National Interest Council resulted in yet another redrafting of the proposal: Draft #11. This was, indeed, the final draft! This proposal is to be found in the Addendum.

In April 1971, at the same time as negotiations were underway with the NEH, the Library's Deputy Director had an opportunity to describe the proposed Project with a member of the staff of the American Association of Junior Colleges (AAJC).[20] That conversation resulted in the AAJC's being provided a copy of the proposal and a subsequent expression of interest in the Project by AAJC. The Library was particularly pleased with the interest of

---

[20]Since renamed the American Association of Community and Junior Colleges (AACJC).

another national body, this a national higher education organization. It was agreed by the DPL staff to add the AAJC to the list of organizations to be represented on the National Interest Council. It should be admitted, too, that the Library hoped that the interest of that national organization would encourage the local community junior college in developing a program of accepting CLEP examinations for credit so that the adults attracted to the DPL Project would have the junior colleges to consider. The membership of the National Interest Council now numbered eight.

When funds to support the proposed Project were granted in June 1971, they came from three sources: the National Endowment for the Humanities, the Council on Library Resources, and the College Entrance Examination Board, the three agencies whose representatives visited the Library in January 1970. NEH advised the Library that it would grant $25,000 the first year to be matched by $25,000 from the CLR and that for the second year it would provide $25,000 outright. The CEEB offered the remaining $25,000 for the second year outright, thus bringing the total funds granted to $100,000. Since, with the reworking of the proposed budget to meet the NEH's requirements, the audiovisual equipment required for the College Information Centers had been placed in the second year's budget, and since the furniture and equipment required to establish the Project Office needed to be placed on order prior to the availability of the funds from the NEH (or, perhaps more accurately, prior to the time — the actual starting date of the Project — NEH funds could be used) the College Board generously advanced half of its $25,000 early so that equipment and furniture could be ordered.

The calendar — revised several times during the year-long period of redrafting the proposal and during the period the proposal was being considered by the funding agencies — now had the Project scheduled to begin in September 1971. Actually, the *Project* began in August 1971 with the hiring of the Project Director and the Project Secretary, and the opening of the Project Office. The Project's *program of service* began in September in the five branch libraries which had now been designated as those to serve as model public libraries. In the few months between notification of the grants and initiating the new service, several things happened concerning the Project. For one, the name of the Project was finally

31

agreed to: the Independent Study Project, most often referred to as ISP (pronounced Issp.)

The ISP Advisory Committee began meeting, and its first action was to invite representatives of the agencies and organizations listed in the proposal and of libraries to serve on the National Interest Council. The libraries chosen to be invited were those which had already at the time been involved in programs of bringing information about CLEP to their communities: the Miami Public Library,[21] the St. Louis Public Library, and the Serra Regional Library System with headquarters in San Diego, California. All the agencies and organizations responded affirmatively immediately, although the American Library Association and the American Association of Junior Colleges took somewhat longer times to appoint since the Advisory Committee had not directed its invitations to specific individuals within those organizations as it had done for the NEH, CLR, and CEEB. In the case of the libraries, the Advisory Committee directed its invitations to individuals at Miami and St. Louis but to the system in San Diego since the person there who had been involved with that library's program of distributing CLEP materials had since left the staff.[22]

An orientation session with members of SMU's faculty was arranged, and representatives from both the College Board and the Educational Testing Service (ETS) joined representatives from the Library to introduce the faculty to ISP and to the idea of the study guides and reading lists they were being asked to produce. Describing the orientation session at SMU in an address to the Dallas Conference on Credit by Examination Through the College-Level Examination Program at SMU on March 30, 1972, David Reich said:

> We asked members of the SMU faculty to prepare study guides that were not to be course outlines of syllabi but *directions* for an adult who probably would not know how to approach the study of a subject. We asked the faculty to prepare reading lists of non-textbook materials, those books the independent student should be able to

---

[21]Since renamed the Miami-Dade Public Library.

[22]A list of the members of the National Interest Council is included as an addendum.

find in his local public library. Now, I suspect that was not a terribly clear assignment; I also suspect that it was not a very easy assignment. After all, we were asking this of rather traditional college instructors, academic professionals who had spent their academic lives involved in traditional, structured, time-slotted learning and teaching. Their first urge, as I recall, was to look at the CLEP examinations and design their study guides and reading lists to fit the examinations. Yet the CLEP examinations, according to our understanding, were themselves devised for the adult who might have learned in a nontraditional way: by watching many hours of television, by reading magazines, by listening to recordings, by working, by *experiencing learning* in life. CLEP exams were not designed to take after six semester hours of classroom lectures and weekly tests.[23]

That rather lengthy statement was not intended by its author to be a criticism of the SMU faculty [Mr. Reich went on in that address to describe similar difficulties with the librarians, who, too, were products of the same sort of structured, traditional higher education] but to indicate the considerable difficulty the Library staff, the Project staff, and even the CEEB and ETS representatives had in teaching the ISP (and the CLEP) concept in those early days of the Project. Not all of the faculty members attending the orientation responded questioningly; one instructor in particular, it is remembered, approached the speakers at the conclusion of the meeting to express his great interest in the effort and his eagerness to help in any way he could.

There was also an orientation session for the librarians who were to provide the ISP services in the five branches. In addition to the ISP Director, the Library's Deputy Director, and representatives from the College Board and ETS, CEEB had brought to the meeting Dr. Margaret Fagin, Director of Programs for Women, Family, and Youth at the University of Missouri-St. Louis. Dr.

[23]David L. Reich, "The Dallas Public Library Independent Study Project: The People's University" (unpublished paper presented at the Dallas Conference on Credit by Examination Through the College-Level Examination Program, Southern Methodist University, March 30, 1972.)

Jose Orlando Toro conducts orientation session for librarians who were to provide ISP services in the 5 branches.   C.D. Bayne, photographer

Fagin inspired the entire group with her description of her successful Circuit Rider Project in Missouri.[24] It must be admitted, however, that, despite the inspiration of Dr. Fagin's remarks, the excitement for the opportunity to provide a new service that came through in Jose Toro's remarks, and the sincerity of the Project Director's words to those who would be looking to her for direction in the Project, the reaction of the librarians was more than a little disappointing. Only a few questions were asked, and no enthusiasm was demonstrated. This slowness to respond plagued the ISP staff for a number of months.

With members of the faculty at Southern Methodist University now working on the study guides and the reading lists, with the public relations consultant arranging for and coordinating news releases, television and radio announcements and appearances, with the ISP Director and Secretary organizing the Project Office and delivering materials and information to the five branches, and with the branch librarians anxiously (in the true sense of the word) awaiting the arrival of who-knew-how-many independent students, the Project fast approached the first of September 1971. During the first few months of the Project a few refinements occurred: for one, it was agreed by the Advisory Committee that the study guides and the reading lists could be produced together as study guides/reading lists and that the format need not be standard for all the guides/lists. It was also agreed that the anonymity afforded other patrons of the public library would be granted the library's new independent students. It was observed that the workshops would have to be initiated by the ISP staff since the early independent students were not requesting them and that some workshops, such as How to Use the Library, regardless of what hopefully-more-inviting title might be used, were not going to draw many takers.

The initial response to ISP (described in other parts of this book) was such that the librarians did, at least, become concerned about the ease of access to the CLEP information and materials and the study guides/reading lists for those attracted to the Project. For a while the ISP staff, the Advisory Committee, and the librarians

---

[24]Dr. Fagin describes her successful experiences in working with CLEP in her article, "CLEP credit encourages adults to seek degrees" in the Fall 1971 issue of *College Board Reveiw.*

entertained the idea of extending the distribution of the materials to all fourteen branches of the Dallas Public Library System and to the Central Library. This was but one example of enthusiasm for the ISP *service* that tended to cause those involved to forget about ISP as a *study*, and it became necessary to draw back and remember that, as a *study*, there were certain built-in conditions within which the service had to be restricted. Another example was the eagerness initially to purchase books and other materials to supplement the collections in the five branches in order to be better prepared to serve the ISP patrons. The Advisory Committee pointed out to the librarians, however, that the Project was designed to determine if the public library is now ready to serve independent students effectively and that buying books before there were normal patron demands for them would be, in a sense, stacking the deck.

It was generally acknowledged that the greatest unknown factor of the Independent Study Project in the beginning was the independent student himself: his age, sex, educational background, etc., even how many there would be. The following chapter describes the developing identification of the ISP student.

BIBLIOGRAPHY

Bradshaw, Lillian M. "Attached Package (14 items)." Unpublished inter-office memorandum to Mrs. Margaret Warren, Mrs. Mildred Williams, Mr. Richard Waters, and Mr. David Reich, Dallas Public Library, Dallas, Texas, February 2, 1970.

Dallas Public Library, City of Dallas, Texas. "A Proposal Designed to Investigate the Effectiveness of the Public Library As a Center For Independent Study Toward Achieving a Two-Years College Education." Proposal submitted to Council on Library Resources, Washington, D.C., January, 1971.

Fagin, Margaret C. "CLEP credit encourages adults to seek degrees," *College Board Review*, No. 81 (Fall 1971), 18-22.

Reich, David L. "College-Level Entrance Examination Board: Library Counseling and Study Center Proposal." Unpublished inter-office memorandum to Mrs. Lillian M. Bradshaw, Dallas Public Library, Dallas, Texas, January 15, 1970.

Reich, David L. "The Dallas Public Library Independent Study Project: The People's University." Unpublished paper presented at the Dallas Conference on Credit by Examination Through the College-Level Examination Program, Southern Methodist University, Dallas, Texas, March 30, 1972.

Toro, Jose A. "The Library as a Counseling and Independent Study Center for Achieving a Two-Year College Education." Unpublished proposal provided the Dallas Public Library, January 7, 1970. Proposal dated October 15, 1969.

Waters, Richard L. "CLR — CEEB, etc." Unpublished inter-office memorandum to Mrs. Lillian M. Bradshaw, Dallas Public Library, Dallas, Texas, February 4, 1970.

Williams, Mildred. "Personnel Employed under a Private Foundation Grant." Unpublished inter-office memorandum to Mrs. Lillian M. Bradshaw, Dallas Public Library, Dallas, Texas, March 12, 1970.

Chapter 3

♠♠♠ ♠♠ ♠♠♠♠♠♠ ♠♠♠♠♠♠ ♠♠

The Independent Student

The concept of the Independent Study Project upon which the proposal was based afforded no description of the student who might be expected to avail himself of the opportunity to continue learning. It was expected that he would be an adult who had experienced varied modes of learning within his life span, whether formal or informal, recognized or unrecognized; that he would be eager for more learning but shy of being questioned about it; and that he would be representative of the neighborhood of one of those five branch libraries chosen for the Project. This meant that he would come from varying spheres of action and represent various background experiences, occupations, and life styles. What had not been anticipated was that the independent student would also come from the neighborhoods served by all of the other nine branch libraries in the Dallas Public Library System and from all of the small suburban communities surrounding the city of Dallas as well as from hundreds of miles away across the state of Texas.

In the Project Evaluator's Report of March 1, 1972,[1] it was noted that the demand for this service was a "stimulated" demand, and, therefore, once the Library introduced independent study through

[1] Betty J. Maynard, "Evaluator's Report: Independent Study Project" (report presented to the National Interest Council of the Dallas Public Library Independent Study Project, Dallas, Texas, March 1, 1972), p. 1.

the mass media, community contacts, and to library users through posters and informational brochures, this stimulus was operable without limitation to geographical area. This "stimulated" demand was to be utilized throughout the Project until the time users themselves became familiar enough with the concept of independent study that they created their own demands. Once the student became independent enough to voice his own needs, a profile of the independent student began slowly to emerge. While, conceptually, the *number* of students involved in the study was not the primary consideration or criteria for measurement of success of the Project, it must be recognized that the *number* of students *did* exert a profound sub rosa influence upon the Independent Study Project throughout its duration.

At the close of the first three months of the Independent Study Project, over 1,000 pieces of CLEP information had been taken from the five branch libraries, and by the end of the first six months the five libraries had received inquiries from 763 individuals, either in person or by telephone. It was of some concern to the librarian that so few interested persons had come to the libraries to make use of this opportunity for continuing learning. It was also of some concern that "Without their reading list in hand they [independent students] are indistinguishable from regular patrons," and that, while the incidence of persons requesting information was small, even a lesser number returned to the library to use materials.[2] Statistical records of the five branch libraries indicated that of those 763 early inquiries, only 53 were concerned with reader's services. At this time the first evaluation report was suggesting that, since the librarian had little or no contact with those persons coming to the library beyond satisfying their informational needs about ISP/CLEP, there was no relationship between student and librarian developing, from which student characteristics might be described. It was also indicated that, perhaps, the user who came to the library to ask questions and to pick up informational materials was apparently not returning to pursue study.

Within the concept and proposal there also were incorporated those special resources which the independent student might need

---

[2]Betty J. Maynard, "Evaluator's Report: Independent Study Project," (March 1, 1972), p. 1.

for help with his study. At the close of the first six months of the Project, 2484 Study Guides/Reading Lists had been taken from the libraries, but no one knew whether any independent student had checked out a book. The Project had also emphasized tutoring as one of the resources available for student use at no charge, but no one had requested this service. The initial concept was that, while individual tutoring should be available for those requesting it, most of the tutor sessions would be preferably in small groups as directed by student demand. With no demand being evidenced by the students, it became the "guessing game" of librarians and the Project Director to assess which areas of study might be of interest and need to the student. Ideally, of course, while the student was directing the librarian to his areas of need, the Project Office would be coordinating with Southern Methodist University. Resources planned for the Project would be offered along with carefully guided directions provided by the librarian so that the student could become independent in his choice and use of the resources. To that end, the first workshops were planned to prepare the student to engage in the process of independent study for learning. The first session was on How to Study Effectively and was conducted by a member of the faculty of Southern Methodist University's Department of Psychology. It remained the stellar performance of the entire Independent Study Project with an attendance of 68 persons. Two subsequent workshops at this same branch library (Audelia Road), one on The Use of the Library and a second on Effective Ways of Reading Books (for study), showed dropped attendance to 20 to 21 persons, and succeeding sessions continued to drop in attendance.

At the close of the first six months of the Independent Study Project not only was the independent student not giving direction as to where he wanted to go, but no one really knew anything about him except that he was excited and eager to study for "credit," he expected to "enroll" in library "classes," and he had great difficulty understanding what "independent" study was all about. He would brook no delay in taking his Study Guide/Reading List from the library, and he seemed to disappear into thin air when he left with it in his hand. It was also noted that this prospective student was eager to talk about himself, particularly when protected by the anonymity of the telephone. The one basic need of immediate urgency each student expressed was to know where to obtain credit for his study; the library could not meet this need. Therefore, the input that had been expected from the student/ librarian relationships was not forthcoming, and the one-to-one working rapport between student and librarian did not materialize.

If there ever were a time at which the Project Office and the Library could have adopted a passive attitude with an "It won't work" response, the close of the first six months was that time. However, there were participants in the Project, even though the number of interested persons was small in relationship to system figures for circulation and registration. If the Library were failing them, the Project needed to define reasons for that failure; if the Library were not failing the students, the Project needed to define the apparent lack of a market or the inability to make contact with the student.

It was, therefore, evident that, if the Independent Study Project were to function as a study which could be evaluated at all, some means of reaching the student for information on his interests and progress would have to be devised. Likewise, if the Project and the librarians were ever to work with the independent student in any meaningful way, some measure of feedback was necessary. It was deemed important at this time to relax the restraints on the evaluation area which had stemmed from the earlier decision not to question the students. Protection of the individual's personal freedom now would rely upon his approval of questioning which he had granted by signing a postcard. At the same time, the risk that such questioning would turn him away from the Project would have to be taken. It was recognized by all personnel involved that, since this was a *study* of a *possible* library service, risks to the service had to be identified and absorbed in order that some measure of "study" could take place.

Throughout the succeeding months of the Project questions usually exceeded answers, one answer leading to further questions in developing and creating growth in the original concepts of independent study. Throughout this same time the suggestions, interest, and advice gained from the Project's Advisory Committee and the National Interest Council were of invaluable help, but all involved with ISP were continually in need of recalling that the Project was a time-limited study. The calendar simply did not allow this new service to develop as a slow, natural, and gradual assimilation into the libraries. Consequently there was not time for the gradual acceptance and understanding of the student, which could have come with normal growth of a service. ISP had to — quite consciously — stimulate demands.

By the close of the first six months' period of the Project, 411 persons had filled out postcards indicating their names, addresses, and agreement to answer evaluation questions. By the end of the ninth month 1,200 persons were on the mailing list to whom a questionnaire[3] was mailed. The answers received from this mailing enabled the Project Evaluator to report a profile of those individuals indicating interest in independent study. During that same period the number and scope of workshops were increased. A Brochure[4] describing how the Project functioned and a monthly newsletter (*ISP NEWS*),[5] which was designed to maintain continuing contact with students, were developed. Branch library statistics[6] indicated that by June, 1972, 4,800 pieces of CLEP information and 3,434 Student Guides/Reading Lists had been taken by interested persons and that librarians had answered 1,786 inquiries, of which 130 were noted as "reader guidance." The number of workshops had been increased to one a month at each of the five participating branch libraries; these covered subject areas which had shown the most activity as measured by the numbers of Study Guides/Reading Lists taken from the libraries.

Through the use of the ISP Brochure and the *ISP News*, industry and business, social organizations, and persons on the mailing list were alerted to specific information about the Independent Study Project and its relationship to CLEP. The *ISP News* provided continuing information on workshops and other community educational happenings and served as a "carrot" for new persons to sign a postcard placing them on the mailing list (this in turn, of course, would provide numbers of interested persons for future evaluation). The *ISP News* also encouraged feedback from the

[3]Addendum

[4]Addendum

[5]Addendum

[6]Addendum

independent student to the librarians at the five branches. At the same time, through the larger number of workshop sessions, personal contacts with the students grew. These contacts provided another source of information on the student and his interests and needs and another place for encouraging the student to provide feedback to the library.

The return on the questionnaire was not large, but statistics on the independent student were reported in the Project Evaluator's report of September, 1973,[7] and those statistics provided the first profile of the independent student. It was interesting to note that these figures related closely to estimated figures on those students attending workshops. The average student in ISP was found to be a female who was employed full-time as a clerical worker. The age range of this average student was from 41 to 50 years of age; she probably had some college experience, but usually had not received a degree.

Over-all statistics from the questionnaire answers are presented in four graphs (Tables 3-1 — 3-4) on pages 46 through 49.

Persons attending workshops also showed the broad age range indicated in the questionnaire, with students from the late 'teens to the 60's. Occasionally, a pre-teen school student came with parents. The median estimated age was 35 to 45 with tapering off at each end of the age scale. Approximately 70 percent were female, and the percentage of minority groups was estimated to be in the 10 percent range. Most of these participants from minority groups were female, in the 20 to 40 year age range. There was variation in library neighborhood minority attendance. Preston Royal and Audelia Road Branch Libraries, both situated in the northern sections of Dallas and both in neighborhoods of middle-middle to lower upper class, probably had a minority attendance of 1 percent. Hampton-Illinois and Oak Lawn, representing neighborhoods of changing residence bordering on both Black and Mexican-American neighborhoods, approximated 10 percent minority, and Crossroads Learning Center, situated in a largely Black neighborhood, drew less than a 1 percent white attendance, the

[7]Betty J. Maynard, "Report to the National Interest Council" (report presented to the National Interest Council of the Dallas Public Library Independent Study Project, Dallas, Texas, September 15, 1972).

An independent student of retirement age pedals her way to the Southern Methodist University library to study for the American Government CLEP examination.

remainder being Black. In this last branch, most of the sessions were attended by all females, but in two instances the attendance was totally male. (These two sessions were one on How to Use the Library and another on Afro-American History, and both sessions drew high interest from those men attending.)

The background experiences of those participants in the workshop sessions were as varied as the individuals themselves. There were free-lance writers, teachers, students, sometimes entire families, professional persons, clerical workers, blue collar workers, veterans, housewives, retired persons, and proprietors of small businesses, and once even a nursing baby. Again, as indicated by the questionnaire respondents, some had a high school education, others had from 3 hours to two or more years of college credit. As interaction with the student became more personal, it was discovered that in *all* five of the library neighborhoods some students did not have a high school diploma. These latter people were of extreme interest in that they were often functioning in responsible supervisory positions over persons with college degrees.

TABLE 3—1

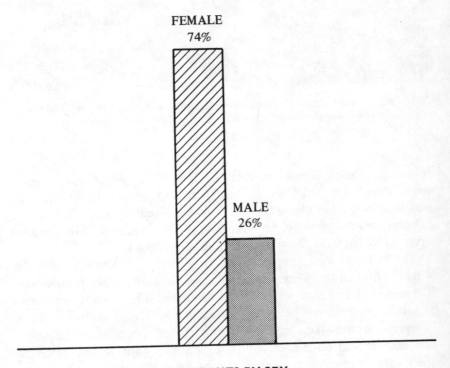

FEMALE
74%

MALE
26%

PARTICIPANTS BY SEX

TABLE 3–2

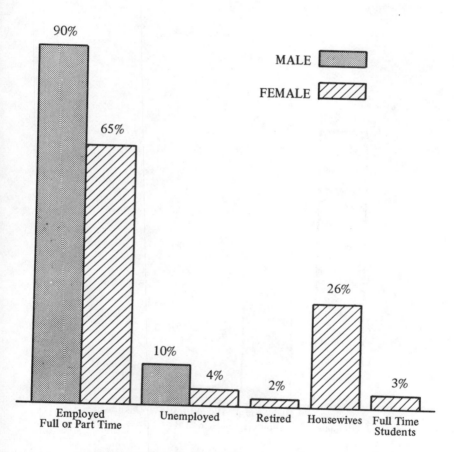

PARTICIPANTS BY EMPLOYMENT AND SEX

TABLE 3—3

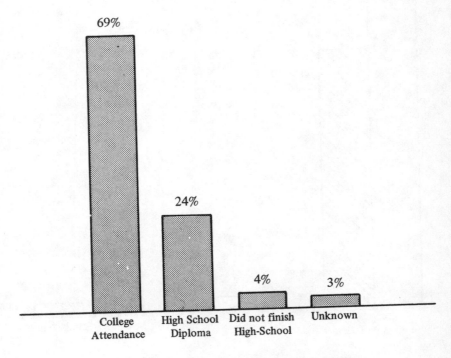

PARTICIPANTS BY EDUCATIONAL LEVEL

TABLE 3—4

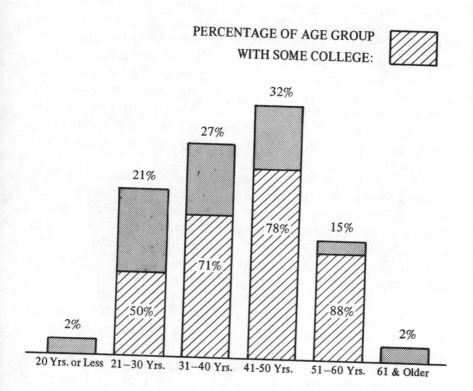

PERCENTAGE OF AGE GROUP
WITH SOME COLLEGE:

PARTICIPANTS BY AGE GROUPS AND COLLEGE EXPERIENCE

While native ability and experiential learning had provided them with the expertise to function in these positions, they felt a lack within themselves and a need for higher education. Personal contacts were to indicate that the lack of education for these persons resulted in a sense of shame, a fear of divulging the truth.

Personal contacts were to remind personnel throughout the Project of the very broad range of ability levels and interests of the students and of the fact that, while ISP might strive to profile the students as to where the majority might stand in age and background, their individual characteristics and needs were as varied as their numbers. While common strands might cross the texture of all the neighborhoods being served, each independent student had to be regarded as an individual and served on that basis. While the study was attempting to identify a group, the service was teaching the librarians that they must always identify with the individual. At the same time, those librarians giving the service must be evaluating and consciously understanding the needs being expressed and how they were aiding each individual within his own learning process.

There were varying goals and expectations expressed by students involved in the Project. Librarians expressed dismay early in the Project at the number who came expecting to "get quick credits." The questionnaire indicated that over 68 percent of the respondents intended to take a CLEP examination for college credit. Seventy-five percent of the remaining students had other goals for which they wished to use this learning opportunity. Fifty percent of them indicated study for personal interests, 10 percent were using the Study Guides/Reading Lists as supplementary aids in formal education courses, and 5 percent were using the Library Project for job-related information.

Those students attending workshop sessions were also indicating CLEP testing for credit as the major end goal, and in most instances the credit or degree was for the purpose of job-upgrading. Other persons, while interested in the degree or credit for job-related purposes, were not actually motivated by economic considerations. One such noneconomic consideration might have been a case as mentioned earlier where the student supervised persons with degrees, was ashamed of his lack of education, which in turn led to doubts about his ability to perform at top level without additional learning. In an other instance, the prospective learner might be the eldest in a family, the first out of high school and into a paying job, who subsequently found himself working to educate his brothers and sisters. Now, perhaps, he could find a way to pursue the formal education he had always wanted. Finances would not permit him to quit his present employment to pursue a full-time education. Moreover, he had been away from formal education so long he might be fearful of his success. The Library offered free resources and a non-threatening atmosphere where he could test his learning wings. Some men in mid-career desired a change in what they found themselves doing; they had begun to see a career as more than an eight to four job. They were seeking intellectual challenge opposed to the daily routine which now was not offering personal satisfaction. Some housewives with small children at home considered the possibility of a future career; women were no longer "stuck" at home in a single role of homemaker for the remainder of their lives. Sometimes a returning veteran found he needed to upgrade his abilities, had found new interests during his service years, or had to upgrade his earlier basic learning to a recognized high school equivalency level via acquiring, through examinations, a General Equivalency Diploma (GED). As one young married veteran described it, "I was too bullheaded to admit I needed an education, but now I know I do." Often, older and retired persons who had never had an opportunity to obtain a formal education liked the idea of trying for a college degree or at least some credit toward it. Others, nearing retirement, were considering preparation for a new career in a small business or in real estate.

Sometimes people were interested in learning about their fellow man, and, while this might be job-related interest, more often it was not. These students were interested in psychology and sociology, sometimes as a backup for volunteer work in which they were engaged. They had a desire to be better informed. Often it was a situation at home which the student did not feel comfortable in handling — perhaps an aging parent or a retarded or autistic child — so there was a need to relate with a greater confidence to the immediate environment. Frequently the need and the goal was to reassert "self" in a more meaningful manner through learning something new and engrossing, a need to get out of the rut of trivia.

Whatever the goal or need which motivated the individual to respond to independent study, he came to the library because this was the place where he was *ready* to start his learning experience. Generally, these were not new feelings of need, but, perhaps, they had now for the first time been articulated. The individual came to the library because it was not a threatening environment. He may have already had a positive experience there, he was under no obligation, and this decision he made was not so final that he could not back out.

Concern was frequently expressed by persons outside the Project that the close tie with a credit program could contribute to the encouragement of false values for some students. It was of interest to note that many independent students had already developed status, had a standing within their local communities, and were not using their learning experiences for reasons of image making. They were not always as impressed with the degree, per se, as one might have expected. Most of them were engaged in working at a job where they felt important, but they felt a need for greater expertise. In actual fact, the majority were quite conscious of the value system. But, if the learning they achieved would aid them to function more capably on the job they were performing, with a minimal time out of a busy life and a minimum of repetition of previous experiential learning, they were pleased. Underlying all of the expressed goals and expectations was the need for self enhancement through growth in knowledge.

The goal distances for individual students were varied. Sometimes the distance was no greater than a single credit course for expertise on the job; at other times it was an associate degree requiring two years of credit representing a step up on the job hierarchy; for many it was in terms of a real life outside employment situation that needed further identification. Perhaps this latter need could be described as a desire to reach a consciousness level for a particular situation, or a need to establish an environment within which one could relate with confidence. The emphasis was not always on the "course" but most frequently the content. Perhaps all of this is telling the Library to be less concerned with decision making and goals *for* the student and more concerned with listening to the concerns he brings to us about his needs for knowledge. Malcolm Knowles, in speaking of "Andragogy versus Pedagogy," states,

The problem-orientation of the learners implies that the most appropriate starting point for every learning experience is the problems and concerns that the adults have on their minds as they enter.[8]

Later Knowles also states,

Learning is described psychologically as a process of need-meeting and goal-striving by the learner . . . an individual is motivated to engage in learning to the extent that he feels a need to learn and perceives a personal goal that learning will help to achieve; and he will invest his energy in making use of available resources (including teachers and readings) to the extent that he perceives them as being relevant to his needs and goals.[9]

The "problem" the independent student brings to the independent learning opportunity may hold an answer to the "structure/nonstructure" of the new "curricula," the content or direction for group sessions. Cyril Houle, in his book *The Inquiring Mind*,[10] speaks of the "goal-oriented" individual whose "knowledge is to be put to use," and he also indicates that the goal includes "understanding." This need for understanding has been most obviously the motivation for the major portion of those who entered independent study; that need to understand has been seen as a desire to function with greater assurance. Houle divides persons deeply engaged in continuing education into three subgroups. As he states it:

They all had goals which they wished to achieve, they all found the process of learning enjoyable or significant, and they all felt that learning was worthwhile for its own sake.[11]

[8]Malcolm S. Knowles, *The Modern Practice of Adult Education: Andragogy Versus Pedagogy* (New York: Association Press, 1970), p. 49.

[9]*Ibid.*, pp. 50-51.

[10]Cyril O. Houle, *The Inquiring Mind* (Madison, Wisconsin: University of Wisconsin Press, 1961), p. 16.

[11]*Ibid.*, p. 15.

Houle's three sub-groups were the "goal-oriented," or those who used education as a means of accomplishing fairly clear-cut objectives; the "activity-oriented," or those who used group learning situations primarily for social contacts; and the "learning- oriented" who had a "desire to know" underlying their continual and varying educational activities. The strength of this "desire to know" was operant in the individual's drive to achieve his expectations independently. In addition to those whom we might consider goal or learning oriented were other individuals who appeared unable to articulate their expectations. Possibly, many of these were the "activity-oriented" mentioned by Houle, who were seeking a relationship which was not content-oriented. Included in this group, however, were persons who undoubtedly had an unidentified need which independent study might help articulate and work toward meeting.

Resources within the library for the independent student were books in the regular collection, special Study Guides/Reading Lists prepared by faculty members from Southern Methodist University, informational materials on the College-Level Examination Program provided by the College Entrance Examination Board, college and university catalogs which were part of the regular library collections, film strip tapes on area colleges specially prepared for ISP, and the availability upon request of tutoring in groups or individually by Southern Methodist University faculty members. Within the Project those users of the library who indicated they were studying in, or were interested in independent study through the use of any of these resources, were described as "independent students" purely for means of identification. In one instance, in referring to those library users as a group, the Project Director designated them as a "student body," simply implying a body or number of persons engaged in studying independently. An independent student, then, was an individual who had identified himself to the librarians in the five participating branches or to the Project Office as being engaged in studying independently.

When it came to needs for those library resources available, the individuals involved in independent study roughly divided themselves into two groups. There were individuals engaged in trying out this new approach who came to the library with enough learning expertise that they were already "independent" learners.

They quickly understood the concept of CLEP, made use of whatever special resources they found applicable to their particular situation, located their own books from the shelves, perhaps took tests and earned credits, and identified themselves months later or not at all. Unless these individuals signed a postcard indicating their involvement with the Project, the libraries had no means of identifying them. Too, names were not always taken at workshops.

The second type of student was more easily identified because he had put himself on the mailing list by signing a card. He told of having taken a test, he called to ask for information or to praise or criticize, or he made personal contact with the librarian, at which time he identified himself as an independent student. While there was a measure of overlap from one group to the other, this second group of students required additional helps because they were less assured, were unfamiliar with academic vocabulary, could not easily find their way around a campus, and often were uncertain of how to delineate goals. Special informational materials on academic information[12] were provided for the librarians at the five branch libraries and for those students requiring help in approaching an academic institution. A minimal amount of in-library counseling was also offered through the services of the Retired Senior Volunteers Program (RSVP). All of these resources were offered in the context of what Illich describes as "convivial tools."[13] They were in the library for the use of the student should he choose to utilize them. The student was free to organize the tools into any form he should direct so as to optimize his particular learning process. The student was responsible for the spontanaeity of the learning process he developed for himself. At no time in the Project should the "helps" take from the student that serendipitous experience when his learning "fell into a pattern," as one student expressed it — that moment of excitement of discovering independently the joy of learning.

The student relied upon the library for information. One form of information within the concept, and described in the proposal, was the College Information Center. The Centers, however, were not

---

[12]Addendum

[13]Ivan Illich, *Tools for Conviviality*, World Perspectives, Vol. 47, (New York: Harper, 1973), p. 12.

particularly successful. The Dallas Public Library system had no expert on varying types of media hardware and software on its staff. Consequently, when the time arrived to use the Centers, it was discovered that the film strips were out of date and the lenses were incorrect for the space available in which to use the projectors (in two of the branch libraries there was absolutely no space available for the projectors). It became clear at once that the films were totally unsuitable for this independent student. He was not at all interested in the usual information about the student union and the swimming pool. The independent student wanted to know exactly how many credits he could earn through CLEP and which courses he must take to earn the type of degree suited to that area of endeavor in which he was interested. To assist the student, the Project Office developed a pamphlet which included all credit information from colleges and universities in the area, the name of at least one sympathetic counselor at each institution, and a glossary of academic terms to help him find his way around a campus.[14]

The Dallas Public Library's Independent Study Project functioned on the principle that information inputs to the student should provide him with a measure of beginning reassurance toward his own information gathering inputs. The Project provided him with such basics as places, people, and vocabulary through which he could learn to assess and locate the types of informational needs he had and from which he could provide decision making inputs applicable to his goals. By the close of the Project, the student was obtaining information from the librarians on CLEP and area credit allowances. Earlier in the Project, however, when credits were either not available at area colleges and universities or were in such short availability that inquiring students were being "given the run-around" at the area academic institutions, the independent student became the successful advocate for granting CLEP credit in the Dallas area.

Steady information and referral which could not be handled at the branch libraries was done at the Project Office. Calls averaged 100 per month on all types of educational information from the General Equivalency Diploma through the Graduate Record

[14]Denver Public Library's "On Your Own Program" later included in an information booklet for use by their librarians even parking conditions on the various campuses.

Examinations. Frequently, this telephone information service became a one-to-one "advising" service. More and more the student was using the librarians and the Project Office personnel to discuss educational problems and to seek reassurance in starting a new learning project. Many persons said they had been seeking such information as ISP was able to give them for periods from two to three months. This customer input suggested to all those involved in ISP that a need for centralized reliable educational information existed within the community. The Library appeared to be the agency which could function as a coordinating center for such one-to-one information needs as were being evidenced. Referrals from area colleges and universities on educational questions which might have been answered somewhere on their own campuses were verifying their acceptance of such a Library centered informational agency.

Judging from the number of Study Guides/Reading Lists taken from the library, the independent student was also relying heavily upon this special resource. By the close of the Project, 6,000 guides had been taken. However, a telephone questionnaire based on a sampling of independent students six months prior to the close of the study indicated that 65 percent had picked up Study Guides/Reading Lists, but only 25 percent were actively pursuing study.[15] It is of interest to note that, while branch library statistics show 6,000 guides taken out, the number of guides remaining at the Project Office at the close of the Project indicated that over 8,400 actually were distributed. While distribution of guides to individuals was discouraged at the Project Office (so that independent students would relate to a branch library rather than an office) that restriction was lifted in hardship cases where an individual could not get to a particular branch library or worked in town and traveled to and from the central city by bus. Allowances for possible branch error and those guides given out at the Project Office could account for the 2,400 additional guides.

Students were also using books in the library. Sixty-seven percent of those respondents to the mailed questionnaire indicated they

[15]Jean Brooks and Betty J. Maynard, "Final Report to the National Interest Council" (report presented to the National Interest Council of the Dallas Public Library Independent Study Project, Dallas, Texas, September 13, 1973), pp. 10-11.

An armed forces veteran checks out books from Hampton-Illinois Branch Library to use in independent study.
Gene Shelton, photographer

were using books from the library,[16] and the Project Evaluator's final report to the National Interest Council showed 40 percent using library books for study.[17] As mentioned earlier in this chapter, the independent student could not always be identified. Spot checks of the library shelves at the five branch libraries indicated absence of books on independent study Reading Lists in many subject areas — mathematics, American history, American government, accounting, and psychology — but these were also books which would have been used by students affiliated with formal educational institutions. The librarians felt that these shortages had no validity in reference to use by ISP students. Statistics showed that only 58 books had been borrowed through inter-agency requests by the close of the Project: 28 by Crossroads Learning Center, 26 by Oak Lawn, three by Hampton-Illinois, and one by Preston Royal. Preston Royal had purchased two books on marketing, and Oak Lawn had purchased two books for ISP, one of which was an English literature anthology. One independent student, in response to the telephone questionnaire at the close of the 18th month, stated, "The books on your reading lists are very hard to locate. Seems there is often a waiting list on many." That same questionnaire indicated that 60 percent of the respondents found the books they wanted, but 13 percent of the respondents indicated they could not.[18] Unavailability of books was a complaint that was heard from time to time in calls to the Project Office or by participants at workshop sessions. Reliance of students upon the library for books was not always satisfied, and some students either bought books they wanted or in some instances had access to an academic institution for resources. For the unaffiliated independent student, the inability to obtain books from the only resource available to him (usually the public library) could totally frustrate his independent study. Additionally, the time needed with books was greater than for the normal user, so inability to renew a much wanted book would also be a deterrent to study.

[16]Betty J. Maynard, "Report to the National Interest Council" (September 15, 1972), p. 8.

[17]Jean Brooks and Betty J. Maynard, "Final Report to the National Interest Council" (September 13, 1973), p. 11.

[18]Betty J. Maynard, "Report to the National Interest Council" (March 8, 1973), p. 4.

THE PUBLIC LIBRARY IN NON-TRADITIONAL EDUCATION

Recognizing that some of the independent students who were still largely dependent upon the library for help needed what would be considered academic counseling, ISP solicited the aid of Retired Senior Volunteers from the newly formed RSVP organization in Dallas. The Project was fortunate in gaining the services of a retired teacher with a Masters Degree in Counseling. Once again, through the *ISP News*, word of this new resource was spread to the independent student. Through this close involvement with a counseling effort, more about the expressed needs evinced by the students was learned. Usually their requirements were simple, but they had need for someone to act as a sounding board as they explored their interests, their abilities, and their experiences. Often, as they vocalized those assets and interests they possessed, it became apparent to them, with careful input of options open from the counselor, what they would like to do. Sometimes, they took more time to consider what had been discussed, but in all instances they made a decision quickly. This type of counseling was time consuming, and usually the individual requesting it had a busy time schedule. The counselor volunteer, because she was retired, was able to adjust her schedule to the convenience of the student and was free to give all the time required. Sometimes the counselor and the student met at a neighborhood library, if it were convenient, and the library they used was not always one of those participating in the study. At other times they met over luncheon or in some other spot convenient to both. On occasion the counselor considered that the next step for the student was to meet with someone at the college or university of his choice. In that event the student was referred to one of those persons on the ISP list of counselors from area colleges and universities. Professors from Southern Methodist University in all subject departments were also available for consultation. In many instances students consulted with these faculty members for help in evaluating their progress in study or obtained help from them over a rough spot in their study.

By the close of the Project, 1,066 persons had attended workshops.[19] It can be concluded, then, that the workshops were one of the library resources which were used by the independent student. The workshops were also used by library users and

19The term "workshop" is used interchangeably throughout this book with the term "help session" to denote group meetings designed to aid the independent student in his study.

non-users who did not intend to become independent students but were simply interested in the subjects covered. In some instances these non-independent students contributed considerably to interest in learning for all who attended. These sessions were offered to the student as a resource through which he might learn more about independent study. At no time were they intended to be "classes" or instruction on subject matter. Subjects covered included the library usage ones mentioned earlier, how to study independently, and how to effectively use books for study. One session on financial aid to students, including bank loans, was done by request for learners at Crossroads Learning Center. Another one, on test taking, was presented at several of the five branches because many of the people preparing for CLEP had never taken this type of computer-scored test. The subject matter of the remaining sessions was spread over the varying discipline areas covered by the Study Guides and the CLEP tests, with one noteable exception. In response to an *ISP News* query, a highly motivated group came together to learn about creative writing, and at the close of the Project they were scheduling their own meetings with the librarian to continue throughout the remainder of the year.

The workshop sessions were conducted in an easy going, informal question and answer format intended to extend the information in the guide about the subject being considered. At the same time the concept was that the needs of the students would be met. If the Project were attempting to offer a broad concept of a discipline which meant slow and careful study, letting interest lead where it might, then student need for areas of subject expertise required by a test was being met in a round about fashion. The student wanted to know how to pass the test; ISP wanted him to acquire a broad knowledge. The first test taker to report back to us had prepared herself for the American History test using the Study Guide/ Reading List. While she recognized the calibre of learning she had accomplished, she reported that she had "overlearned" for her purposes, which were job related, CLEP oriented, and time limited. That student did deserve a measure of interest directed toward her immediate goals, and the Project had to accept the fact that individual goal expectations might not always coincide with the broader goals of ISP. The more capable student might be using valuable time in over-learning beyond his goal achievement. Once again, those involved in independent study had to be reminded that the student was to be free to choose how he would use his learning; ISP's job was to give him the input he needed.

As the Project developed, the librarians, the SMU professors, and the Project Director found that the student was directing them as to his needs in tutoring and that not everyone who attended a workshop or help session was motivated nor equipped to study independently. One help session ran through four meetings, growing as it went along, but by the end of the sessions not one of the individuals in attendance had made any effort to read between meetings so that he would be better able to ask questions and discuss the subject. Some of the students thought they were being *taught*, but they were not stimulated enough to start studying — and *learning* — on their own. An article on the University of Maryland experiment with the British Open University Concept has this to say:

> On a weekly basis, students and tutors met together to view the film, to air the tape, and to discuss the week's assignment. Lively discussions, long pauses, and puzzled silences occurred at the sessions. Soon the tutors learned not to lecture, and the students learned to question, discuss, and argue.[20]

Too often the help sessions on a particular subject, which students requested for a series of three meetings, ended up with the student listening, followed with long pauses when he was encouraged to contribute. The students wanted to be "told," and they were not interested in putting forth effort to contribute on their own. Involvement of the student himself, it might be concluded, depends to a large degree on his desire to independently learn. The British Open University has a structure on which the student builds; the Dallas learning situation was self-directed by the student. If the student were not self-motivated, and the stimulus of the help session did nothing to arouse motivation, the help session was merely a group meeting where everyone had a good time. But few, if

---

[20]Betty Jo. Mayeske, "Open University Experiment: University of Maryland Reports on British Transplant," *College Board Review*, VI, (Summer, 1973), p. 5.

any, students started a true learning process. Other sessions operated on a good question and answer exchange with an obvious interest in continuing the experience by learning more on the subject. The group session as a learning resource needs careful study.

Tapes of some of the workshops were prepared, but use of them was minimal. Two Study Guides were taped for a blind man who studied in the Project, and subsequently books for his study were taped through coordination with the Regional Library for the Blind and Handicapped. Tapes are surely resources which might prove valuable in this type of studying, but those persons working in such a program as ISP would require orientation to the use of such resources to assure that they became accustomed to their use. Perhaps in programs where academic personnel were not available to the student, tapes would be more acceptable. In ISP, however, the personal contact with the faculty member was very important to the students, and the tape player did not replace it.

It is clear that the librarian was important to the independent student. Inquiries on all phases of his study were directed to the Adult Librarians who worked with the independent students. From them came the referral to other sources of information. Students also used the librarian to help locate those books they wished to take from the library, and all but one respondent to the telephone questionnaire indicated they had received all the information they required.[21] By the end of the Project the librarians had answered inquiries from 3,272 students, had helped them choose 6,000 Study Guides, and had talked and related to the independent student much of their limited disposal time as possible. Also, the student who was critical of librarian attitudes toward him in the first six months of the Project was stopping by during his last period of the Project to talk with the librarian and to report progress in his study.

In general, unless an independent student had a problem with which he needed help, the librarians and/or the Project Office did not hear from him. Size and other obligations of the branch staff normally did not allow for calls to the student to inquire into his progress. Some few students did call or visit a branch library to

---

[21]Betty J. Maynard, "Report to the National Interest Council" (March 8, 1973), p. 3.

express their gratitude for the Independent Study Project. Some wrote letters or postcards or called in to report a successful CLEP test result or acceptance into a college or university with hours of credit earned on their own. In many instances students called to let the Project Director know that a tutoring session had been held and to express their pleasure at a good experience; others reported they were going to take a test. There seemed to be a desire on the part of many of the students to maintain a personal contact because they had had a rewarding experience.

At the close of the two-year Project in September, 1973, the total number of persons on the ISP mailing list had reached 2,300. Since it is certain there were others, the exact number who might have been touched in some way by the Independent Study Project is not known. Response to the Project was always excellent, eliciting responses such as "It's great;" "It's beautiful"; "Why didn't I know about this before"; "It has changed my whole life"; "It's the realization of a lifetime dream". Admittedly others "couldn't get started," "didn't have time," or "started to college instead." For many the interest ran high and appeared to be continuing. In August, 1973 the *ISP News* carried the item that September marked the end of Project funding and that, unless other sources of funding were obtained, the Project would close. Following that message several calls came to the Project Office requesting six to eight Study Guides/Reading Lists in case the supply ran out before the students had completed the goals they had set for themselves. Many who answered questionnaires who were not studying at present liked knowing that the Independent Study Project was there (perhaps it was part of the great American dream). And, there was always that time element of something they would get to later. Often a caller would state, "I am Mr. X, you remember we talked together about three months ago." Coupons from a paid advertisement on ISP came in six, eight months, and even over a year later, apparently pulled out of a safe place where they had been kept until the time was "right." One hundred persons a month had signed cards showing an interest in independent study. During the last six months of the Project there had been no publicity, and still around 60 persons per month were signing postcards indicating their interest in ISP. The news was now traveling by word of mouth.

Achievement of goals was almost necessarily measured by the taking of a CLEP examination because ISP could check test takers against names on the mailing list. At the end of the Project it was known that 105 persons who had taken CLEP tests were also on the ISP mailing list. A total of 257 tests were taken in 27 subject areas; this was the equivalent of 1,205 credit hours. Translated into years of credit, independent students had taken CLEP examinations equivalent to 40 years of college credit at an approximate cost to all students of $3,285.00. Quoting from the *Final Report to the National Interest Council,*

> It was noted that the time of entry into ISP until examination date was in the range of 1 month, 2 months, 6 months, 3 months, 5 months, and on up to 1 year or more for some individuals . . .

> The following table will illustrate test-takers from entry into ISP in relation to test period broken down into 6 months' periods. Those who took several tests within one 6 months' period are not repeated.22

TABLE 3—5

Time of Test	Test—Takers	Time of Entry
First Six Months	2	First Six Months
	Total: 2	
Second Six Months	6	First Six Months
	12	Second Six Months
	Total: 18	
Third Six Months	5	First Six Months
	10	Second Six Months
	15	Third Six Months
	Total: 30	
Fourth Six Months	4	First Six Months
	5	Second Six Months
	24	Third Six Months
	25	Fourth Six Months
	Total: 58	

22Jean Brooks and Betty Maynard, "Final Report to the National Interest Council" (September 13, 1973), pp. 4-5.

Other students indicated rewards or achievement of less measureable goals, such as the discovery of the excitement of a breakthrough into the realization of the learning process, the ability to relate better to fellow workers, the pride in the fact that they could study independently, and the knowledge that this was an engrossing way of life which was "fun." Branch librarians were reporting visits from students who had "brought a friend," and sons and daughters of students were becoming involved with ISP. Most important to those involved in the Independent Study Project at the libraries was the recognition of the desire of those who had had a good experience to come and share it with the librarian. Often a conversation would open with "I just had to let you know" — a sharing of an educational or learning experience which is not the usual behavior for people who are continuing learners because it tends to make them appear "different."

In the library situated in a predominantly Black community CLEP was not proved successful, probably because the rewards were too distant. Achievement was largely for economic gain, and the experiences which were necessary to achieve on CLEP examinations were rarely relevant to the experience of the individual in that neighborhood. These students, as others across the five branch neighborhoods, had expected from CLEP promotional literature that their past experience would have prepared them to take and do well on the tests. They came to the library to find out how to get those "instant credits" only to find out that most of what they had learned in life was not "curriculum" oriented. Some became discouraged and dropped from the program, even though the librarian spent time helping them to learn. Others tried the tests and found their scores were not acceptable for credit. They felt betrayed by a promise. One student worked for eight months and did achieve a creditable score on a CLEP test, and at the end of another eight months was prepared to take another CLEP examination. The not inconsequential achievement of a few was that they gained enough confidence to enter a formal institution where they could receive the continuing backup and support they required. Through the Library they were introduced to formal education; at some later stage some of them may return as continuing learners.

THE INDEPENDENT STUDENT

The need of many of these people was for the basic tools which were developed in the General Equivalency Diploma program. GED workshops were developed by a Committee consisting of two Retired Senior Volunteers, both former teachers, a 21 year old young man who, engaged in independent study himself, volunteered to help tutor, and the Project Director and Secretary. From the workshop sessions a "guide" to studying independently for the GED evolved. Several of the participating learners took their tests, passed them, and came back to share their experiences with the other learners. Later, one of these students volunteered to tutor at the library and eventually had a group studying for the GED and for Civil Service Examinations. Through independent study the student was enabled to assess where he was, where he wanted to go, and to achieve his goal. From there he was free to choose whatever level of learning he desired to pursue.

As the Project moved, more individuals from the community came to offer volunteer services to help someone else learn. Some were teachers who were employed full-time, lawyers, an electrical engineer, and a college professor; all who wanted to become "involved" in their community. During the last summer of the Project students home from college volunteered their services, and the Project was able to fill most of the tutoring requests at both GED and CLEP levels through the help of these volunteers. The Independent Study Project, through the five branch libraries, was reaching people in the community who had a desire to learn. It involved them with each other and with others in the community who wanted to help further a community of learning. Numbers might have been small, but the impact of individual expressions of excitement and involvement with studying to learn was continually growing, and it was strong. The Library and the librarian in cooperation with the academic community were functioning as a learning unit. Weaknesses in meeting student needs were apparent, but those weaknesses were pointing to new ideas for support services which could offer the student more of a continuum of aid and a broader range of resources relevant to his needs.

BIBLIOGRAPHY

Brooks, Jean and Betty J. Maynard. "Final Report to the National Interest Council." Report presented to the National Interest Council of the Dallas Public Library Independent Study Project, Dallas, Texas, September 13, 1973.

Denver Public Library's "On Your Own Program" later included in an information booklet for use by their librarians.

Houle, Cyril O. *The Inquiring Mind.* Madison, Wisconsin: University of Wisconsin Press, 1961.

Illich, Ivan. *Tools for Conviviality.* World Perspectives, Vol. 47, New York: Harper and Row, 1973.

Knowles, Malcolm S. *The Modern Practice of Adult Education: Andragogy Versus Pedagogy.* New York: Association Press, 1970.

Mayeske, Betty Jo. "Open University Experiment: University of Maryland Reports on British Transplant." *College Board Review,* VI (Summer, 1973).

Maynard, Betty J. "Evaluator's Report: Independent Study Project." Report presented to the National Interest Council of the Dallas Public Library Independent Study Project, Dallas, Texas, March 1, 1972.

Maynard, Betty J. "Report to the National Interest Council." Report presented to the National Interest Council of the Dallas Public Library Independent Study Project, Dallas, Texas, September 15, 1972.

Maynard, Betty J. "Report to the National Interest Council." Report presented to the National Interest Council of the Dallas Public Independent Study Project, Dallas, Texas, March 8, 1973.

Chapter 4

❦❦❦❦ ❦❦❦❦❦❦❦❦❦❦ ❦❦❦❦❦❦ ❦❦

The Library

Five Branch Libraries of the Dallas Public Library System were to serve as "environments" for independent study which would be representative of a welcoming atmosphere conducive to a relaxed and informal continuing learning situation. The libraries would be the ground against which the librarian would serve and come to know the needs of the independent student. Here, also, the student engaged in studying on his own would come to seek help and use the resources he required for his learning experience. There was a wide range in size, materials budget, and number of volumes among the five participating branches, and the neighborhoods and population sizes and makeup they served were also varied.

PARTICIPATING BRANCHES

Agency	Bldg. Size Sq. Ft.	Staff*	Collection Bks.	Pers.	Mtls. Bdgt.	Served**
Audelia Road	13,100	14	58,100	165	$47,100	38,400
Crossroads*** Learning Center	3,800	5.5	23,900	80	15,200	22,200
Hampton–Illinois	11,200	14	67,000	160	36,300	53,300
Oak Lawn	3,200	7	31,900	91	18,000	23,400
Preston Royal	12,400	13.5	76,300	162	40,600	50,100

*FTE (Two Pages = one full–time)
**Population served —— NOT population in service area
***Does not include The Learning Scene, a mobile unit.

TABLE 4–1

The five libraries would be the physical environments, the facilitating agencies in which the students would have their introduction to the concept of independent study and which they would use as their Learning Resource Centers. Each of the participating branches had a good general basic book collection which would serve as the primary resource for the student. No additions specifically for ISP were to be made to these collections unless student demand indicated a need,[1] but the participating branch libraries were free to borrow from agencies in the total library system (nine other branch libraries and the Central Library). In addition, the book collections of the five branch libraries engaged in the study were representative of needs expressed within those neighborhoods they served, and book selection policies were broad enough to allow for this branch library autonomy. As mentioned in Chapter 2, the branch libraries were described in the proposal as "serving different socio-economic communities" but, as noted in Chapter 3, since many independent students came into the five participating libraries from all sections of the city of Dallas and surrounding suburbs, the five branches often served only an orientation function for the students. Gradually, as the Project progressed, some differences in library use indicative of each library's neighborhood did begin to emerge.

As shown in Table 4-1, each branch library working with ISP, differed in size: the *Oak Lawn Branch Library* was the smallest.[2] Through the all-glass front of the library the outlook was toward a heavily traveled, six lane thoroughfare bordered with business establishments. The library itself was next door to a large grocery store, and, since there was no parking available at the library, patrons used the grocery parking lot. The neighborhood which Oak Lawn Branch Library served was rapidly changing in character. Once-lovely, old homes were being torn down to make way for modern apartment houses and condominiums, and the neighborhood proximity to central Dallas made the Oak Lawn area a prime choice for young people working in the city. A park and the Dallas Theater Center were near the library, and the community Oak Lawn Branch Library served boasted a sprinkling of young adults

---

[1]The decision not to "stack the deck" is described in Chapter Two.

[2]A new, large facility is currently in the design phase for this Branch.

living in their chosen free style in close proximity to beautiful park-like estates. During one summer a Free University flourished in the park. There also was a large Mexican American neighborhood within the Oak Lawn service area (10,000 or 22% of the Oak Lawn population[3]); so the library expressed that cultural need within its book collection. There was not a large Black population within this neighborhood (10% of the Oak Lawn population), but some Black families were beginning to move into apartments and homes there, and there was a Black community within the larger service area of the Branch. There were a large number of young people with college educations in the library neighborhood (census tracts in the area show median number of school years completed running from a low of 8.1 to a high of 13.3), and many of the shops were decorating, art, and antique establishments. Consequently, many of those who lived in the locale of their stores were designers, illustrators, antique collectors, and, as in all artistic neighborhoods, a number of actors. The transient character of the neighborhood was demonstrated by the number of telephones disconnected or of persons who moved away — addressee unknown as illustrated by ISP questionnaire returns.

The Oak Lawn Branch Library was also on a travel route taken by commuters to and from work in the downtown business district of Dallas. During the first six months of ISP, those persons inquiring for independent study information at this branch library came largely from this group of clerical workers who stopped at the library on their ways home to the suburbs. The demographic statistical profile shows that within the Oak Lawn area 36% of the workforce was in sales or clerical occupations, 17 percent in craftsmen-operative occupations, and 12 percent in service type work. The median family income was $6,400. It was noted by the branch librarians that there were many questions regarding credit beyond the CLEP level of the first two years of college. ISP also drew a few of the retired persons living in this neighborhood, some of whom were described as "the regulars" by the librarian. Those who were new to the branch appeared to be in their late 40's

---

[3]Statistics in the branch library profiles used here and below in this chapter come from the "Final Report to the National Interest Council," by Jean Brooks and Betty J. Maynard (September 13, 1973), pp. 20-29.

THE PUBLIC LIBRARY IN NON-TRADITIONAL EDUCATION

TABLE 4—2

CITY OF DALLAS AND OUTLYING SUBURBS

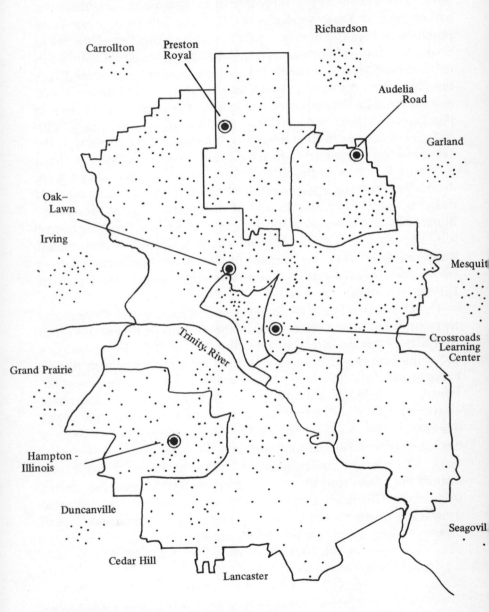

Key -- straight lines represent city limits of Dallas
1 dot equals 2 independent students

72

through the 50's, a few were drop-outs, and most of those interested in independent study were looking for a way to job advancement. There were always one or more Black and Mexican American participants at workshops at Oak Lawn, and the librarian found some who were interested in CLEP. The two librarians who worked with ISP felt that few neighborhood persons had shown interest in independent study. The librarians suggested that this might be because those persons in business and living in the area had a cultural background above the average. The demographic profile suggests that, if it is assumed that ISP/CLEP is potentially for everyone except college graduates, some 20,000 persons in the Oak Lawn service area were potential users.

The Oak Lawn Branch Library did not have an auditorium or meeting room of any sort. There was a staff room which doubled as a supply and work room, but workshop sessions were not feasible in that location of the library. There were two tables for adult patrons and two smaller round tables for children in the library. When independent students met for workshops at Oak Lawn, there was no way in which informality could not reign because everyone sat around the children's tables in low chairs. With 18 or 20 in attendance at a help session, close involvement with the group was inevitable. One of the librarians at this library described the Oak Lawn Branch as a "small town library" since everyone felt at home there. The librarians were on a first name basis with many of their users, checking on them if they learned they were ill or in the hospital. The environment was ready-made for the relaxed and informal atmosphere considered "comfortable" for the independent student. At the front of the library were four lounge chairs, and during the day and evening these chairs were often occupied by one or more of the elderly persons who lived in the Oak Lawn area. The librarian mentioned that some of these people came in day after day, often just sitting quietly without even reading a book or a magazine; they found it a pleasant and companionable place to be.

There was no space available at Oak Lawn Branch Library for the DuKane Projector without utilizing one of the tables at which library users studied. One independent student did spend time at the branch using tapes on a workshop session she had missed, but she was slightly deaf, the tapes were not of top quality, and no earphones were available. The resulting two hours of "listening" experience proved to be a shattering one for librarians and other library users. Space-wise, Oak Lawn was using every spare inch of room it had available, and there was no way to shift space usage to gain another inch.

Books available to the independent student were fewer in number at Oak Lawn than at some of the larger libraries in the ISP study, and (as noted in Chapter 3) the librarians there requested 26 books from other branch libraries in the Dallas Public Library System and added two English Literature anthologies to their collection for use by the independent student. If the number of students studying independently grew large, Oak Lawn might have found its collection needing support, but the small physical size of the library appeared to be no detriment to the students.

Statistics kept by the branch librarians showed that 840 pieces of information on CLEP and 1,050 Study Guides/Reading Lists were taken out of the library. The librarians answered 312 inquiries on independent study during the two years of the study. During that time 21 students took CLEP tests; only four were from outside the Dallas area. These figures on test takers would indicate that many of the "new" users noted by the librarians were unquestionably from the Oak Lawn service area.

Interest in ISP started very slowly at this branch library, and there were no test takers until the second six months' period of ISP with the number gradually increasing to 14 in the final six months of the Project. No one who entered the Project in the first six months from the Oak Lawn Branch Library had taken a test by the end of the Project. The average time from entry into ISP to test taking was three months, and for some few a year. Workshop attendance at that branch library was slow to start, too. The numbers in attendance were also always small, often from 5 to 7; several times no one attended. This small attendance number was not exceptional; programs at Oak Lawn rarely drew many people. The last workshops were on business law and had attendances of 18 to 20 with requests for more sessions in the fall. The top five Study Guides distributed were English Literature, English Composition and Grammar, American Government, American History, and Western Civilization, with Human Growth and Development following close behind. But the workshop attendance was highest at those sessions on business subject areas. The librarian considers that this may indicate a need within the Oak Lawn community for study sessions directed toward the business sector of the community.

Crossroads Learning Center (CCLC) was another small library as shown in Table 4-1. It was a store front library next door to a barber shop with headquarters of the Southern Christian Leadership Conference upstairs over the library.[4] The branch library also faced on a heavily traveled main artery with minimal parking available. The neighborhood served was largely Black, and the library was not heavily used by the adult population. The librarian considers difficulty of transportation part of the answer to the minimal usage by adults, but more importantly she called attention to the historical background relating to the use of libraries and those persons over 30. "You must remember," she said, "these adults grew up in a period when they did not consider they were welcome in the library, and use of the library is not a part of their cultural heritage."

There was a good sized meeting room available for help sessions at Crossroads Learning Center, and space for study was adequate for the numbers served. The atmosphere of the library was open and light, giving a feeling of space and freedom. The staff was Black, so relationships with those who used the library in no way were constrained, but rather were also free, open and relaxed. The book collection had the basic, well-rounded core and was heavily supplemented with an excellent and thorough Black studies collection. Crossroads library also found it necessary to borrow from other branch libraries in the system, and (as reported in Chapter 3) they requested 22 books for the use of persons studying in ISP. Eight hundred and eighty Study Guide/Reading Lists were distributed by Crossroads Learning Center along with 783 pieces of CLEP information. The top subject area interests illustrated by the number of guides taken were American History, English Literature, English Composition and Grammar, American Government, Sociology, and Business Management. The librarians answered a total of 207 inquiries of which 125 were in-depth discussion types; there were only 20 reader guidance requests. The

---

[4]A new, large facility for this branch is currently under construction.

majority of those persons showing continued interest were businessmen and working women between the ages of 30 to 50, but, as indicated by the number of in-depth discussions, they all required time-consuming support.

CLEP did not work well at Crossroads Learning Center, not because the student was incapable of using it, but because helps for these students required personal one-to-one continuing contacts which the existing small staff could not satisfy and still continue to meet their commitments to other library users and the community. The students were not dismayed by the need to study, they were eager to learn, and they had a profound determination to learn, but they could not function alone. Some who started with ISP gained sufficient confidence to enter structured classroom instruction at one of the colleges of the Dallas County Community College District. Others came to General Equivalency Diploma workshops at the library to learn those basic background areas of knowledge which would enable them to move up into college level work. Contacts with others were lost to the Project because the transient problem was even more acute in this locale than in the Oak Lawn area. While tutoring was available through ISP, it did not cover the very basic needs of the individuals in this community. Only 30 percent of the population 25 years of age and older in the Crossroads area has a high school diploma, and the overall median educational level is 9.9 school years completed. Approximately 16,500 persons between the ages of 20 to 34 are not enrolled in any educational institution, with the total rising to 40,000 with the addition of those persons over 35 years of age. In this Crossroads area there are 7,879 persons who are high school graduates.

Some of the librarians themselves considered CLEP beyond the capabilities of most of the people given the disadvantaged conditions of prior years. They also often felt that the eventual $15 test fee would financially eliminate many. In view of the fact that the median family income in the Crossroads area is $4,060, their assumption as to the test fee appears plausible. The one Black college in the Dallas area never accepted CLEP scores, although they continued to study its value to their students. Cost-wise, then, that student of very low income who wished to go beyond the high school level might find CLEP the least costly route, but if he could not use the credit at the Black college and could not afford the

THE LIBRARY

Community College fees, he could have realistically been deterred from entering ISP.

During the first eight months of the Independent Study Project, workshops on CLEP subject areas were held at the Crossroads Learning Center, and attendance usually numbered nine or ten persons. These sessions included both Black students from the community served by the library and a few white students. All of the Black persons in attendance were working women, ranging in ages from the 30's through the 50's, and at the end of that eight months' period attendance had dropped off to a point where the librarian asked that the workshops be discontinued. The move into the GED sessions resulted in a group of 21 working at the library on high school diploma studies and Civil Service examination preparation with the help of a volunteer tutor from the Crossroads neighborhood. When this tutor was no longer available, this learning situation also ceased.

A session on the use of the library which was presented by the librarian drew an all male attendance from the business sector of the neighborhood. A workshop on Afro-American History drew a total of three men; one said, "This is a very important subject for

Faculty member from Southern Methodist University conducts learning session on the humanities at Crossroads Learning Center.
                                        Bob McCown, photographer

77

my people to know about, but why is it being held here in the library instead of out in the community where the people go?" For Crossroads Branch Library, then, ISP pointed out that the library did have something important for the community, the people were eager and determined to learn, and personal contact was the way to get the message "out there." Perhaps there was a need for one librarian who could have the time to make follow-up telephone calls and who would always be free to give time to the interested student. Outreach into the community to reach target groups needed more time, and other than book media supports for the beginning student were needed. Three students from the Crossroads Learning Center took CLEP tests. One of those students was unsuccessful in attaining acceptable scores in the five general examinations; she subsequently enrolled in the community college. The second student was successful in achieving creditable scores on the five general examinations and later successfully took the examination in Western Civilization; the third student had just taken the five general examinations at the close of the Project. The average time from entry into ISP to examination was 10 months for these students; the first two students came into ISP during the first six months of its existence. In the Crossroads area there are an estimated 27,000 persons over 25 years of age who could be considered users of a program such as ISP.

Hampton-Illinois Branch Library was one of the larger libraries engaged in the Independent Study Project. The library was situated in a large shopping center on a busy intersection in South West Dallas, and parking facilities were available at the entry to the library. This library was inviting in appearance with a good, spatial floor plan with several lounge areas surrounding tables for study. As in all the libraries in the Dallas Public Library System, there were large windows giving a sense of openness. This library had an auditorium which allowed for large group programming, and workshop sessions were generally well attended. The book collection was large enough to accommodate the many persons served daily and, in addition to the basic collection, Spanish language and Black literature was being added to accommodate changes in the neighborhood needs.

The community served by Hampton-Illinois Branch Library was largely middle to lower middle socio-economic in character.

THE LIBRARY

The core of persons who had lived in the area for many years was conservative and fundamentalist in attitudes. The demographic profile shows that the population is still largely Anglo, with 9 percent Mexican American and 3 percent Black. But it is also a rapidly changing neighborhood with a steady growth in minority group representation. The neighborhood has a high concentration of workers in the lower paying occupations such as clerical, sales, craftsmen, and operatives. The median family income is $7,949.

In spite of the fact that Hampton-Illinois was an extremely busy branch, the librarians could identify characteristics of interested ISP users, many who were new to the library. The larger number were white, lower middle class women who had married early and, now that their children had grown and gone from home, had the opportunity they had never had before to continue their education. Three librarians at this branch worked with the ISP students; one of them described contacts with the students by saying, "They were really interested. They wanted to talk with someone, really wanted a kind of on-going relationship with the college professor; they had a desire to explore thoughts." Other younger women who still had children at home came, and they often brought the children with them. They expressed a need for involvement, but they had little time to pursue formal education classes and saw ISP as an opportunity to learn at home on their own. The librarian at Hampton-Illinois felt that the independent student wanted to know someone by name, wanted a continuing source of personal contact within the library. He also felt that the library needed to offer more aids to the student who left the library with a Study Guide and books, but probably did not have the expertise to work purposefully with the resources. Attendance at workshops was generally good at Hampton-Illinois Branch Library. And in several instances enthusiastic groups exchanged names and telephone numbers, planning to talk together about their learning experiences. More men came to help sessions at this library, and in many instances children came with the parents. Even though Dallas Baptist College and Mountain View Community College were close to this branch library, it appeared that these people who had "stopped out" of education to raise families now chose the public library as their learning center. It seemed to the Hampton-Illinois Branch librarians that the library could now expand its involvement in community learning through more personal helps and special resources for these people.

The need for personal help was demonstrated by the fact that statistics from this library showed 554 inquiries, of which 309 were in-depth discussions. Eighteen hundred and fifty-five pieces of CLEP informtion were taken from the library along with 1,570 Study Guides/Reading Lists. English Composition and Grammar, English Literature, American History, American Government, and General Psychology were the top ranking guides in popularity. Persons who took tests numbered 23 from this branch library, and at least one who entered the program in the first six months of the Project tooks tests each succeeding six months, indicating a continuing interest in learning over the two years' period. A personal conversation with one of the CLEP test takers from this neighborhood elicited the following statement: "This has given me a whole new outlook on life. I read three psychology books before I recognized a pattern, and then the fourth book had some different opinions which made me question. This is the most exciting thing that has ever happened to me; I am enrolled in college now and have taken three more psychology courses." The demographic profile indicates there are 62,000 potential library, ISP/CLEP users in the Hampton-Illinois area.

Preston Royal Branch Library was in the northern section of Dallas in an upper middle to upper socio-economic neighborhood. The library was larger in square footage (Table 4-1) than the three previously discussed, but the overall impression was one of intimacy rather than large space. There was an auditorium as in Hampton-Illinois, and parking space was readily available around the library. It was situated in a pleasant residential neighborhood, next door to a day care school, and within easy access to a North-South Tollway and a large shopping area. The book collection was excellent, exceptionally well designed to fit the needs of CLEP students, although the library did purchase two books on Marketing for ISP students (as mentioned in Chapter 3).

In the Preston Royal Branch Library the three librarians working with ISP students found it difficult to differentiate the IPS student from other students — and non-student patrons — it had always served. Those interested persons who made initial inquiries were usually housewives, sometimes with a few college credits, usually with small children at home so that formal education was not possible at the time. Often there were inquiries from students engaged in formal education, and frequently they had been referred to ISP by a college professor. Others were working women, and many were older women whose families were now grown and had left home. Statistics from this library showed that 1,497 pieces of CLEP literature and 1,640 Study Guides/Reading Lists were taken from Preston Royal Branch Library. The librarians answered 659 personal inquiries, of which 65 were for reader guidance. Still, the librarians could report no distinct profile of the independent student (possibly because adults using the library had always been engaged in some type of continuing learning). American History was the Study Guide most often taken, with American Government and English Literature next, and English Composition and Grammar and General Psychology rounding out the top five choices. Students from the Preston Royal Branch Library known to have taken CLEP tests numbered 23.

The mean family income in the Preston Royal neighborhood was $21,802, and over 50% of those employed were in professional or managerial-proprietor positions. Fewer women in the Preston Royal Library service area were employed than statistics showed for the remainder of Dallas, and the median number of school years completed was 14.7 with one census tract showing a median of 16.0. In spite of the high educational level of the neighborhood, the total potential for ISP/CLEP students came to almost 40,000 persons. Since, however, formal educational advantages were not out of reach of the economic standards of the type of population represented in the neighborhood, it was conceivable that independent study would be more used by the working woman or the young mother at home, both who did not require the personal help needed as in the CCLC and the Hampton-Illinois Branch Libraries.

Audelia Road Branch Library was one of the newest libraries in the Dallas Public Library System, and it was the largest in square footage of the ISP libraries (Table 4-1). Like Preston Royal Branch it was situated in the North of Dallas, farther to the East than Preston Royal. Immediately surrounding the library were large homes, an elementary and a high school, and vacant land where cows grazed (rather surprising within the city limits). The branch was easily accessible from three super highways, and there was a large parking lot available to library users. By the close of ISP some of the vacant land where cows had grazed was being built up with town houses and apartments. The neighborhood library user was in the middle to upper middle income level (median family income was $10,973), he was a relative newcomer to the neighborhood; and the number of elderly and retired was few (41 percent of the population was under 20 years of age). The average age level of the library user was in the 35 to 45 range. While there were some apartment dwellers, most of the library users were family people with very traditional standards. They were hard workers and strong believers in traditional education. The median educational level was 13.2 years of formal schooling. Workshops at this branch library brought complaints about smoking, unfeeling language used by faculty members, and meeting night conflicts with church activities.

The library was large and so arranged that it gave an impression of space and light. The collection was broad and excellent for the independent student. Audelia Road Branch Library did not require books for their collection. ISP students took 1,087 Study Guides/ Reading Lists, almost the same number as those taken out from Oak Lawn, and only 200 more than the number taken at Crossroads Learning Center. The two largest subject area interests were American History and English Literature with almost a 50 percent drop in interest to the next three in popularity — English Composition and Grammar, Sociology, and General Psychology. Librarians at Audelia Road Library answered 794 inquiries, of which 397 were considered to be in-depth discussion types of questioning. It was possible that, since the Audelia neighborhood resident was oriented to traditional education, explanation of the concept of independent study could have been more time-consuming. The number of reader guidance inquiries was 90, the largest number at any of the branch libraries participating in the ISP study, and the 27 test takers from Audelia Road Branch was also the largest number identified with any of the five participating libraries.

The three libraries working with ISP at Audelia Road Branch Library reported that they could not identify any particular type of individual for whom they answered inquiries. One of the librarians said that attempts to identify students always ended up with those persons questioned identified as students in formal classes at the nearby community college. Observations at workshops indicated that those in attendance were interested in a "new" offering but were probably the "activity-oriented" learners described by Houle.[5] They wanted to hear "about" knowledge, but they rarely had motivation to become actively involved on any long term learning basis. Many of them were problem-oriented, desiring information rather than learning, and many came to every subject workshop offered. As the Project progressed, most of them dropped off, and those attending workshops usually were persons from other areas of Dallas and the surrounding suburbs who were studying for credit. Calls for information on ISP received at the Project Office from persons located in the Audelia Road Branch Library neighborhood were usually from young apartment dwellers, new to the community. The opening of a Community College campus within close proximity to the library opened traditional educational opportunities with which persons in this neighborhood were more comfortable. There is a potential of 13,200 community college or library independent study users in the Audelia Road Branch Library service area.

In each of these libraries, it must be emphasized, many independent students came who were not from that particular neighborhood, and many of them may have used the Study Guides/ Reading Lists at other libraries in the surrounding areas of the city and county. Since there was no way in which the users could be limited to specific neighborhoods, it is interesting to note that a pattern of difference in acceptance and use of ISP could still be partially defined for each of the libraries serving as "models." In each of the five libraries, size and number of books in the collection did not appear to make any significant difference in the use of that particular library as a learning center. In actual fact, minimal use was apparently made of all of the libraries by those persons who had expressed an interest in independent study. In view of the minimal demands being made upon their collections, the libraries were well prepared for the independent student. There were

[5]Cyril O. Houle, *The Inquiring Mind* (Madison, Wisconsin: University of Wisconsin Press, 1961), p. 16.

problems with scheduling of times for workshops, but the Dallas Public Library System allowed for flexibility to make special arrangements whenever possible. There were complaints about books not readily available on the shelves, the library not being open enough nights or on the nights certain individuals were free to use them, and the libraries closing too early. There were requests for a special book section for the independent student and for the purchase of special programmed paperback books for the independent student. But these were not new requests nor new complaints for the libraries; students engaged in informal education had voiced many of them before, the business man could not always find the book he wanted, nor could the car repairman or the housewife working with decoupage. Usually, however, all of these persons were given material which they *could* use and which would satisfy their needs even if it were not the precise book they may have requested. The concept operating in independent study, it should be remembered, was that the student could use any book on a subject which the library owned; he was not limited to one particular text. In this context of library usage, the library was

Independent student studies at Audelia Road Branch Library
Bob McCown, photographer

prepared, since the sophisticated student described in Chapter 3 who was familiar with the learning process functioned well within the availability of library personnel, books, and special materials planned for independent study. In some instances, persons who could not be considered sophisticated students also functioned well with available library resources.

Lee J. Cronbach states, "A person's readiness consists of the sum-total of response patterns and abilities he possesses at any time."[6] The independent student was invited into the library to engage in independent study. He was a mature adult who accepted this invitation to learning because of his own personal need at that time, and he might have been a "re-entering" or "beginning" student for whom the most personal help, most time spent, most "different" resources were requested. He might have been that student who stood, Study Guide and Reading List and three books from the library shelves in hand, and asked, "Now, how do I begin?" The Independent Study Project would now involve the library as the primary facilitator in arranging those aids to study which would be provided by Southern Methodist University. From this time on, for those students whose "response patterns" and abilities did not provide the readiness to proceed with their study alone, special supports would be necessary. It was also at the point of entry of Southern Methodist University into the study that, while those special helps designated in the proposal would be utilized, the possibility of other supports for the student would be the object of study. Recognition of special needs of independent students which might overlap with needs of other library users but which were not considered as part of the proposed "study" could be considered as "findings" only. Differentiation of study from service often proved difficult, but study could lead to the possibility of future refinements. If the student were not able to function with what the library made available under the charge of the "study," these findings could lead the Independent Study Project to a better service in the end.

The independent student often would accept no substitute books because he had been assured by his faculty tutor that a certain title

[6]Theodore L. Harris and Wilson E. Schwahn. *Selected Readings on the Learning Process*, "A Description of Active Learning," by Lee J. Cronbach reprinted and adapted from *Educational Psychology*, pp. 46-51, (New York: Oxford University Press, 1961), p. 9.

was "the best" for his study. In many instances this particular book might be one which the library did not own, but which the faculty member felt the library should purchase. Some of the independent students purchased their own copies of faculty recommended books, but in other instances they simply registered their dissatisfaction with the librarian and accepted a substitute or left the library without a book. Such demands were small in number. But they did exist within the Project. And, while at this stage of evaluation of a new service, purchase of new volumes might not always appear feasible to a branch library, such requests did present an issue for future consideration. Equally as important for future consideration were the requests for special programmed books expressed as a need by students who were finding difficulty in directing their independent study. Sheffield, Margolius, and Hoehn employed the film "implosion" technique in teaching an assembly task where parts of a subassembly were spread out, each one "jumping" into place in proper sequence. They described it as a kind of "perceptual blueprinting."[7] While this technique is not described as programmed learning, the principle of breaking subject matter into sub-units, where each sub-unit "jumps" into place in proper sequence on a page approximates an "implosion" concept. Hilgard and Bower state, "properly designed programmed books can serve about the same purpose as the simpler forms of teaching machines,"[8] and Skinner notes marked similarities between programmed materials and individual tutoring.[9] For that student who did not choose to attend tutoring or help sessions, or on a cost basis for the library as compared to tutoring cost, such programmed materials could be a possibility for the future. In the Independent Study Project, the Study Guides/ Reading Lists often incorporated some of this type of sub-unit approach or advice on ways to begin the study, and the library also had available books which dealt with the subject of how to study, so there was information available within the library on this subject. In addition, toward the end of the Project a short

[7]Ernest R. Hilgard and Gordon H. Bower, *Theories of Learning*, (3rd ed.; New York: Appleton-Century-Crofts, 1961), pp. 551-52.

[8]*Ibid.*, p. 556.

[9]Ernest R. Hilgard and Gordon H. Bower, *Theories of Learning*, p. 556.

guide on reading and using books for study and a guide on ways to approach independent study had been prepared for the ISP student.

The student who was totally dependent upon the resources of the library for his study helps, and was without a furnished textbook for his sole use, often required a longer period of time in study with one book. If renewal were not possible because some other user had reserved the same book, the student would find it necessary to change reading matter mid-steam. Library subject collections were available to all students, traditional and non-traditional, and budget allocation for duplication of copies of one particular title multiplied over many subject areas could cut into needs of other users which could be considered just as important for service. No "special" area was set off within the library for books for the independent student although several users suggested such an arrangement. The Independent Study Project considered that part of the student's independent learning would stem from his growing ability to choose books from the total collection. College catalogs were in a separate area within the library, and, when ISP materials especially prepared for the Project were no longer being used for statistical records, they too could be incorporated into the college information center. Paperback racks with books of special interest to the independent student might be a consideration for the future.

The proposal and subsequent contract with Southern Methodist University allowed for workshops and tutoring for those students who found difficulty starting study. Conceptually, as described in Chapter 1, the student himself would initiate such call for assistance. However, it was felt that certain basic areas of general assistance should be undertaken at once to guide the student into study competence. The five branch libraries engaged in the study were open two nights each week (covering a span of the three opening nights of each week) and it was concluded that nights would be the best times for these sessions. At a later date in the Project, student and library commitments indicated the scheduling of some daytime workshops. Prior commitments of participating libraries to system programming sometimes produced limitations on times available for ISP workshops. Nevertheless, the five participating libraries, working through the Independent Study Project Office, coordinated 112 workshops for 1,087 independent students before the Project ended. Time of the Project Office in coordination of faculty members' free hours, students' expressed subject interests, and library free time was extensive. Sometimes very few students attended a session. In fact, this could occur at any time since the "unstructured" approach taken by ISP did not *obligate* anyone to use resources offered by the library. At other times there were two or three requests for help in a subject on which a workshop had just been held. With a choice of 20 to 28 subject areas for which help sessions could be held, meeting needs within the library was difficult. On occasion, a branch library in the system other than one of those participating in the study was used, and in some instances the SMU campus provided the meeting place. Individual tutoring was often done out of the participating branch libraries because it was a continuing process involving one to five students who often met at hours the library was closed. Often the time and place for the next meeting was set up at a tutoring session. But this did not allow time for coordination with system programming. Admittedly, set times could have been allocated to ISP by the branch libraries, but time was needed to be flexible enough to adjust to schedules of both faculty member and student. The library did not always have a quiet spot free at busy times. But the concept of ISP was to fit the services as much to the convenience of the independent student as possible, so either the Head Librarian's Office or the Staff Room frequently doubled as a meeting place.

Within ISP it was felt that, while individual tutoring needs were important, group involvement for idea exchange was also a good learning experience for the student who might find it difficult to study by himself. A "group" could begin with one interested individual or more, added to as calls came in from others interested in obtaining help in that particular subject, and reduced through drop-off of those who had achieved their goal. This type of arrangement worked well in ISP, and it resulted in several long term groups involved in learning.

Embarked on collecting resources and establishing a philosophy of working with the independent student, the Library recognized that it needed to reach out into the community to inform the prospective user about the learning opportunities available to him. Opening publicity, carried in all forms of local mass media, announced the availability of an alternative educational opportunity for those adults in the Dallas community who wished to continue their learning through the use of library facilities. The opening months of the Project did bring in prospective students, but the number (800 in the first four months) was not considered to be significant in view of the total population who might have made use of this type of service.

While it was agreed within the Library that numbers were not the important issue in a service such as independent study, it had to be recognized that lack of numbers could be interpreted as lack of interest in view of the potential users in the communities served. Money with which the taxpayer supported a public service expended on a program of little interest to the public would appear to be an unaccountable expense. The function of the Library in ISP was to offer all those resources it could muster to afford alternative ways of action to the adult interested in entering or re-entering the mainstream of education at whatever depth or level he chose. The student who came to the library was free to choose his own path to whatever goals he saw as desirable and/or possible for himself. The Library would serve as a resource center not only for materials to use in study, but also for other informational inputs required for the student to prepare himself to make the best decisions possible. Informational exchange from and to the community was, therefore, necessary on a continuing basis. Since media publicity could not reach everyone, contacts with business and industry, local government agencies, local service organizations, and labor unions to reach the potential user of the service and to obtain information which the user could apply to his informational pool where required. Often, in the search for information needed by the independent student, the story of ISP was spread. And, when ISP contacted organizations to describe the Project, career and educational information came from the community to the library. Over all, in introducing ISP to the community, the Library projected a new dimension of its image. In turn, the Library introduced — to many independent students — cultural activities within the community in a new light, tying them in as part of a total learning process. The Library became an active agent in presenting the concept of an open learning community.

THE PUBLIC LIBRARY IN NON-TRADITIONAL EDUCATION

Dissemination of information and publicity had an effect on interest demonstrated in the Project which is illustrated in Table 4-3.

TABLE 4–3

| Time Period | Inquiries | CLEP Information | | Study Guides/ Reading Lists |
		All Pieces	Exam Booklets*	
First 6 months	947	3,056	390	2,054 (Opening Publicity)
Second 6 months	1,373	2,579	837	2,162 (Paid Advertisement)
Third 6 months	673	1,450	350	1,122 (Minimal Publicity)
Fourth 6 months	280	688	210	662 (No Publicity)
Totals	3,273	7,773	1,787	6,000

*CLEP booklets describing the subject and general examinations.

It would be assumed that during the fourth 6 months' period of ISP, word of mouth was beginning to carry the Project.

ISP found that the Library could function as a meeting place for those who had a need and a desire for education and in so doing could reach out into the community as an educational resource. The Library could function as a learning center regardless of its size, possibly without a great outlay of money. The Library discovered that coordination with another educational institution was possible, and that in such a cooperative effort both agencies were strengthened. The Library could take the initiative in presenting an alternative to formal education to its community and through such an undertaking gain the support of the formal educational institutions. While not all independent students were "new" to the library, through ISP some learned to use the library in a different and often more meaningful way.

Independent students meet informally in the library following workshop session.
Bob McCown, photographer

Other libraries across the country were also emphasizing the learning function. One such program was the Denver Public Library's "On Your Own" project which, while serving the adult interested in CLEP, gave a broader scope to independent study by bringing in that library's "Right to Read" program under the umbrella of independent study. The Denver project covered a large regional area of libraries and listed 17 state, regional, and local educational bodies as sponsors. The Denver Public Library, in Colorado, Miami-Dade Public Library in Florida, the Serra Regional Library System in San Diego, California, and the St. Louis Public Library in Missouri, all have CLEP information available, and both Denver and St. Louis have prepared reading lists for the use of their learners.

Study Unlimited, jointly operated by the Chicago Public Library and the City Colleges of Chicago, houses learning centers in three public libraries where students are learning through the use of videotaped courses and television monitors and are receiving counseling from professional counselors. There are no tuition charges for Chicago residents, but courses taken for credit do have a charge. The Illinois Junior College Board is financing this venture. The independent student is free to use this learning situation for whatever purposes he chooses without charge. If he wishes credit toward a college degree, he can pay a tuition fee or alternatively elect to use his knowledge to take a CLEP examination.

The Dallas Public Library System is now offering instruction for the General Equivalency Diploma Tests in eight branch libraries where professional teachers and para-professional tutors offer one-to-one help to students. The Dallas Independent School District is funding the effort, and it is open at no charge to the student who wishes to make use of it as a learning resource regardless of his goal or purpose. Placing the learning situation within the library opens the door to the use of the library in future learning situations, particularly since the special guides prepared during ISP will also be available to participants so that they may study on their own with library materials. The move of the educational institution out into the library can serve as a support to his independent pursuit of knowledge.

As can be seen by the library outreach programs offered in Chicago, Dallas, Denver, Miami, St. Louis, San Diego . . . and elsewhere, "independent study" is a broad enough "slogan" to cover most any learning project.

Many times the Independent Study Project was queried about the cost of such a service to the library. The following table delineates the cost of the Dallas Public Library Project.

TABLE 4—4
PROJECT COST

$55,900.56	Salaries for full-time and part-time services of Project Director, Project Secretary, and pro-rated time spent by Branch Librarians
10,875.00	Preparation of 29 Study Guides/Reading Lists
7,000.00	Tutorial Services
4,250.00	Evaluation
2,000.00	Public Relations
9,574.00	Supplies and materials (includes DuKane Projectors and telephones)
$89,599.56	**Total cost 2 years***

$25.60 cost per student based on an estimate of 3,500 students total.

*This total excludes cost for office furniture, equipment, car and travel expenses.

The total number of students is based on the number of *CLEP May Be For You* booklets given out since the booklet is the basic informational pamphlet on CLEP which was given to each questioner at the five branch libraries. If the cost were to be figured on the known number of test takers, it would have been $853.32 per student. At 40 years of college credit possible, it would amount to $2,239.93 per 30 hours of college credit. Assuming that students continue to study and take tests, these last figures could be expected to drop. But, as in any service which would be costed out on an individual basis, the number served would decrease the cost per individual. It also must be recognized that the test takers numbered by the Project were those who could be identified through the mailing list; there was the possibility of others unknown to ISP. The individual costs do not represent other students who might have achieved different goals than test taking. Cost for libraries would rely upon resources a library had to start with, what student needs were encountered, and how many of these needs the library felt it important to meet. Much has been said about re-allocation of priorities. But in the Dallas Public Library System, priorities are people. In short, a need for any one of the persons who comes to use the library, even though it may not *appear* to be a learning need, is important.

The physical features of the library in which learning occurs are only the backdrop against which a comfortable learning atmosphere is achieved. The student will find the atmosphere comfortable for learning only to the extent that he feels the library is making every effort to meet his particular personal needs. Kathleen Molz describes such a learning site in this manner:

> Because the term "library" is specifically associated with books, the broader and newly directed activities of libraries have acquired a nomenclature of their own: community learning centers, library learning centers, neighborhood learning centers, student learning centers, and others. These novel and informal enterprises, often located in poor areas of the inner city, focus on providing an environment that not only is hospitable to the learning process but that offers space inviting the visitor to study, to browse, and to discuss ideas with others. They are

indeed educational 'halfway houses,' in which fact often yields to interpretation, and insight is imparted along with information.10

BIBLIOGRAPHY

Brooks, Jean and Betty J. Maynard. "Final Report to the National Interest Council." Report presented to the National Interest Council of the Dallas Public Library Independent Study Project, Dallas, Texas, September 13, 1973.

Harris, Theodore L. and Wilson E. Schwahn. *Selected Readings on the Learning Process.* "A Description of Active Learning," by Lee J. Cronbach reprinted and adapted from *Educational Psychology.* New York: Oxford University Press, 1961.

Hilgard, Ernest R. and Gordon H. Bower. *Theories of Learning.* 3rd. New York: Appleton-Century-Crofts, 1961.

Houle, Cyril O. *The Inquiring Mind.* Madison, Wisconsin: University of Wisconsin, 1961.

Molz, Kathleen. "Halfway Houses to Learning." *American Education.* (May, 1972).

10Kathleen Molz, "Halfway Houses to Learning," *American Education,* (May, 1972), p. 1.

Chapter 5

The Librarian

If the library is the key to an environment suitable to independent study, the librarian is the viable element within that environment. If the key cannot move the lock, the environment will remain closed. How well the library can create and make use of the environment required by the independent student is totally dependent upon the responsiveness of the librarian. The librarian, then, needs to "feel" the needs of the user he serves as those needs relate to the goals of both the library and the user.

Within the five branch libraries serving as model public libraries for the Independent Study Project, there were a total of 13 adult and assistant adult librarians. Both those service librarians and the prospective independent students were involved in an undertaking which was new to them. As it has been suggested in earlier chapters in this book, librarians have always given guidance to users interested in one form or another of continuing education, whether it be how to repair a car, how to do macrame, or what books are the best for someone who wants to learn about the history of art. In such guidance, the librarian offers advice from his knowledge of the library's resources or the knowledge of the availability of other resources in the community. And, when the librarian needs to augment his knowledge, he has access to bibliographic tools which cover the whole range of knowledge and ideas of man.

In the case of the independent student, while the librarian still has all of the resources suggested above plus the special materials prepared for the ISP student, the librarian has an added responsibility. That responsibility has to do with the complete reliance the independent student has on the librarian and the rapport the librarian develops with the student. According to the concept, the excitement of this new learning adventure should of itself establish immediate rapport between librarian and student. In providing library service to students from formal institutional settings, the learner and the library have had the backup of a set curriculum and an instructor. In the Independent Study Project, on the other hand, the librarian became responsible for directing the reading of the student who came to the library for his help. If the learning desired were for self-enrichment, the librarian's responsibility was merely to present reading materials for general background. If, as was more frequently the case with ISP, the student were working to learn for the purpose of gaining academic credit, the librarian had to assume the rather awesome responsibility of suggesting books which would prepare the student in the total area of his learning normally presented in the classroom. There was no way of measuring whether a particular book would prepare him adequately; there were no quizzes after each chapter, no term paper based on reading within assigned subject areas, no instructor delivering facts he would expect to be recalled for a test, etc.

The librarian's first steps toward a relationship with the independent student were, therefore, somewhat cautious and tentative, if not fearful. And, this approach of the librarian was matched by that of uncertainty on the part of the student. The student needed information on the total concept of studying by himself, what subject to begin his study with, and where and how he could earn college credits. Most of the librarian's time was spent in providing explanations of these basic concepts, and, as it happened, the librarian most often began responding to the student by almost immediately referring him to a college or university in the area. Too often these referrals resulted in telephone calls from particularly highly motivated prospective learners to the Project Office for information, and, as a result, the Project Office assumed some of the informational role it was expected the branch libraries would provide. Consequently, the librarian in the branch noted — and sometimes complained — that, after the first encounter, the independent student never returned to the library.

Concommitant with these first attempts to create the appropriate environment and to establish rapport went the lack of accreditation for CLEP examinations in most colleges and universities in the area. The librarian was uncomfortable both with the information (and lack of information) he had to offer to the student and awkward in his approach to the student. And, it seems clear, the librarian had little or no confidence in the student's ability to become independent. It seems clear, too, that, if the librarian could not assert some independence from the structures of the traditional educational system himself, certainly he could not relate to a student who was willing to accomplish this but did not quite understand how to go about it. In many instances, it is suspected, the student's willingness to try to study for credit on his own translated to the librarian as an attempt to get credit without really working for it.

It should be admitted that the librarian had had no specific preparation for working with ISP except an orientation by the College Entrance Examination Board on the particulars of CLEP. The Project Office soon recognized that information needed to be prepared for the five participating branches which, as a result, would expedite information input to the student. Additionally, it was quickly recognized that the librarian's relationship with the student would have to be put into a perspective that would be acceptable to both. Gradually a positive librarian/student relationship began to develop which made it possible to work toward a solution for the individual who came to the library for help. The *Independent Study Project Brochure's* cover statement prepared the student for an initial understanding of the basic concept of the type of study in which he would chose to engage. A booklet which provided current information on credits, counselors, test centers, and varying education options gave both the librarian and the student good informational input at hand. And the *ISP News* continued to keep the student informed with current information. In addition, by the end of the first year, students were able to obtain the promised two years of college credit at many of the area colleges and universities. The necessity to "shop" for credit allowance was alleviated.

As the librarian's confidence in the library's informational resources grew, he was enabled to impart a more relaxed approach to the prospective independent student. In turn, the prospective learner became more open in his relationship with the librarian. What had been initially an encounter became a partnership. The librarian had come to understand that the first meeting with the new user could be the deciding point for his entry into independent study or re-entry into continuing learning.

The librarian learned not to judge the motive of the student for his interest in independent study. Some students might have thought this an "easy way out," but even that motive was not suspect. Rather, the librarian learned that he was there to impart all the information possible to the questioning individual, to be a knowledgeable resource. From the pertinent information, the student could be guided to use his own mind. With the needed information, the prospective student could decide what his most immediate goals might be. He could consider alternative actions. This began the process of decision making which would facilitate the learning process. The librarians began to draw on their personal experiences for examples of the kinds of decisions which could be made. They could point out what had worked and what had not worked for them. In turn, the prospective student presented his personal problems, time, responsibilities, and desires. Both student and librarian began to examine the level from which the student was starting. Goals could be examined with recognition that self-pacing of distance of goals helped. If the goals set were too distant, results could appear minimal; steps toward the distant goals could be maximum achievements. Working together this way, it was possible for both the librarian and the student to be more confident of the ability of each other. The earlier sense of impatience each had with the other was diminished and the librarian began to feel satisfaction in his input to the student.

In the interim, the librarian began to worry less about numbers as a total and more about students as individuals. While it never became a negligible factor in the service aspect of the Project, as long as the numbers game was foremost, indifference to the individual appeared to rule. As the truism tells it, disinterest is contagious. If a library program appears to be popular and draws many people, the librarian reacts in a positive fashion. There is, on the other hand, a sense of disappointment and embarrassment at presenting a program which is attended by only a few persons because of the planning and preparation time and effort consumption that went into it. Success in libraries is most often expressed in numbers, a show of public approval. If that approval is not evidenced by attendance numbers, then spectacular feedback results must take its place. Lack of one or both, with large blocks of time spend on a few individuals resulting in no sense of achievement on the part of the librarian, leads to a vicious circle of despair. "It doesn't work; it won't work; why should I knock myself out for an unrewarded job." The same set of fears which goads the librarian into taking responsibility for the student's "failure" operates in the fear of being coupled with a program that fails. The librarian rarely sees himself as the positive force which makes a program "good," and the initiative of saying "this is a good program" is lacking unless many patrons say it first. Sometimes "good" does not depend upon it being a "lot of good," however, and this might be said for the Independent Study Project.

Because ISP was a study, numbers were important only in respect to answering the questions of what were the reasons for the small numbers and were there ways of increasing the numbers. Had the library reached all the needs out there, or was the library failing in its role when some went away and did not return? If few or none came to help sessions, were there measurable reasons for this? The librarian now needed to give a total response to smaller numbers, and he had to recognize the importance of each individual. Perhaps this was a harbinger of change which was worthy of library time; perhaps this was a quality service which would be important enough to ignore the numbers game. The librarian was faced with the problem of making value decisions. Had the Project brought in overwhelming numbers, the librarian's learning process might not have been so thorough. In the end, the relationship between librarian and student could only profit from the smaller numbers. The librarian was now committed to quality service to a diverse range of a limited number of persons attracted to independent study rather than to a formal institution (for whatever his personal reasons.)

The librarian had expected to be confronted with ready-made independent students. Those who fitted that category came to the library, picked up study guides and reading lists, took them home, probably took out books, and in some instances prepared themselves and took examinations. The librarian had little or no contact with them because they knew what they wanted and how to achieve it with little or no aid from the library other than the resources available. The others — the less-than-independent students — relied heavily on the library for information and reassurance which would give them confidence to pursue independent study. Above all else, the librarian was to help these individuals understand that the library was a resource center for learning which was not dependent on a set curriculum presented at a set time in a set place. Books were on the library shelves from which a reader could enjoy a lifetime of learning. The difference from the traditional library approach was that the student would be consciously learning, and the librarian would be consciously helping him choose materials designed to further his learning experiences.

To aid the student in becoming independent, so that he could learn on his own or prepare himself to take CLEP examinations, the resources available within the library were there for his free use. While the Project made every effort to let the community know of the availability of this (ISP) educational opportunity, once individuals came into the library expressing interest in learning more about it, the resources and aids to learning were presented for their choice. No one was pushed into independent study. The desire to maintain an unstructured approach to learning provided that the prospective user be introduced to the learning aids available for his use should he wish to take advantage of them.

The librarian was the guide to those resources the library had within its own walls, the resources offered through Southern Methodist University, and the counseling resources available from colleges and universities in the community. The initial contact with the librarian was generally for information about CLEP, college credits, and the general concept of independent study. The initial source of aid to the student, therefore, was CLEP information and interpretation of the concept of independent study. And, this proved to be time consuming for the librarian and a service which the librarian found dull to perform. The student who needed more help usually was not in any way familiar with the academic structure and even the academic jargon. Speaking to him of hours of credit, credit which must appear on a transcript to be official, and courses required in degree programs was introducing a new vocabulary. Explanations often needed to be repeated in more than one way until all the facts were understood.

It has been suggested by some who observed the Independent Study Project that, perhaps, such a full explanation was not necessary when the new inquirer came to the library. It has also been suggested that so much information might have discouraged some persons from starting the learning process. But, when the librarian was bombarded with the questions — and they normally came all at once on the very first visit to the library — he tried to answer them as they came. The preferred but admittedly slower procedure was for the interested individual to take the printed information home and then return to ask questions and plan for his next steps. Rarely was the new independent student interested in the slower method. Most often he also had time limitations, and he wanted as much information as he could obtain within the initial visit to the library.

Librarian at Oak Lawn Branch Library assists independent student in use of the card catalog.
Bob McCown, photographer

THE PUBLIC LIBRARY IN NON-TRADITIONAL EDUCATION

Among the resources the librarian had for the independent student were the Study Guides/Reading Lists, and these were used more often than any other resource. The guide was an overview of the subject area designed to provide the student a broad study range. The reading lists contained some books which were not in the library collections, even though the original preference of the ISP Advisory Committee had been for the materials to be those in the public library or available inexpensively in paperback form. The lists, however, were merely to serve as suggestions for reading from which the learner could pick and choose. The librarian was also free to recommend any other books the library owned. Part of the librarian's service to the independent student was to encourage him to browse and select on his own those books which may or may not have been on the reading lists. It became known that, in subject areas with which the librarian had less expertise, both the student and the librarian were dependent on the lists rather than independent. The librarian also recommended fiction and biography where such might be applicable to a subject area. At no time was the aim of the library — or the librarian — to narrow the reading to a test situation.

The reluctance of the librarian to recommend books and to rely on information from area colleges and universities in serving the independent student has been noted. Perhaps traditional library training could be considered partly to blame; the librarian is taught to always have a reliable reference for whatever information he gives a patron — always document! The librarian had not seen any of the CLEP examinations, yet he was asked to recommend books for persons who wanted to study to pass those examinations. The ISP concept was that, if the independent student knew a subject thoroughly, he could pass any test, whether CLEP or one developed by a local college or university. In theory, this is believable, but the librarian felt that, in reality, the examinations could express viewpoints different than that of the particular book he recommended.

This philosophical problem was not resolved until word of the first CLEP examination passing came in through feedback from an independent student. The student informed the librarians that she had "overlearned" and that the study guide she had used was "excellent." She did add that some of her study was a "waste of time." But, with that ISP philosophy now justified, no one could feel too dismayed with that student's observation. It did point out, however, that, if the Project were to serve the needs of the user, the librarian might choose when to narrow the sights of the learning experience resources. If the student's need were for one particular examination result by a specified time, it was incumbent on the librarian to give him any information available from CLEP on that particular examination and to approximate the exact information needed with the requisite books. In his choice of books, the librarian would be guided by the starting point of the student, his immediate goal, and his past experience. For the best service to the independent student the choosing of reading material by the librarian became true reader's advisory service.

In some instances the librarian felt quite responsible for the student's learning and was, therefore, fearful that books he recommended might not insure the passing of an examination. This, too, may be a valid concern on the part of the librarian, but, it should be remembered, the Independent Study Project offered only the opportunity for the student to study independently — the library was not offering "teaching." The librarian was not teaching. He was attempting to guide the student to resources through which the student could self-teach himself or direct his own learning. It was hoped that, through properly chosen reading materials and the suggestions in the study guide, the student could self-pace his learning process. The librarian served as the guide to the use of these materials.

Of course the student wanted the "best" book for his purpose. The librarian became an artist in leaving the choice up to the student, but often the beginning learner was not ready to make his own choice. The librarian needed to be able to say, "This is the best book with which to start." Faculty members conducting workshops (help sessions) did just that, and in some cases the student deferred to the opinion of the faculty members over that of the librarian. This was due, in part, to the hesitancy of the librarian to commit himself to only one book recommendation as the faculty member was able to do so easily. It should be noted that, since the reading lists were quite long and most of them were not annotated in a semi-graded fashion, choice was, for most students — and librarians — difficult. Even with the list, if the choice of the student were not on the shelf, shifting to a book "just as good" was an unpalatable decision for most. The librarian was extremely reluctant to work without the reading lists. But with them, he was put in the position less of recommending and guiding than of mollifying and substituting.

As the Project progressed, both librarian and student learned to work with the reading lists satisfactorily. However, experimentation without set reading lists might prove in the end to be less of a problem for the librarian. In the General Examination area there were no reading lists until the end of the Project when one on the Humanities was prepared. A broad based subject of this type allowed for a wide variety of reading with a maximum of approaches to the literature. The librarian felt freer here, and throughout the Project more known learners worked in this subject area than in any other. Moreover, there were many successes on CLEP examinations. Perhaps this was an indication of the freedom of curricular approach translating itself to both learner and librarian.

Also noted was some reluctance on the part of the librarian to provide the student with the college and university information source materials. If the student used a college or university catalog and verified it with the institution, the librarian felt safe. The booklet of information prepared by the ISP Office contained materials gathered from the area educational institutions, and all the information was re-verified to insure its correctness. The five branch librarians knew this, but most of them were still reluctant to share that gathered information with the prospective independent student. There was somewhat less reluctance in letting the user leaf through the book himself, however. The librarians indicated that personal experiences in the past left them wary of college and university information; most of them at one time or another had had a bad experience with course requirements, which, in their words, "are constantly changing." They believed, therefore, that credit information for CLEP would also be inaccurate. This proved to be unfortunately true in a number of cases, but, with the aid of the Project Office as advocate, the student was warned to recheck his information frequently with the library for the latest information. Eventually the interest shown by concerned individuals at the colleges and universities' testing and counseling centers eased this problem.

THE LIBRARIAN

The workshops/help sessions, it was expected, would provide the opportunities for the librarian to meet and talk with the independent student in an informal and relaxed setting. Unfortunately, few of the librarians at the five branch libraries had time to attend the workshops, and rescheduling of staff was not considered practical, if even possible. The branches of the Dallas Public Library were extremely busy during evenings when most of the help sessions took place, and staff available was sufficient only to cover the service desks. If the five branch libraries had directed time to working with the independent student as conceptually planned, regular patrons would have received no help or staff members would have had to work overtime. The former is not tenable, and the latter is not the policy of the City of Dallas. Even if work schedules had been rearranged, the time blocks needed still coincided with the normal rush hours, so, again, regular users of the library would not have received service. The librarian felt that he had no choice in this dilemma, if he were to try to serve all of the individuals who come to the library. However, the faculty member who conducted the workshop and the Project Director, who attended most of the sessions, were available to the independent student.

The few librarians who did find time to attend at least the question-and-answer portions of the sessions found it easier to relate to the student afterward. They also found it helpful in judging the student's needs which might not be met by the faculty member. A number of the librarians prepared collections of books to be displayed at the sessions, but few of the materials were ever checked out by the students. The librarians were dismayed, but that phenomenon has at least one explanation: since the time for the workshops was short, the sessions usually ended outside the front door of the library with informal conversations still going on — the student simply had not time left in which to check out a book. In other instances, the faculty member, judging the abilities of his audience, would recommend paperback programmed materials or beginning texts which the library did not own. This tended to put the librarian in a somewhat awkward position, too. Faculty members were careful to point out that any library book the librarian recommended would so as well, but, rather than settle for a substitute title from the library collection, the student would frequently opt to buy his own book.

A result of the inability of the librarians to work with the students in the help sessions has been alluded to above, that is the relationship which should have developed between the independent student and the librarian frequently developed instead with the Project Office staff. It seems obvious that it took a considerably longer period of time in the Project for the student to develop the habit of going to the branch library — rather than to the Project Office — for personal help than it might have if the branch librarians had been freer to give more time to the independent student.

Much has been discussed already about the relationship between the librarian and the new student. This aspect of the Project has been stressed because of the importance of the new user's need for a measure of reassurance and self-confidence about an undertaking which was unfamiliar to him. Because of that need, the librarian was placed in the position of having to encourage the student, and, obviously, an aloof professional manner was not at all applicable. Such an attitude suspected of some librarians was translated as indifference by the students. In an article on Neighborhood Information Centers in the Summer 1973, *RQ*, Linda Crowe and Carol Kronus stated:

> It is unnecessary to reiterate the crucial role that staff attitudes at all levels play in affecting the success or failure of any project.

While classifying librarians as "closed," "open," or "neutral," the authors verify the experiences of the Independent Study Project in the statement:

> . . . it is necessary for librarians to accept and respect the community and people, even though they may have less education, different life goals and methods of survival.[1]

They add that the librarian needs patience and a willingness to work and wait for acceptance by the people served. Help is less

---

[1]Linda D. Crowe and Carol L. Kronus, "The Neighborhood Information Centers; Staff Attitudes," *RQ*, Vol. 12, No. 4 (Summer, 1973), p. 346-7.

important, those writers suggest, than the offer of something worthwhile.

It is clear that the ISP approach demanded that the independent student be accepted and respected where he is now. His desires to change must also be respected as justifiable and acceptable. Value judgements which stem from "better" education or insincere acceptance are at once suspect. The warmth of true interest cannot be misunderstood, and it is this warmth that is normally part of every public librarian's attitude toward his clientele that should make him the right person to help the independent student. It is recognized, nonetheless, that not all librarians can nor would even prefer to achieve the ability to develop the sort of one-to-one (and, it must be admitted, time-consuming) relationship with an independent student.

For ISP to work, the librarian involved in service to the independent student should be fully committed to the philosophy of the Independent Study Project and all of its elements. The librarians in the Dallas Public Library's five ISP branches were not, for the most part, fully committed to the Project. They gave time, and they worked hard at producing informational input to the study aspect of the Project.[2] For some, their efforts gradually developed into more attention to the service for the student, and they let the services provide information for the study as a by-product. As one observer of ISP, a member of the Project's National Interest Council, remarked, "The dichotomy among the librarians is very obvious." One might classify that dichotomy in terms of "positive" and "negative." Those who grew with the Project developed a positive attitude, which in some cases they were able to translate into service to all users. Others, those whose attitude was negative, still felt at the end of the Project as one librarian, who expressed to the Project Director, "I am glad it's yours and not mine." The librarian who was committed to serve the user within the concept of independent study began to recognize that, if this service were no different than the service he had always given, then, perhaps, all aspects of his service could profit from what was being learned here. The librarian who never evaluated the

---

[2]Perhaps this lack of hesitation to work toward providing informational input to the study stems from the apparent natural (trained) tendency of librarians to gather statistics.

service to the new user in any way other than his normal performance level remained negative. If he were negative about service to this new user, then he must have recognized a difference in the service (perhaps a greater difference that what there actually was); possibly he was negative to change in any form.

Much consideration has been given to the training of the librarian for user-oriented and one-to-one service. Ervin J. Gaines, in a paper on the urban library, opines:

> Training evolves rather naturally from perceived short-coming. Such awareness may arise from within the librarian as a challenge to his own self-fulfillment, or it may come from a group recognition that a library should haul up its socks . . . because it needs to embark on a new enterprise. In such eventualities, training is ad hoc and tailored to the particular situation. I find myself in sympathy with radical educators who incline to the opinion that people learn because of their own inner drives, not because of schooling.[3]

Those librarians within the Dallas Public Library's Independent Study Project who were challenged functioned as part of a learning process.

Perhaps challenges for new types of services should be introduced at the library school level before the professional librarian enters his profession. Perhaps the library science student is not being — or has not been — apprised of the well-known-by-practicing-public-librarians-fact that libraries cannot remain static within a changing world. Above all he should be taught that, if he is to work with the public, the "system" does not destroy nor seriously hamper his ability to serve the individual to the best of his ability. The librarian is, after all, the "system."

The branch librarian serving within the smaller community is the advocate for his users. Experience trains him to assess the needs of those users, and commitment challenges him to translate those needs to those for whom he works. It might be difficult to imagine

[3]Ervin J. Gaines, "The Personnel Needed for Tomorrow's Main Libraries," *Library Trends: Current Trend in Urban Main Libraries*, Vol. 20, No. 4 (April, 1972), p. 742-54.

training for motivation, but it is possible to illustrate by example or model ways in which change can occur without total disruption. It is also possible to illustrate by example varying approaches to work that could be applied by an individual. Surely it is possible to train people to look at themselves as "closed," "neutral," "open," "positive," or "negative." Perhaps it is even possible to illustrate that being one or the other can result in better or lesser service within a library. The desire to take up the challenge comes from the librarian himself, and necessary change can come as readily from his personal experience.

Self-learning is often more gratifying, more fully understood, and more generally applied than learning superimposed through teaching. Starting with the concept ISP did made it impossible to forsee what aspects of training would be needed for the librarians beyond an understanding of the concept of unstructured independent learning and training in the informational aspects of CLEP. Only through experience with the Project were the librarians and the ISP staff able to work as a group together to evaluate and consider attitudinal changes with which everyone might work. Expertise with the available materials did not loom as a great need for training beyond stressing the need for familiarity with the book resources of the library. Study of the CLEP materials, the guides, and the books in the collections would be one training area which could have been accomplished prior to the Project's opening. It was presumed that this would be a natural accomplishment on the part of the librarians, if they were to properly prepare themselves to function well in the new undertaking. This could be incorporated into a planned course of training, of course, but it actually involves individual preparation on the part of the librarian himself and, once again, is closely tied to challenge, motivation, and commitment.

The one-day orientation to CLEP mentioned in Chapter 2 was not thorough "training." It barely scratched the surface for the librarian. Since the Project involved just five of the Dallas Public Library's fourteen branches, only the personnel in those five branches at the time of the start of the Project received the CLEP orientation. Changes in personnel in the branch libraries happens quite naturally, so, as personnel changes occurred, an orientation was given at the Project Office for librarians new to ISP. Those who would not be working with ISP were given a one-half hour overview of the study, and those who were to be involved with the Project were given an hour and a half orientation. The Project Director met with Branch Heads of the five branches to discuss problems of service and to exchange ideas and suggestions for service. Personal visits were made from the Project Office to each of the branches for the same purpose. Continuing coordination was maintained by telephone between branches and the Project Office. The Office of the Chief of Branch Services and the Project Office communicated constantly and personally as well as by telephone concerning areas needing clarification. Information input with suggestions for its use was continually updated and sent to the five branches from the Project Office. And, all personnel working with the Project cooperated in evaluating ways of meeting needs of the independent student. As new questions arose, solutions were determined, and the new information was disseminated to all concerned. In this way, there was a continuing cross-training going on within the Project.

The librarian was faced with the question of service priorities in relation to independent students, . . . individuals who required much more time than the average user if to be served adequately. For some time there appeared to be fathomless contradictions in the librarians' input: there were not enough students showing interest in the Project; the librarians did not have enough time to give all the help the students needed; there was not publicity enough to bring in more students; those who did come to the library never checked out any books; but the students always wanted the books on the reading lists and would not be satisfied with substitutions! There were also complaints of no feedback from the students, and there were those who were disappointed because there were "no fresh, young minds." Still, when questioned, the librarians denied being "burdened." It was not easy to understand that the librarians felt that they could not serve those "few" adults who took advantage of ISP without cutting back on service to the younger students who were affiliated with formal education programs at even lower levels. When this question of priorities of service was discussed with the librarians, some of them seemed quite unabashed about their preference to serve the traditional student they had always served.

A time-consuming and careful study of librarian input, coupled with statistical information gathered at the five branches, suggested some reasonably accurate answers to the apparent contradictions mentioned above. Inquiries were divided into three sections: directional, readers guidance, and in-depth. Statistics showed that the greatest number of all inquiries were coming into the branches both in person and by telephone during the time block of 2:00 to 6:00 p.m. It was learned that that same time was also the busiest for all branches in the entire library system. The prospective independent student waited his turn with others seeking information from the librarian, and there were often four or five patrons waiting at each librarian's service desk. The telephone rang constantly, and some questioners on the line were also asking for ISP information. The majority of those who came to the library at that particular time of the day were there because transportation was available only on the way home from work, after the children returned from school, or the breadwinner came home from work and the housewife was on her way home from the grocery store. Most of those library users were unable to come for books and/or service during the hours of the day when the library was less busy. ISP students fitted into the crowd quite naturally.

With so much demand on his time, the librarian was forced to deploy smaller amounts of time to reach all questioners. The independent student, needing a quiet place to sit down and consider a new concept and its implications for him, was necessarily allotted the same amount of the librarian's time as everyone else. Often it was time enough for him to pick up initial informational pamphlets to read by himself at home. If he were deeply motivated, he returned to the library for further information and resources. If he already had some knowledge of the educational system, he could move independently into study with little or no further help from the librarian. In the case of the newcomer to unstructured learning, there was, quite understandably, a far greater need for much personal exchange. The librarian knew this, but he had to make every effort to serve all the publics for which he recognized responsibility. There were few times the librarian could give one patron more than relatively quick information from which the unsophisticated learner had then to extract the best he could. The librarian learned that often the new ISP student did not return to the library. Therefore, he hoped that more persons would come into the library because he knew that, among those who did come, some would be retained or would come in at hours when better service could be afforded them. The librarians, in general, eventually recognized and admitted that the greatest amount of their time was spent in information-giving rather than in reader's guidance, which was usually what formally educated "fresh young minds" needed. It does appear that, in the sense of this partial explanation of the contradictions, the service to the independent student was a burden to the librarian because of not-enough-time at certain periods of the day and because of the type of service required at all times. Too, the librarian, partly because he was rushed, was not comfortable with the reassurance role and the slow deliberation of the new user who must understand and weigh the possibilities offered in independent study.

Interestingly enough, however, the librarian himself was often more adaptable to small changes which he felt would offer better service to the novice continuing learner than was the library as a whole. The librarian started the process of evaluating those changes which could be made while working within the library structure. When the Project began, the librarian was not ready to provide the new service; at the close of the Project there were still some who did not feel that the endeavors had proved to be appropriate services of the public library. But, even those librarians most doubtful were willing to help plan a new phase of independent study. All of them saw aspects of the Independent Study Project that were felt worthy of being incorporated in a new effort. And, all of them saw cooperation with the local community college as an answer to providing services and resources not completely satisfied in ISP. Some applied concepts of independent study were seen in the planning of programs for branch libraries, making space provisions for independent study in future library buildings, and for cooperative planning with other educational agencies to offer educational opportunities at the GED level within the service area of each branch library.

THE LIBRARIAN

BIBLIOGRAPHY

Crowe, Linda D. and Carol L. Kronus. "The Neighborhood Information Centers; Staff Attitudes," *RQ*, Vol. 12, No. 4 (Summer, 1973).

Gaines, Ervin J. "The Personnel Needed for Tomorrow's Main Libraries," *Library Trends; Current Trend in Urban Main Libraries*, Vol. 20, No. 4, (April, 1972).

Chapter 6

ㅎㅎㅎㅎ ㅎㅎ ㅎㅎ ㅎㅎㅎㅎ ㅎㅎ ㅎㅎㅎ ㅎㅎ

The Tools

In order to facilitate study for the user who might elect to use independent study as a vehicle for organizing his knowledge in preparing for CLEP tests, certain special helps were conceived and included as part of the Project's proposal. As the Project progressed, other helps appeared to be needed, and differing types of aids were developed to serve as additional supports for the independent student. In total, these tools would provide information and subject matter from which the individual could start and with which he could continue his study plan. They would be provided as guides to help the student direct his progress toward those goals he had decided were of value to him. They could also provide the librarian with informational inputs with which he could offer more informed guidance to the student. In turn, many of these tools resulted from demonstrated direct needs of both librarian and student as they worked together.

The Study Guides/Reading Lists were prepared by faculty members of Southern Methodist University. While designed to help the student organize his knowledge and, where necessary, enlarge upon it for CLEP tests, they were not narrowed to the test requirements. It was expected that the Study Guides would present the discipline covered in an informal, easy to read and understandable way which would excite the interest of the student and motivate him to learn. From the guide, it was hoped, the student would gain an overview of the area of knowledge being presented, an understanding of its place in relation to other disciplines, and a description of its relevance to the individual who taught or learned within the subject area covered in the guide. The student could be expected to learn what a historian did and how he approached his area of expertise and to understand ways in which a study of the subject area might be relevant to the interests of the student himself. Each one of the 20 subject guides prepared was somewhat different from the other, but, in all, the major emphasis was on a broad outline of the discipline to be covered. Differences stemmed from the subject matter treated, the writing style of the faculty member, and the writer's interpretation of the appropriate learning approach to the particular subject. All of the guides included a Reading List, either incorporated within the body of the guide or as a separate selective bibliography at the end of the guide. It had been expected that the Reading Lists would contain a good number of "light" reading citations including fiction where applicable, and it was expected that annotations would encourage interest in the reading matter.

The Independent Study Project's Advisory Committee, which was composed of members of the University faculty and Dallas Public Library staff, spent a great amount of time considering the format of the guides and reading lists. Members of the National Interest Council were also concerned with the efficacy of this particular aid to the independent student. There were user complaints, librarian complaints, and Project misgivings. In essence, after careful study, the complaints appeared to be universally directed to the reading lists: they were too long, the books were not in the library collections, the independent student was being frightened away from independent study by the heavy reading lists. Cries of "too academic" were being heard across the land, while within the ranks of the Project were pronouncements that one could earn a graduate degree from the knowledge gained from some of the reading lists. All of it was true. Some of the books were not in the library, the lists were in general very "academic" and in many instances quite long, and one could indeed be well on the way toward a profound knowledge of a subject area if he were motivated to complete the reading list. The complaint that came from the independent student was somewhat valid because he did not understand that he was not "required to read every book on the list!" Early in the Project, it was interesting to note, a few librarians did not understand that books other than those on the list *could* be recommended. That misunderstanding served to emphasize that the tools were only as good as the ability to use them with a measure of discretion.

The Reading Lists which accompanied or were included in the Study Guides were SUGGESTED readings only. The student was not expected to be overwhelmed by them, nor was he expected to walk out of the library with an initial sense of defeat because he could not find a listed book on the shelf — the reading lists were meant to be but a part of his introduction to the excitement of learning. In this aspect, the Lists often failed. In this aspect, too, they were often heavy and beyond the experiential levels of some of those persons who entered the Independent Study Project. For some independent students the reading lists were not useable without help from the librarian. The Project's Advisory Committee spent a great amount of time considering the format of the guides and reading lists since the proposal designated revision of 10 of them for the second year of the Project. Two revisions were done by faculty members, resulting in not much more than watered down versions of the originals. Moreover, attempts to "create" a model proved fruitless.

As the first students began to come back into the Library with excellent test results and high praise for the Study Guide/Reading Lists, it had to be conceded that they were excellent tools for those who used them as intended. For the less sophisticated student, time was needed to guide him to their proper use, and tutoring or help sessions were expected to continue his guidance into self directed study. Interestingly enough, those general subject areas where there were no study guides, or where several subject guides were necessary to cover a subject area, were the areas CLEP examinations were most frequently attempted. There were, for instance, many student requests for a guide to the humanities. While the student was more comfortable with a reading list, since it served as a support encouraging him to study, it also served as one of the resources which made the Project a little less than completely "unstructured." In balance, the consensus of opinion in the Dallas Project over the period of the first year's trial was that the reading lists met an expressed reader need and should continue to be offered as a resource.

At the close of the first year of the study, the decision was made to prepare 10 new Study/Reading Guides rather than attempt to revise the original 20. By this time not only were independent students using the guides, but college and university students were using them as extra-curricular resources. Some college faculty members were recommending them for class use, some test centers were referring students to the libraries for the guides, and a university librarian had asked for sets to place in the college library's reserve collection. The Study Guide/Reading Lists were successful, and they did serve students at all levels and depths of study. In fact, one independent student complained that they did not go far enough.[1]

The following guidelines for preparation of the new Study Guides/Reading Lists were outlined from suggestions of the Advisory Committee, librarians, and students:

TABLE 6—1
Guidelines for Study Guide/Reading List

A. Introduction
  1. What the subject is about (i.e., history) — place it in its relationship to the world of knowledge.
  2. What the expert in the field does (i.e., the historian).
  3. What the study can give the student — breadth of knowledge for personal interest or to use for testing — for CLEP or *any other testing*.

B. How to study format
  1. Break subject into study units.
  2. Write as a running commentary.
  3. Embody readings within body of the guide with *good* annotations.

---

[1]Another student, it might be remembered, reported that she had "overlearned" with the Study Guide/Reading List (Chapter 3).

4. Include references to use of library materials and help of librarian.
   a. Familiarization with card catalog subject areas.
   b. Familiarization with books on shelf — general browsing.
   c. Call on librarian for suggestions on reading material and help in learning use of library.

C. Reading List
   1. Incorporate suggested readings within body of the work.
   2. Make the readings guided in range of difficulty (comment whether materials are introductory, light reading, popular).
   3. Incorporate light readings (popular), philosophy of field, criticism and fiction where possible.
   4. Keep reading list short — may add additional *short* suggested reading list for deeper study at end.
   5. All books *must* be in Dallas Public Library.

D. Style
   1. Keep easy-going but not folksy.
   2. Avoid disciplinary jargon which could dismay a lay person.
   3. Use clear and simple language and ideas.
   4. Speak to a broad audience.
      a. Sophisticated student perhaps with some degree of college experience and good background.
      b. Student with little or no background who needs stepping-stone reading guidance.

E. Implementation
   1. Coordinate with Dallas Public Library subject area librarians, and with branch librarians.
   2. Submit rough draft to Project Office for presentation to Advisory Committee.

F. Points to keep in mind.
   1. The independent student wants the Study Guide to tell where and how to start his study and where and how to progress.

2. This means, if possible, the guide incorporates some possibility for self-evaluation.
3. Make clear that books listed are only samples — ask the librarians for others like them.

Those items listed in the guidelines were descriptive of weaknesses noted in some of the earlier guides. A copy of the guidelines was sent to each faculty member preparing a new Study Guide with requests for his criticism and evaluation of his ability to work within them. One criticism was that "It can't be done," and another by the same faculty member was a flat NO to the essay format; he preferred an outline form. For his subject matter, Fortran IV Computer Language, the format proved to be a valid objection, but he did, nonetheless, the impossible by writing the guide in simple and direct language, although he confessed to great difficulty in this accomplishment. Each faculty member was given a three months' period in which to complete his task, and the final Study Guide/Reading List came into the Project Office for reading, possible revision, typing, proofing, and reading list check against library holdings nine months later. It did take time to write a thorough knowledge of a subject area without great detail or a normally erudite language. In addition, while some faculty members did consult library holdings, most of them were busy with classes, students, and research with extra time was very limited.

The new guides were generally shorter in length, and the reading lists were broader in levels of expertise required. Each still differed from the other in style and approach, but almost any one of them could have served as a model for someone else who wished to prepare a Study Guide/Reading List. The Study/Reading List for Afro-American History had been eagerly awaited by both librarians and students. The guide came in as a lengthy bibliographic essay, which the Project Office and members of the Advisory Committee felt was too long. The guide was turned over to the Assistant Chief of Branch Library Services and the Branch Head of Crossroads Learning Center for their criticism. Both of these librarians asked that not one work of the guide be changed; it spoke to the Black community. The readings listed ranged from picture books to more erudite volumes, and the two librarians considered it an offering of Black literature of significance for their people.

THE TOOLS

Not every subject fitted into a set form, so the guidelines were adapted to suit the subject matter treated which indicated to ISP that the search for a "model" Study Guide/Reading List was not realistic. The Independent Study Project did consider that one guide could serve varying levels of student expertise if the reading list were broad in range and if the less sophisticated student worked closely with the librarian in choosing reading materials. Perhaps the most viable element of the guides was the academic knowledge, the lifetime of teaching experience, and the affinity to the subject area which came across. This academic flavor enhanced the guide, in the eyes of the student, as in no other way. When, therefore, the faculty member reached the point of maximum accommodation to the guidelines for the preparation of his Study Guide/Reading List, the Project Office gracefully accepted his decision.

The original agenda of Study Guides for the final 10 had included three new subjects in the area of medical technology. A co-author of one of the actual CLEP examinations, as it happened, taught in a Dallas medical school, and her initial response to preparation of Study Guides/Reading Lists was favorable. Later, following further careful consideration, she admitted to grave doubts about such material being offered to the public in general. The initial thrust for these subject tests had been to answer needs of veterans who had served as medical corpsmen, had clinical experience, but required the background subject knowledge for credit purposes. Checks with two other medical schools in the Dallas area elicited the same response, and the Project Office decided not to produce guides in these subject areas. The decision was based on actual need in the community versus the possibility of misuse. At a later date in the Project there was one request from a veteran medical corpsman who subsequently agreed that ISP's decision was well founded.

The Project Office then filled those slots with two other subject areas guides. From the community had come a request for a Study Guide/Reading List on Voluntary Action for the training of volunteers and supervisors of volunteers. In cooperation with the Dallas Voluntary Action Center and a Community Services Instructor at one of the local community colleges, such a guide was prepared. This was not a CLEP subject area, but it was an independent study need expressed by community agencies, and it was accomplished at no cost to the Project. Plans for the future include incorporating the use of that guide, seminars at the Community College, and use of the library for individuals enrolled in the Community College or who are studying on their own. In effect, the library will have a special community resource available for those who wish to use it. Colleges and universities across the country are presenting courses and seminars for volunteers, and in some instances credit is being considered. This is a multi-disciplinary study which lends itself well to independent study, bringing together varying types of reading materials in a variety of subject areas.

Another aspect of the Study Guides which was noted as the Project progressed was the need for self-pacing helps. The guides which broke the study into units of learning were often easier for the new student to use. The presentation of the subject matter in "units" of learning enabled the independent student to approach his reading with more confidence than if he were confronted with a total subject area in which he had no idea where to start. It was again being demonstrated by the student that some measure of structured help was necessary until he reached that plateau where he could master his own pacing.

Some students took more than one Study Guide/Reading List, and a few were studying in a multi-discipline fashion, combining a study in American History with American Literature, or Psychology with Sociology. Often, in the beginning of the Project, some students took entire sets. Final statistics showed that, while 6,000 Study Guides/Reading Lists were taken from the five branch libraries, only 191 tests were known to have been taken by independent students, as shown by Table 6-2.

The wide difference between the number of guides taken and test taking numbers led the National Interest Council at the final meeting in Dallas to the conclusion that more study should be done on the value of the Study Guide/Reading List in independent study.

While the Study Guides/Reading Lists were intended solely for the student, other informational resources prepared by the Project Office had a two-fold purpose. The *ISP Brochure* was prepared, as mentioned earlier in this book, to introduce the Project to the community (business, industry and membership organizations) as well as to describe for the independent student exactly how the

THE TOOLS

TABLE 6-2

Study Guides and Reading Lists		Tests Taken
English Literature	599	6
American History	533	21
English Composition	504	35*
American Government	442	36
General Psychology	352	7
Western Civilization	328	6
Introductory Sociology	319	3
Human Growth and Development	315	0
College Algebra	295	3
Introductory Accounting	278	4
Introduction to Business Management	255	3
Biology	228	2
Analysis and Interpretation of Literature	217	13
Introductory Economics	217	2
Computers and Data Processing	213	2
Introductory Marketing	203	3
Educational Psychology	167	0
General Chemistry	160	3
Geology	158	2
Statistics	148	1
Elementary Computer Programming FORTRAN IV	36	1
American Literature	22	3
Money and Banking	12	2
History of American Education	10	1
Tests and Measurements	9	0
Introductory Calculus	8	0
Afro-American History	7	0
Humanities**	3	30
Introductory Business Law**	2	2
Total	**6,000**	**191****

*Includes test takers for subject and general examinations
**Not available to students until September, 1973
***Does not include general examination test takers listed below who might have used a combination of subject study guides.

Natural Sciences	23 test takers
Social Sciences	22 test takers
Mathematics	21 test takers

program functioned. The *ISP News* was prepared, as also mentioned previously, to maintain contact with the student.

When the Project opened, each Branch Library maintained an individual list of those persons signing postcards, and as workshops were scheduled, each branch library mailed an invitation to the persons on its list to attend the workshop.[2] As the lists grew, time available at the branches was too limited to allow for this procedure, even though the Project Office prepared and provided mailing labels. The process of card exchange to Project Office, typing of individual lists, return of cards and mailing labels became a complicated and unsatisfactory operation. Also, as more workshops were scheduled, independent students began to travel from one branch library to another to attend a subject area workshop which they had missed at the branch they normally used. Circulars were prepared which announced the monthly workshop schedule, but, if the student did not happen to reach the library at the right time, he might miss the announcement of a help session he wanted to attend. With the advent of the *ISP News* also came the opportunity to computerize the master list of all students who had signed postcards indicating they wished to be kept informed of upcoming help sessions. The newsletter was also mailed monthly to Dallas businesses and industries where it was posted on bulletin boards. Copies were also made available at all branches and the central library. There was no indication that the change from the postcard invitation to the *ISP News* resulted in any change in the size of workshop attendance, but more information was available to the user and to the librarian.

The information booklet prepared for use at the five participating branch libraries was also intended for use by both the student and the librarian. Through continuous up-dating it was always current, and, when the librarian might be occupied with another patron, the interested user could leaf through it himself. When the librarian was free to help him, he would have questions formed and ready for answer. During the second year of the Project this informational booklet was developed as a pamphlet which could be taken out by the student. This pamphlet was of prime interest to both librarian and student since it provided information on a community-wide credit offering for CLEP.

2See Addendum

THE TOOLS

When the Project first opened, workshops were scheduled to orient the student to the concept of independent study itself and to those techniques which would be helpful to the student who chose to study independently. Basic routines of time budgeting, breakdown of subject areas into workable units, setting of goals, ways in which books could be read most effectively, and library usage were discussed in the first sessions. These sessions were scheduled at each of the five participating branches over the first six months of the Project. By this time requests were coming to the librarians for sessions on particular subject areas, but the number of persons interested in one subject was small, and the range of subjects was large. The Project Office then began scheduling workshops at each branch, based upon the librarian's report of those subject areas most often requested.

The problems of library hours was discussed in Chapter 4. Taking those nights open at each branch within a month's period, with a list of subjects desired at each branch, the Project Office charted future sessions, verifying time and date with appropriate faculty members. The subject to be offered and the date of the

Faculty member conducts help session for independent students on How to Study Independently.

Bob McCown, photographer

session was verified with the librarians at each of the five branches, and poster work was arranged with the Library's Exhibits Office.

Work done by the Library's Exhibits Office artists required seven weeks' advance notice, so scheduling of workshops was manipulated within a situation which allowed for little flexibility. As mentioned in Chapter 4, when the Branch Office developed its own system wide scheduling of programs, the advance time schedule for ISP sessions grew to seven month's prior notice. As far as time slots were concerned this prior notice was manageable, but ISP could not possibly predict what subject areas would be of concern at which branch seven months in advance. Through coordination with the branches, the Branch Office, and the Public Relations Office, the Project Office was able to maintain the flexibility necessary to schedule workshops at the need of the independent student. Tentative scheduling of subject areas to be covered was done six months in advance, but the chart on which the Project Office set up tentative and "set" help sessions showed many changes.

Workshop scheduling had to be kept fluid so that pushes for certain subjects or desire for a continuation of certain subjects could be handled. Many times requests for art work went in to the Exhibits Office way under the deadline, but the personnel involved always came through for the independent student with flying colors.

When it came to the set arrangements, a date, a place, a time, and a subject area, the ISP Office made contact with the faculty member, and, if he were not free, arrangements were made with another person to whom he referred the Office. Scheduling of faculty was time consuming, because they often had evening classes, and the Project could not guarantee attendance on a particular night far in advance. Once arrangements had been made with the instructor, a letter was mailed to him confirming the date, and a week prior to the scheduled session a postcard was mailed. Frequently a follow-up telephone call was made the day of the help session. This latter exercise was not done out of any real belief in the "absent-minded" cliche, but one workshop session did end up without a faculty member, and, while he sprang to the rescue a half-hour late, the Project Office was wary of a repeat performance.

If six or more independent students indicated a desire for a group session in the same subject area, scheduling was set up wherever

THE TOOLS

there was an open time slot at one of the five branches. Meeting sites were later extended to other branches, if location proved to be a problem, or to the Southern Methodist University if that location was indicated as best serving the purpose. Often, through the newsletter notices, what might have started as an individual tutoring session ended up as a continuing series of group sessions. Workshop sessions appeared to work well when they resulted from a request of one or more of the participants.

These student/faculty member sessions were variously named workshops, help sessions, tutoring groups, or groups meeting in a particular subject area. This diversity in nomenclature was not by accident; it occurred because the Project, the National Interest Council, the Advisory Committee, and the librarians together could find no suitable special title. These sessions were designed as informal, question and answer sessions, in which general aids on how to study for a particular subject area might be covered. The student could be helped to evaluate where he was and how much progress he had made, or general informational needs might be met. At the close of the Project, 112 workshops had been scheduled for 1087 independent students. The following table lists all workshops for the two years of the Project with attendance numbers and branch locations.

TABLE 6–3

Independent Study Project Workshops

Workshop	Date	Attend-ance	Br.*	Avg. Attend-ance
Accounting	May, 1972	4	PR	
	July, 1972	7	AR	
	August, 1972	7	OL	5
	February, 1973	6	PR	
	March, 1973	4	OL	
Afro-American History	April, 1973	6	CCLC	
	April, 1973	5	CCLC	4
	April, 1973	2	CCLC	
American Government	May, 1972	4	PR	
	July, 1972	7	AR	
	August, 1972	7	OL	5
	February, 1973	6	PR	
	March, 1973	2	OL	

127

American History	April, 1972	2	HI	
	June, 1972	5	OL	
	September, 1972	11	AR	5
	October, 1972	2	PR	
	January, 1973	6	PR	
American Literature	January, 1973	2	HI	2
Analysis & Interpretation of Literature	January, 1973	8	HI	8
Business Law	June, 1973	7	OL	
	June, 1973	12	OL	
	July, 1973	18	OL	14
	August, 1973	18	OL	
	August, 1973	18	OL	
Business Management	October, 1972	5	OL	5
College Algebra & Trigonometry	July, 1972	2	OL	
	January, 1973	6	PR	
	January, 1973	9	PR	1 5
	February, 1973	2	PR	
	February, 1973	5	PR	
Computers and Data Processing	August, 1972	5	AR	
	November, 1972	6	HI	
	January, 1973	1	AR	
	April, 1973	0	SMU	
	April, 1973	21	SMU	
	April, 1973	14	SMU	
	May, 1973	12	SMU	9
	May, 1973	12	SMU	
	May, 1973	12	SMU	
	June, 1973	8	SMU	
	June, 1973	8	SMU	
	June, 1973	9	SMU	
Creative Writing	May, 1973	10	WH	
	thru	9	WH	
	August, 1973	18	WH	
		11	WH	
		8	WH	
		9	WH	
		12	WH	
		10	WH	
		10	WH	10
		9	WH	
		8	WH	
		10	WH	
		13	WH	
		11	WH	
		14	WH	
Educational Psychology	September, 1972	6	AR	
	November, 1972	4	PR	
	November, 1972	3	PR	3
	November, 1972	1	PR	
Effective Ways of Reading Books	January, 1972	17	AR	
	April, 1972	6	CCLC	9
	August, 1972	13	HI	
	November, 1972	0	CCLC	

128

THE TOOLS

English Composition and Grammar	July, 1972	0	CCLC	
	September, 1972	5	OL	2
	March, 1973	3	PR	
English Literature	April, 1972	6	OL	
	May, 1972	8	PR	
	June, 1972	6	AR	6
	July, 1972	10	HI	
	January, 1973	2	OL	
Financial Aids	August, 1972	8	CCLC	8
General Chemistry	March, 1973	1	AR	1
General Psychology	April, 1972	26	AR	
	May, 1972	24	HI	14
	September, 1972	1	CCLC	
	November, 1972	5	PR	
How to Study Effectively	October, 1971	68	AR	
	November, 1971	9	CCLC	
	February, 1972	14	HI	25
	April, 1972	22	PR	
	May, 1972	11	OL	
How to Use the Library	December, 1971	26	AR	
	March, 1972	6	CCLC	10
	March, 1972	0	OL	
Human Growth and Development	May, 1972	11	AR	
	June, 1972	11	PR	9
	September, 1972	6	HI	
Humanities	February, 1972	8	CCLC	
	March, 1972	2	HI	
	June, 1973	38	HI	21
	June, 1973	35	HI	
	June, 1973	25	HI	
Marketing	September, 1972	13	PR	
	September, 1972	9	AR	12
	October, 1972	10	AR	
	October, 1972	15	AR	
Organizing Essays	February, 1972	4	AR	4
Psychology of Testing	April, 1972	21	AR	
	May, 1972	5	CCLC	
	June, 1972	17	HI	10
	November, 1972	6	OL	
	October, 1972	0	CCLC	
Sociology	June, 1972	3	CCLC	
	October, 1972	4	HI	
	November, 1972	6	AR	4
	January, 1973	5	AR	

		January, 1973	5	AR	
		January, 1973	5	AR	
Tests and Measurements		May, 1973	8	PR	10
		June, 1973	12	PR	

*Key to Branch Library abbreviation:

AR	— —	Audelia Road Branch Library
CCLC	— —	Crossroads Community Learning Center
HI	— —	Hampton-Illinois Branch Library
OL	— —	Oak Lawn Branch Library
PR	— —	Preston Royal Branch Library
SMU	— —	Southern Methodist University (Computer Center)
WH	— —	Walnut Hill Branch Library

The individual tutoring sessions were handled through the Project Office, either directly from student request or by referral the student from the branch library. From the student the information on subject area desired, times and places most convenient, and general reasons for requesting tutoring were obtained. This information was referred to the faculty tutor along with the telephone number of the person to be tutored. Specific arrangements for the session were then decided between the two parties involved. Often the sessions, as has been previously noted, evolved into group sessions which continued for some time with students coming in and out as their needs dictated. Sometimes the requests were for student evaluation and counseling, and in some instances a telephone conversation with the faculty member could answer a problem.

These "special aids" or tools for the independent student became increasingly used as the Project progressed. It is quite possible that this use was due to the fact that the librarians became more familiar with their value to the student and were able to impart that fact. The tools were examples of aids to learning which cooperative library/academic institution arrangements could offer to the people of a community. They demonstrated that such cooperative offerings could take place at either institution or at both without losing one iota of the individuality of the cooperating units. The library might have been that agency in which independent study was supposed to take place, but, once it started, it could move anywhere into the community and still retain its identity with both the library and the academic institution.

Faculty member conducts informal tutoring group in American History at Hampton-Illinois Branch Library.

Bob McCown, photographer

The library was circulating ideas; new ways in which learning could take place, new places in which non-traditional learning occurred.

Chapter 7

ᕫᕫᕫ ᕫᕫ ᕫᕫᕫᕫ ᕫᕫ ᕫᕫ ᕫᕫᕫ ᕫᕫ

Academia

Cooperation with the colleges and universities in the Dallas area was excellent once the academic institutions overcame their apparent initial shock of finding the public library actively pushing non-traditional education. Southern Methodist University, with considerable experience in teaching the adult student in its extension division, Dallas College, did not see this cooperating venture with the Dallas Public Library as a threat but rather as an extension of its existing services. The Library also viewed the Independent Study Project as another option to learning for the adults in the community. Early in the Project it was felt that, perhaps, other academic institutions in the Dallas area might consider the Library's efforts in independent study for credit as an intrusion in areas where it did not belong. As information was exchanged and the Project began to develop, such fears, if they had ever existed, were allayed, and the Library became recognized for the services it could offer to the non-traditional student. The Independent Study Project came into being at a time when educational change was taking place across the country, so acceptance of the library as an institution where directed learning could take place was not as "far-out" as it would once have been. Certainly, many of the members of the Library's staff and the college and universities' faculties learned to understand the respective community roles better as the Library and the academic institutions worked together with — and for — the unaffiliated student.

The major areas of cooperation with Southern Methodist University had been discussed throughout this book as the very backbone of the aids to the independent student. Dr. Fred Bryson, Dean of Continuing Education, and Dr. James Early, Associate Dean of Faculties, School of the Humanities and Sciences, were members of the Independent Study Project's Advisory Committee and, as such, were continually consulted on tutoring and the Study Guides/Reading Lists by the Project Director. The Project Evaluator, Dr. Betty Maynard, Chairman of the Southern Methodist University's Department of Sociology, worked closely with all of the personnel in ISP. The cooperation of the faculty members who wrote guides and personally helped students was always complete and willing.

All of the academic personnel involved in ISP also worked fulltime as faculty members, but they still found time to counsel ISP students, help them evaluate their progress, and preside at workshops where they provided an informally erudite atmosphere. They were always on call from the Project Office, and they never turned down any requests for assistance. They enjoyed their move out into the community, and the independent students enjoyed them. The services of the faculty members to the novice learner was an important factor in helping the student gain self-confidence to continue his learning. The student had great respect for the expertise of the faculty member, and the close relationship with the members of the academic world lessened the student's fears of moving out into traditional education.

The Project Evaluator helped those who worked in ISP bring their efforts into focus, and her evaluation visits were always a stimulation to the staff. When asked by members of the National Interest Council for a description of the evaluation model for ISP, the mutual decision of the Project Evaluator and the Project Director was that the "model" consisted of the refining of the biases of the branch librarians, the Project Director, and the Project Evaluator. In the process of learning which took place for all of those concerned with the Project, each learned from the other; each learned about the working situation of the other, and this resulted in a team effort which functioned well and smoothly.

Other colleges and universities in the Dallas area began early in the period of ISP to recognize that ISP was not a competitor, and community wide cooperation became a reality. Each college and university in the Dallas area made available to the independent student through ISP and the five branch libraries the name of at least one on-campus individual who understood the problems of the older unaffiliated student and who would serve as a counselor. Letters came from some of the educational institutions offering any aid they could give, and occasionally a faculty member from an area college or university visited a workshop and talked with the students. Test centers asked for copies of the Study Guides/Reading Lists to use as resource referral materials for students, and credit information was freely given to the Project.

When the Project opened — and for approximately one year following — credits allowable for CLEP examinations in area colleges and universities were few and far between. Students informed the Project personnel that they could not even obtain reliable information on credits available from Southern Methodist University. The students, if they could get any credit granted at all, were placed in the position of shopping from institution to institution. If they located one college where credit might be granted, they again found it necessary to shop for a college or university which would accept the credits on transfer. College-Level Examination Program publicity was being disseminated by radio and television in the Dallas area announcing the availability of two years of college credit through CLEP examinations. At the same time branch librarians were running out of polite ways to explain why this was not true. In March, 1972, David L. Reich, then Deputy Director of the Dallas Public Library presented a paper, "Independent Study Project: The People's University," at the Dallas Conference on Credit By Examination Through CLEP, which was held at Southern Methodist University. Administrators from all the area colleges and universities were present, and the program was presented by the College Entrance Examination Board. In his paper, Mr. Reich presented the Independent Study Project dilemma to those present:

Our librarians are able to tell the adults the schools we know for certain do accept CLEP, that schools differ in which examinations they accept (that is, subject exams or the general exams), and that schools differ in how much credit they give. The librarians can and do direct the independent student to the colleges for information we cannot provide, but this can be a frustrating experience. A couple [of] examples:

One of our local universities reported recently that it had received a number of telephone calls following a period of some particularly good news coverage. The calls came to the Office of the Dean of Continuing Education, where the adult asking about that school's program for accepting CLEP and granting credit was referred to the Admissions Office, where the caller was referred back to the Continuing Education Office, where, this time, the caller was referred to the university's Testing Center, where no one could answer any questions about credits granted. And, amazing as it may sound, there seemed to be no one in the Admissions Office who could help. We would have to agree with the person who reported this to us that "people are getting the runaround."

My second example concerns the same university. A student at that university took home to his mother a CLEP brochure. She called the Dean of Admissions, who referred her to the Testing Center, who referred her to our Independent Study Project Office. But her question was "How many hours credit can I get and in what subjects?"

The really confusing thing about those two examples is that the university is one that has made a particular point of publicly announcing that it does grant credit by examination through CLEP. And we are really up against it when we run into those colleges and universities who prefer to keep their credit-by-examination programs and policies privileged information, even from prospective students.[1]

[1]David L. Reich, "The Dallas Public Library Independent Study Project: The People's University," (Unpublished paper presented at The Conference on Credit By Examination

Later in the same paper Mr. Reich adds:

> It seems reasonable to us — and to our National Interest Council — that the public library, which is a free information source for all citizens, could be a central place where such information for all the schools in the area can be obtained. In addition, the librarians need to have the name of an individual in each admissions office who understands the philosophy of CLEP, who knows his own school's program concerning CLEP, and is sympathetic to the adult who is trying to approach higher education through independent study and credit by examination — and, I should not forget to add, who is a potential degree-seeking student for his school.[2]

After several such vivid descriptions from students of the "runaround" they were experiencing on campuses, one faculty member suggested at a workshop that the students approach the heads of departments. The Project Office also informed students that it was up to them to help in the pressure for credits. At the meeting at which Mr. Reich presented his paper in March, 1972, the University of Texas at Arlington announced that it would be accepting CLEP scores for credit and requiring only 30 hours of on-campus credit. Perhaps Mr. Reich's words to the college and university administrators, added to the announcement by University of Texas at Arlington and reinforced by student requests, led to the opening of CLEP acceptance by area colleges and universities a few months later. At the same time the unaffiliated student was able to find an understanding counselor on campus, and, if he had any problems, he learned to come back to the Library for help. If the Library called a campus to plead a student's cause, the response was such that the institution made great effort to find a solution of benefit to the student.

Perhaps the most difficult problem for the academic world was the acceptance of the library's entrance into the CLEP area of

Through the College-Level Examination Program (CLEP), Southern Methodist University, March 30, 1972), pp. 14-15.

[2]*Ibid.*, p. 16

Southern Methodist University instructor describes the Skinner Box at a Psychology workshop at Audelia Road Branch Library.
Bob McCown, photographer

education. At no time was the library attempting to encroach on the job that the formal educational institution was better equipped to do: *teaching*. The library was open to those individuals within the community who wished to *learn*, had, perhaps, the "impossible dream" of a degree, but would not (or could not) attend a college or university at the time. As individuals who entered ISP gained the confidence to move out into the formal educational institutions, it became obvious that the library might be serving as an open door to a formal learning situation.

If there were any *teaching* at all, it was done by the faculty member who, working with the Project, often found himself in situations where he had to improvise. In most instances such improvisation was done on the basis of the classroom situation, that is, the instructor (as he now became) transferred the classroom mode to the library. It was quite recognizable that the use of the CLEP subject areas was in itself a somewhat limiting and structural factor. As the Dallas study indicated and as hypothesized in the Report of the Ohio "Extended Learning Program," the university connection "tends to perpetuate the traditional subject areas even though the delivery of the course is changed."[3] The Ohio report also notes the revision of college courses in other colleges and universities "according to thematic and/or problem-solving experiences." The Ohio report states, "These interdisciplinary approaches lend themselves to creative thinking and offer intriguing alternatives to traditional divisions of study."[4] But in a later statement it is noted that "Only a handful of students expressed an interest in inter-disciplinary or thematic studies," and, further, "it appears that the demand is for specific courses rather than broad areas of knowledge." The report hypothesizes that the "majority of ExL (Extended Learning) students are mature enough to know the career objectives they want and therefore seek courses that relate to their employment goals."[5] ISP students were *self-oriented*, their needs were very personal whether problem or employment-directed, and while it was the "intriguing

---

[3]*A Report to the Ohio Board of Regents,* Extended Learning Program, (Athens, Ohio: Ohio University, June, 1973), p. 37.

[4]*A Report to the Ohio Board of Regents,* p. 36.

[5]*Ibid.,* pp. 36-37.

alternatives" which the Dallas Public Library's Independent Study Project was seeking to offer the independent student, it was also recognized that the offerings had to be relevant to the student's needs. Transplanting the classroom out into the community was not an answer. It was hoped that subject areas could relate to the student and his immediate needs and from that point broaden out to cover the subject area and its relationship to other disciplines.

ISP expected that the Southern Methodist University faculty member would be challenged by the varied levels of experience and competency he would find in the independent students. It was expected that the faculty member would involve the student in meaningful exchange of ideas about a discipline which would impart the excitement of learning more through reading and study. The faculty member was interested in and intrigued by the experience of outreach into the community, but in the major portion of instances he referred to the librarian following a session to ask, "Did it go alright?" The student in turn felt great awe and respect for the instructor's erudition, and in some instances a good rapport developed between students and faculty members. In most cases, however, the faculty member did not see this student as a valid learner as *compared* to students on campus. The student usually was not well versed enough in a subject area to effectively communicate thoughts and ideas, and he too was accustomed to the teacher/student relationship of a structured classroom.

The concept of the independent student help effort was that it would not always demand the presence of the faculty member himself. In fact, the Project Office always suggested that a graduate assistant would be most welcome. It is to the credit of those faculty members who agreed to conduct help sessions themselves. (It might be mentioned here that the stipend of $50.00 per session cannot be overlooked as a slight motivation.) On those few occasions where graduate assistants were utilized in the role of "tutor" the effort to relate to and aid the student frequently appeared to function at a level of greater involvement of time and personal relationship on the part of the assistant. The graduate assistants, too, often recognized the lack of background of the student, but, perhaps because they were still "learners" themselves, they were more positive in their "belief" that the student might eventually achieve his learning goals.

ACADEMIA

It seemed that the instructor who worked on campus with young people, while he was attracted to helping the new independent students, viewed them with some disappointment. Their base of entry into the learning situation often appeared to be so low that it suggested a lack of ability to function at higher levels of learning, and few of the independent students showed any potential for becoming a scholar. In the instance of the independent student, he had not yet reached the plateau of learning where his relationship to any type of "average" could be exhibited. The faculty member was accustomed to working with a-grade-for-degree oriented student who produced or was dropped. The independent student had no obligation to "work" at his learning beyond his individual desire to learn. If the faculty member did not bring forth the commitment to learn, the fault could be laid at the door of the student himself. It could also be, though, that this is not at all the correct rationale, and that more careful study of the teaching material is in order.

Often, the independent student was problem-oriented; something in his personal or family environment caused a need for greater understanding, advances and changes in his working situation were leaving him behind, or societal pressures were beyond his understanding. The complexity of meeting such needs within the framework of credit "courses" to satisfy the simultaneous needs of the student studying for CLEP examinations was the problem. Perhaps ISP was involved in an insoluble situation; faculty members in the majority felt this to be the case. Possibly differing program types for differing audiences would be a better answer, and perhaps some type of programming with a combination of disciplinary approaches could be designed to meet needs of more than one type of student. Even within the classroom varying students must be challenged unless the faculty member takes carte blanche to present "as he sees it," with no attempt at relevancy for his audience. It is suspected that, because he had this other obligation to the student on campus as his top priority, and because that was a full-time job, the college professor had little time to spend on consideration of a special curricular approach for the independent student.

The initial objection by the faculty member to the use of the CLEP examination accreditation route was the academic distrust of the information tested. A recent report by Edward Caldwell also suggests misgivings about some of the CLEP tests. Caldwell was particularly disturbed at the number of two and four year colleges in Florida using a cutoff score for granting college credit "at or below the 25th percentile. Even more alarming than the low cut-off levels," Caldwell continued, "is a content analysis of the tests done by subject matter specialists . . ." The concern was directed toward the CLEP general examinations, and the specialists found that "In two examinations (mathematics and natural science), most items were judged to be at high school level. In the other three the proportions were not so extreme . . ."[6] Fears of Southern Methodist University faculty members were allayed when cutoff raw scores for granting credit were set at or above 50. Since there was always a degree of material covered which might be considered of high school level in freshman college courses, the higher cutoff score on the CLEP test assured that the student would need a broad background knowledge to achieve success. Other colleges and universities in the Dallas area did give credit for the general examinations, but Southern Methodist University used only the English Composition and the humanities examinations in conjunction with a subject examination. Individual SMU faculty members taught within a very personal formula, but the Project concept of a broad learning base within a subject area discipline seemed to overcome any misgivings they had about student preparation for CLEP examinations. The faculty members attempted to approach the workshop sessions with the broad view of the subject area. However, for many months faculty members referred to the Study Guides as *syllabi* and to the study areas as *courses*. They often also closely related their discussions of the disciplines to the usual classroom definition of course content. As they worked with the independent student, they did begin to recognize the need for different approaches, and most of them made an effort to be less formal in presentations.

As reported in Chapter 6, the Study Guides/Reading Lists also reflected the academic bias toward vocabulary and often heavy reading matter. While this approach was valuable to some students, it had a tendency to intimidate the beginning student with little

[6]*Report on Education Research* (September 12, 1973), pp. 7-8.

background. As the ISP continued, the faculty members began to recommend books other than those on the Reading Lists, books which the faculty members considered might be less intimidating to the independent student. While the Project attempted to prepare the student to use the Study Guides and Reading Lists prior to his initial approach to them, operation in a completely "unstructured" manner left the student totally independent in his decision as to the direction and speed of his study. Within a more closely guided situation, the student might be encouraged to move forward in the study at a pace more closely related to his individual needs. It might have been expected that such self-pacing guidance would be accomplished through the Use of Study Guides. Special help sessions on how to learn or read, or study, unless offered on a continuing basis, would always miss some newcomers to the Project.

The time-consuming efforts involved in arranging faculty/student meetings were also discussed in Chapter 6, and procedures outlined there were utilized in order to expedite getting the service to the student. Calls from five separate libraries to faculty members, it was felt, might result in fragmentation of efforts resulting in confusion within the study. Synchronization of efforts appeared to dictate that a central location could best handle such requests. As with other efforts involving faculty members, the academic member and the branch librarian were thus separated by a third party, the Project Office staff member. If the faculty member had time available to make visits to the branch libraries to acquaint himself with the personnel and the environment, such artificial separation might have been lessened. Throughout the study, however, both academic members and branch personnel looked to the Project Office as the spokesman through which communication might be initially relayed to the student. Only those students who attended workshops or tutoring sessions really had the advantage of any close relationship with the faculty members.

As the Dallas Public Library's Independent Study Project progressed, colleges and universities across the United States were becoming engaged in developing independent study programs of their own, consoritums of Universities Without Walls, and varying forms of Open Universities. The names varied, but they were all options for persons wishing to learn at the academic level. The majority of these innovative approaches to post-secondary learning seemed to be primarily directed to the young adult, but in all instances the older adult could also take advantage of them. The student within the Independent Study Project was generally the older adult, settled within the Dallas area, not desirous of changing residence in a free-wheeling search for learning. He was apprised by the Project of all of the educational opportunities open to him, but only a few gave promise of meeting needs in a manner he would find applicable. Perhaps, because it, too, offered credit via the CLEP examinations, the Regents External Degree Program of New York stirred considerable interest in the Dallas independent student.

The Regents External Degree was established as an alternate route to a college degree as described in the following excerpt from the Regents External Degree; Handbook of Information for Candidates:

> Specifically designed for those individuals who choose to learn on their own, the program is based on the philosophy that what a person knows is more important than how he learned it. Thus, on-campus residence or classroom attendance is not required in order to earn a Regents External Degree.[7]

In September, 1973, 531 persons, some of whom had never set foot on campus, were awarded Associate of Arts degrees through the University of the State of New York Regents External Degree program's third commencement exercises.[8]

The Thomas A. Edison College in the State of New Jersey also offers an external degree and works in close coordination with the New York Regents External Degree program. For the Dallas independent student, the New York program was of particular interest because it enabled him to achieve an Associate in Arts external degree totally through testing without moving out of the Dallas area. If the student could travel to New York for testing, there was also the opportunity to work toward an Associate Degree

---

[7]The Regents External Degree: Handbook of Information for Candidates (New York: University of the State of New York, August, 1972), p. 1.

[8]Phi Delta Kappan, November, 1973, p. 209.

in Nursing and a Bachelor's degree in business, both of which incorporated both CLEP and assessment testing.

The University Without Walls, a program of the Union for Experimenting Colleges and Universities was described as:

> . . . an alternative form of higher education. It seeks to build highly individualized and flexible programs of learning and makes use of new and largely untapped resources for teaching and learning. It moves toward a new faith in the student and his capacity for learning on his own, while at the same time providing close and continuing contact between the student and the teacher.[9]

On occasion a younger independent student was interested in the type of an educational experience offered through the University Without Walls, and each of the five ISP libraries had information available on this option to higher education.

Also in New York, SUNY-Empire State College offered degrees through varying optional methods, one of which was independent study, and the Nassau County Public Libraries were engaged in conducting 12 free informational sessions on this option to learning. In a booklet entitled *Increasing the Options*,[10] John R. Valley listed 28 new programs in existence in 1972, with 30 proposals for other programs. Cyril O. Houle's book, *The External Degree*[11] traces the history of the external degree, describes similarities and differences in existing programs, and discusses their possible meaning for education in the future.

There are several other alternatives for education which may have significant implications for libraries. These include, among others, the British Open University which relies heavily on the public libraries of Great Britain. The University of Maryland has utilized a public library as a learning center, but from all reports to date, the reading materials are programmed texts, supplemented by films and tapes specially prepared for that particular program.

---

[9]*First Report, University Without Walls* (May, 1972), p. 1.

[10]John R. Valley, *Increasing the Options: Recent Developments in College and University Degree Programs* (New Jersey: Educational Testing Service, 1972).

[11]Cyril O. Houle, *The External Degree* (San Francisco, Jossey-Bass, 1973).

The same approach appears to be operable in two new mass media learning options which have recently been opened to the Dallas community. The educational television station is running a series of programs on *Man and His Environment*, which were prepared by Miami-Dade Junior College in cooperation with the community colleges in the Dallas-Fort Worth area. The learning materials offered are specifically planned for the course and are available only to those students who register with the community college. The second mass media offering is that of the Copley News Service which offers courses by newspaper under grants from the National Endowment for the Humanities and the Exxon Foundation. The course was developed by the University Extension, University of California, San Diego. It offers an optional kit of learning materials and an optional course for credit from a participating university in every locality where the series appears in the newspaper (in Dallas, Southern Methodist University). For the independent student who wishes to learn without credit, the public librry may serve as his resource center. Other TV presentations which consist of courses, such as those presented by Sunrise Semester, emanating from Chicago and New York, can be utilized by the independent student to augment his study whether for credit or for personal enrichment.

Along with the growth in numbers of educational opportunities opening to the community is a move toward changes in the academic calendar allowing students to accelerate learning and/or learn on their own. Westminster college operates on a 5-4-1 calendar. The short term (1) allows the student time to take an added course during the month mid-April to mid-May, and he may elect to take the course at any one of the members of a seven college "spring term consortium" or through enrollment in off-campus courses. Each student is required to take three short term courses during his four years. Saint Louis University has developed the 1-8-1-8 Plan, whereby bright students take college level courses in high school and complete one year of college while still in high school, and a number of students are selected each year to skip eighth grade, moving directly from seventh to ninth grade. St. Louis University allows credit for those college courses taken at the high school level. The university feels that this approach allows "freedom from repetition and drudgery which these students experience . . ." and that it also allows them to "expand their educational horizons by additional electives at a later stage in their careers."[12] It would appear that colleges and universities are actively engaging in opportunities to "turn the student on" rather than to turn him out, and this can only reflect in a positive way on library usage in the future.

The move of the formal educational institution out into the community has exciting implications for the public library. However, the financial base of each entity (the academic institution and the public library) realistically influences its ability to function in cooperative services to the new adult student. The college and university are dependent upon student fees for their financial existence, but moving the classroom situation out into the public library (or even introducing a new instructional approach into the public library) which limits attendance and resources to paying students negates the public library service philosophy of free and open access to *all* library users. The public library is a tax supported public service, librarians serve the total community, and library resources are available for choice to all users. Ivan Illich suggests,

> We must conceive of new relational structures which are deliberately set up to facilitate access to these resources for the use of anybody who is motivated to seek them for his education.[13]

The faculty member and the librarian, aside from their realistic financial bases, are dedicated to learning — one through his expertise in teaching, the other through his expertise in encouraging the use of resources for learning. In its coordination with Southern Methodist University, the Dallas Public Library, through ISP, brought together services from the academic community and the library to maintain an unstructured, free, and open learning resource center for its users. Financial bases for such new "relational structures" which could incorporate the strengths of both the public library and the academic community in service to *any* unaffiliated learner emerge as needs for the future.

[12]James A. Duplass, an unpublished report (Saint Louis, Missouri: Saint Louis University, N.D.), p. 4.

[13]Ivan P. Illich, *Deschooling Society* (New York: Harper and Row, 1971), p. 78.

BIBLIOGRAPHY

A Report to the Ohio Board of Regents. Extended Learning Program, Athens, Ohio: Ohio University, June, 1973.

Duplass, James A. An unpublished report, Saint Louis, Missouri: Saint Louis University, n.d.

First Report, University Without Walls. May, 1972.

Houle, Cyril O. *The External Degree.* San Francisco: Jossey-Bass, 1973.

Phi Delta Kappan, p. 209, Nov. 1973.

Illich, Ivan P. *Deschooling Society.* New York: Harper and Row, 1971.

Regents External Degree: Handbook of Information for Candidates. New York: University of the State of New York, August, 1972.

Reich, David L. "The Dallas Public Library Independent Study Project: The People's University." Unpublished paper presented at The Conference on Credit By Examination Through the College-Level Examination Program (CLEP), Southern Methodist University, March 30, 1972.

Report on Education Research. September 12, 1973.

Valley, John R. *Increasing the Options: Recent Developments in College and University Degree Programs.* New Jersey: Educational Testing Service, 1972.

Chapter 8

🔒🔒🔒 🔒🔒 🔒🔒🔒🔒 🔒🔒🔒 🔒🔒 🔒🔒🔒 🔒🔒

The Future

I ndependent study meant change to the five branch libraries of the Dallas Public Library System; some changes for which they were not fully prepared; some changes for which the Library was not fully prepared even at the end of the Project. It was recognized early that the concept of ISP in its simplest form would work, and the five branch libraries did function as resource and learning centers for 105 known individuals. In the traditional sense of an appropriate library function, the library had been effectively serving as a learning center for years. But, in the sense of guiding students to total independence and self motivation in the learning process and often simply in helping students become receptive to learning, the close of the Project left much to be tried. Admittedly, as a study, ISP had been a learning situation for all who worked with it, and while student numbers were small in comparison to the numbers already using the library, the library administration recognized the need for further study of some areas of service which appeared to be emerging as possible "new" roles for the library. The students to whom these roles would be directed were those who had needs for more aids to start, self-direct, and motivate their own learning experiences. For others, it was "seeking" some type of more meaningful learning experience for self-enrichment which they could not clearly define. The importance of the Southern

Methodist University inputs to ISP students indicated needs for even greater academic institution back-up on a continuing basis. The emphasis would be on independent study in the sense that the participant would be aided to reach a stage of personal independence in pursuit of whatever form of continuing learning he should choose. To that end, any further study would become more structured where such support was deemed necessary, while allowing the individual to move at his own pace into independent study.

The Independent Study Project had made impact upon the community. Success stories, personal interest stories, and word of mouth passage of the message could attest to that. Up to the final weeks of the Project persons calling in would say, "I just heard about this; why haven't I heard before?" Those working in the Project were certain that ISP had not reached "all those out there" who would be interested in this non-traditional educational opportunity. All personnel concerned with the Project also recognized that a need for one-to-one educational information hitherto unrecognized in the Dallas community had been identified and, to some degree, met through the Project. Some who worked in ISP felt that a movement had been started within the community to make use of the library for learning, that the growth was slow and the numbers were small, but that the potential for a meaningful service and growth was there. The two years of study had brought the Project to the point where findings were indicating ways to move into a possible second phase, implementing those plans seen as needs for the future.

The librarians had been assured at the beginning of the Independent Study Project that service to the independent student would be no different than any service to students they had previously performed. But it was different: many of the independent students were looking upon the librarian as their mentor. In the usual practice of his profession when a user came to the library and asked for a book on how to repair the carburetor of his car, the librarian was readily able to locate a book which gave him the precise information he required. When the user left the library with that book in his hand, the librarian did not worry about his ability to successfully repair his car utilizing the library resource. When the student from a formal educational institution came to the library for information on one particular aspect of a broad subject area to use in preparing a paper or passing a test, the librarian was able to locate for him all the information he could use and was careful to avoid "doing" the research for him. The librarian was offering the traditional student resources with which to do independent study, and, when the student left the library, the librarian did not worry about his ability to perform this function.

When the independent student came to the librarian for help in studying the entire field of sociology on his own, the librarian was quite capable of locating all the information the library had available covering the subject area, starting the student at the level he needed, and guiding him to books at higher levels as need arose. This type of help was reader's guidance which was part of the librarian's professional capabilities. But, often, when the independent student left the library with a Study Guide/Reading List and books in hand, a sense of worry and responsibility for his success or failure remained with the librarian. The librarian was not comfortable working in what was his normally unstructured manner when the user's goal was an acceptable score on a test over a complete subject area based on an unknown, albeit structured, curriculum approach. The faculty member might know the "one best book" to use, but the librarian did not. Yet the student was to rely upon the librarian's advice in choosing his books. The librarian, working with the ISP student, recognized that it would be the rare individual who could and would find studying alone a successful route to the CLEP goal. Still, the library had offered an open invitation to would-be students to use the library for just that purpose. As one of the librarians working with ISP stated to the Project Director, "Please make it clear that it was that very professional library commitment to quality service to the user which made us uncertain about the concept of independent study except for the very few."

As the Dallas Public Library Independent Study Project continued, it became clear that CLEP credit was not the goal for everyone and that with the varying reasons for learning went differing needs. Some persons appeared to be seeking ways in which they might prepare themselves to become better contributors to the changing society in which they lived. As the educated and the less well educated mixed in society, those who lacked formal background knowledge, though having a fund of "hands-on" experience, began to recognize their educational limitations. They often felt that, with a better understanding of the basic disciplines and an improved vocabulary, they might be better equipped to communicate ideas which could contribute to meaningful solutions for the problems of society. They were thinking people who had a need to better express themselves. And, when the opportunity came to achieve that end, the public library was the place they were now familiar and comfortable with. Later, as their learning progressed, they might move on to other sites, but the public library was the place to begin; the open door to the learning community. Other persons in the community came to the Project Office offering their services as volunteer tutors because they too wanted to become involved in a more meaningful way in their community. Perhaps Marshall McLuhan describes this beginning interest best when he states,

> To be able to dialogue with modern people caught in extremely complicated situations requires precisely the encyclopedic range of awareness of the ancient humanist. That is, the complexity of the contemporary world demands a non-specialist preparation of awareness which is almost poetic in its scope and sensitivity to pattern.[1]

For other students who expressed a desire to learn through independent study, the librarian recognized needs for help in the actual process of studying which were not being completely met in the Project. Workshops could not reach all students, and some students did not find the workshop approach attractive. Needs for learners at the GED level had been indicated since, for some learners, existing commercial programmed materials were often too confusing to use independently. There were needs for incentive and rewards recognition — a continuing sense of moving on and up rather than continual striving for a distant goal. For some of those working with ISP the word *study* invoked unhappy connotations, and not far into the Project the word "learning" took its place. It is

---

[1]Marshall McLuhan, *Take Today: The Executive as Dropout* (New York: Harcourt Brace, 1972), p. 292.

so, of course, that the student applies his mind to *learn* about a subject, and he searches out meanings and pays attention to detail in order to understand the subject matter, and these make up the basics of *studying*. While the book sufficed as the learning resource for many ISP students, there were other adults, often those most eager to learn, who were not yet ready to use the book as their sole resource from which to study. McLuhan states,

> The TV eye is not a convergent focusing eye but an environmental scanner that works at speeds which reveal the hidden patterns that demand programming. The same speed-up technology creates ecological configurations that end the old classifications of knowledge. The shift is from concept to percept.2

It is possible that the careful combination of other than print media with the book could ease the transition from mere study to learning, from concept to percept. A report from the Stanford University School of Education published in 1968 stated,

> Among educational experimenters . . . there is growing awareness that instructional technology must be conceptualized as some combination of learning theory and individual differences . . . 3

The report emphasized that aptitudes or "individual differences in interaction with instructional-media variables" did exist and that little attention had been given to this aspect of instructional media. In addition to these individual differences, it was noted in ISP that not all of the adult learners were familiar with the use of tapes, television, and other forms of media instruction as study tools. Learning to learn with these forms of media, or incorporating them into learning experiences, was a need of ISP students. Illich describes "convivial tools" as

2Marshall McLuhan, *Take Today: The Executive as Dropout,* p. 14.

3Richard E. Snow and Gavriel Saloman, *Aptitudes and Instructional Media* (Stanford, California: Stanford University School of Education, 1968), pp. 2-3.

> . . . those which give each person who uses them the greatest opportunity to enrich the environment with the fruits of his or her vision.[4]

And, he goes on to say,

> At its best the library is the prototype of a convivial tool. Repositories for other learning tools can be organized on its model, expanding access to tapes, pictures, records.. [5]

Needs exhibited by students in ISP suggested that the transition from "concept to percept" might be more easily affected through the use of a broader range of "convivial tools."

Some librarians working in ISP felt they were not giving all the time their professional commitment required to help the independent student, and, consequently, some students might have become discouraged and did not return to the library for further help. These librarians considered that one person in the library should be free at all times to work with the independent student. One of the librarians commented, "My natural store of warmth seems to dissipate when I have four people standing in front of my desk waiting for my attention." This same librarian indicated that, unless enough time was given this new learner, he could be lost to independent study and that what he needed was one person to whom he could relate and whose name he would know, there in the library at any time he wished to make contact.

In addition to worries about time available, a problem with the semantics of the word "counseling" had been with the Project from the time of its inception. In the performance of reader's guidance, librarians had always engaged in a form of counseling; the traditional librarian/user relationship was a one-to-one exchange which resulted in very personal relationships with some users, often covering spans of years. The librarian usually was well trained in the art of eliciting the wants of the user so that he could be well served. "Counseling" of the independent student also often called

---

[4]Ivan Illich, *Tools for Conviviality*, World Perspectives, Vol. 47, (New York: Harper and Row, 1973), p. 21.

[5]Ivan Illich, *Tools for Conviviality*, p. 21.

for a measure of academic guidance which could be gleaned from college catalogs and, therefore, was well within the realm of reader's guidance. Added to this type of guidance for the ISP student would always be the suggestion that "at some time" in the planning for his long range goals the student should check with a counselor at a college or university to avoid error due to possible changes in academic policies. Further, evaluation of an individual's abilities, personal aptitudes, and accreditation for work experience would be done on an individual basis at the college or university. These were not in any way considered to be a reader's guidance function, and were not, therefore, considered the kind of counseling appropriate for the librarian. Such counseling was referred to one of those academic counselors on campuses in the Dallas area who formed the resource pool for ISP. Regardless of where the cut-off in reader's guidance/counseling came, for the librarian working with the "dependent" student this was a slow, time-consuming process in which answers must be thoroughly understood by the student if he were to proceed with assurance.

Often, when the student understood what was offered through ISP, he wanted to pursue alternative routes which also were not within the expertise of the librarian to guide, and, if the student's desires for alternative action and his readiness for referral did not coincide, referral might stop the process of entering the learning situation. If the student were highly motivated and the referral went smoothly, the student could be on his way to a new learning experience. The librarian was placed in the position of differentiating levels of readiness for referral while at the same time satisfying the eagerness of an individual student's response to a learning option. Once, again, if the library could offer within its doors the primary aids to the self-direction process which encompassed academic expertise, it was considered possible that more of the new users might be encouraged to continue on toward successful independent study.

During ISP there was the use of tutoring and group help sessions by those persons who came to learn about learning. But the variations in levels of knowledge and interest patterns indicated a need for variations in types of sessions, including groups which encouraged motivation through learner involvement and programs for self-enrichment.

Expressions of concern from local business, government, women's organizations, and educational institutions in coordinating information on educational options open to traditional and non-traditional students emphasized the need to expand and strengthen information and referral resources on a coordinative basis within the community. Indications that there was some consideration of a very small consortium of colleges with plans for a possible external degree program and a credit bank in Texas contributed to the recognition of a future need for a central location in Dallas for a one-to-one educational information exchange. The same need for one-to-one information in business organizations is pointed out by John Price, Manager of the corporate information center of Exxon Corporation.

> . . . businessmen he serves do not like to use libraries. . . . The typical library image held by the average business-man is that of the community public library catering to housewives and school children.[6]

Mr. Price adds,

> . . . when an executive needs an answer to a question that has just come up, he wants it immediately, before the subject he is dealing with changes — not after a leisurely library search.[7]

The staff members and the information client enter into a dialogue where the client's problem is discussed, and the staff member locates the information for him. Mr. Price states that he and his staff have found that,

> . . . most people are reluctant to seek out adequate infor-mation even when the need is substantial — only a minority of exceptionally motivated individuals develop the initiative to search aggressively for information.[8]

[6]Paul Doebler, "Profile of an Information Buyer," *Publishers Weekly*, (August 20, 1973), p. 71.

[7]*Ibid.*

[8]*Ibid.*, p. 72.

THE FUTURE

This same reluctance to seek out information, even when the need exists, might be considered to be true of the independent student. But in too many instances the student *had* sought information and had either been unable to locate answers sought or had received unreliable information. Roger Morris opines,

> Institutions best serve those who seek them out . . . it seems a safe bet that people who want and need library service will eventually show up at the checkout counter.[9]

In a subsequent letter in response to critiques of some of his previous statements, Mr. Morris adds,

> It is laudable that a library makes its user aware of all educational programs . . . After all, how independent (or capable) is a student who cannot seek out the proper CLEP or university officials for counseling once the library has made him aware of the program? Are we simply rounding up students who are marginally interested and marginally academic?[10]

The Independent Study Project was no more prepared than Mr. Morris for the numbers of capable businessmen, business women, college instructors, and housewives who used the ISP information services because of inability to locate adequate information and counseling on campuses or elsewhere in the community.

Mr. Morris also deplores the practice of "recruiting" students and wonders how many there were who wanted help.[11] Publicity, which might be considered "recruiting," was the only way in which ISP also could make some estimate of how many there were "out there" who did not know of learning options open to them. Cost of a program which served large numbers of persons would most certainly be far more easily justified than one which found little interest from the public. As Mr. Morris defines it,

[9]Roger Morris, "Keep the Independent Student Independent," *American Libraries*, (July-August, 1973), p. 421.

[10]Roger Morris, Commentary, "Libraries in the Education Game," *American Libraries*, IV, (October, 1973), p. 533.

[11]Roger Morris, "Keep the Independent Student Independent," p. 421.

I suppose the ultimate worth of the Dallas program will be judged on whether it has helpèd genuine students who would not have been helped otherwise, whether the cost is compatible with that of existing educational programs, and whether the project will continue its full-fledged counseling and teaching functions once the funding has dried up.[12]

ISP did not maintain "full-fledged counseling and teaching functions," as has been clearly explained throughout this book. However, Mr. Morris' question of cost is valid and pertinent to the Project. The cost of the Project has been presented in Chapter 4 and evaluation of student needs for the future has been presented in the preceding paragraphs of this chapter. The Dallas Public Library System cannot maintain the services offered by Southern Methodist University; the Library cannot afford to carry such costly resources for the use of its patrons. The Library can offer the CLEP information and those special tools prepared for the Independent Study Project in all of the 14 branches of the Dallas Public Library System. The professional staff members of all 14 branches can be informed on the use of these materials and oriented to the concept of independent study. Programs and publicity can be incorporated into the on-going functions of the library system. When the existing supply of specially prepared resource materials is exhausted, copies can be maintained at the branch libraries for reference. The librarians can continue to serve the user to the full capacity of their time allowance and can offer reader's guidance to aid the independent student in his learning.

The sophisticated student could function well within the services which the library could offer as such services become assimilated into the system. Because maintenance of current reliable information on college and university credits and counseling referral sources and volunteer tutoring capabilities is so time consuming, there is question about the ability of the library to continue such services. For that student who was less-than-independent and for whom hitherto unrecognized needs have been defined by ISP, the Dallas Public Library System could

---

[12]Roger Morris, Commentary, "Libraries in the Education Game," *American Libraries*, IV, (October, 1973), p. 533.

not function without support, yet this was the student who was not affiliated in any way with another educational institution. In addition, this student frequently was not learning even on a "random basis,"[13] often at the age of 30 considered himself "too old to learn," and would not have re-entered the learning process without the library's encouragement. The next step for ISP was to consider ways in which services could be offered to this new user. The working unit to which the Dallas Public Library System turned for help in considering a possible new phase for study was the Dallas County Community College District, (DCCCD) which, like the library, has as its primary goal service to the community. While this second phase has become more structured where need for support was indicated, at the same time the variety of learning opportunities has been enlarged to allow the student freedom to move from one aspect of study to another as his interest and motivation directs him.

Those areas where ISP had indicated needs for added support to the learner were basically continuing personal assurance and special materials. These are being met during a new phase of study within learning centers at two branch libraries in the Dallas Public Library System. These centers are manned full-time by DCCD counseling and para-professional counseling staff, and special materials resulting from joint experimentation by DCCD/DPL staff members are available. Audio-visual equipment, packaged kits, and programmed materials supplement and enrich the tools which had been available to the student during ISP. Once again, emphasis should be placed upon the understanding that these serve as "convivial tools," tools for learning which the student can utilize in whatever pattern he chooses. With the book as a guide, the student *can* devise his personal curriculum for learning; he can be the decision maker as to where his learning interest lead him. If he is credit oriented, perhaps his choices would be more limited, but he might also come back to the library at a later date to pursue an area of interest for personal enrichment.

Accessibility to counseling and information services is now maintained for all libraries of the Dallas Public Library System through the use of a telephone hot-line. In addition, the Dallas Public Library's *Learning Machine* works in conjunction with the

[13]Roger Morris, "Keep the Independent Student Independent," p. 423.

Dallas County Community College District's *Up With Education* mobile counseling unit to reach out as far as the Crossroads Learning Center (South Dallas) neighborhood. Programming for help sessions has achieved a broader range with the added expertise of the community college's community services departments. DCCD also has moved into the television arena, and independent students during ISP had used their original TV program on American Government as a supplemental learning resource. Now, with the *Man and His Environment* TV series, DCCCD has recognized the need for student feedback and group contact which is accomplished both on campus and at a library learning center. The Dallas Independent School District GED classes being held at the public library are supplemented with the resources at the library learning centers.

The story of ISP is merely a description of the efforts of one library system to study the implementation of a concept, independent study. Much of the service involved in independent study was not new to libraries, but, as demands upon resources grow and coordinative efforts with other educational entities increase in number, it is quite possible that new professional commitments will be encompassed by the library profession along with new approaches to cooperative resource funding. What appears to be a "role" for one library may not always be the role another library will be called upon to play, for, just as the neighborhoods in Dallas displayed different interests and needs, it is quite possible that the larger geographical "neighborhoods" across the country will present their own individualities. Differences in "independent" and "dependent" students could be expected to disappear in the future, and, wherever independent study takes place or in whatever form it appears, it seems probable that students of all types will exert increasingly greater impact on libraries (of all types) and librarians.

The Office of Library Independent Study and Guidance Projects, funded by grants from the National Endowment for the Humanities, the Council on Library Resources, and the U.S. Office of Education, has been established by the College Entrance Examination Board to aid libraries and librarians who may wish to work with independent study programs. Training seminars will be held for library systems which will cover all aspects of such a library program. In addition, the Office plans to prepare models for librarians in the areas of adult decision making, learning, and evaluation. The Council on Library Resources has just funded a fellowship "to research and design criteria for a role for urban public libraries in non-traditional study programs."[14] From these two programs alone, one would have to admit, it looks as though the "handwriting is on the wall," and many libraries will become more deeply involved with independent study in the future.

The National Association of Educational Broadcasters describes radio and audio technologies which could have educational impact in the future. The Association's premise is that "The stage, in radio, is the listener's imagination,"[15] and

> In future years when shopping, banking, and other similar activities may be carried on electronically through a home reception and transmission center, education must also be included in the console if lifetime learning is to take place under the circumstances of the future.[16]

Cable television audio technologies are also included under this blanket description of radio, and the implications for educational programming to and from libraries stagger the imagination. The computer is also being studied as a teaching tool, some aspects of which have direct application for library/community coordination. Northwestern University's Computer Aids to Teaching project is utilizing the concept of Illich's learning web as

> . . . a network of people and information within which learners may work. In one way it is like a giant library in which people (as well as books and other resources) are cataloged — He [Illich] sees the learning web as a dynamic catalog — changing with the people who use it.

---

[14]"The Council's Grants: May 1 - June 30, 1973," *CLR Recent Developments*, I, p. 4.

[15]The National Association of Educational Broadcasters; National Educational Radio Division, "Radio's Role in Instruction: Report and Recommendations of the Instructional Radio Task Force," Washington, D.C., September, 1972, (Spec. pre-publication copy), p. 30.

[16]*Ibid.*, p. 40.

It would possess the ability to schedule people who were interested in learning about or discussing specific topics. A small community could accomplish this with a bulletin board and a card catalog . . . 17

In the future, the computer can also be put to use by "users searching for learning peers,"18 which was done in ISP via the telephone and a card file.

For the independent student all or any of these new forms education is taking are important inputs for his future planning. From some he can learn directly for the aspect of independent study he is pursuing; from others he can learn of alternatives for the future. The total community becomes a learning resource for the individual who wishes to learn on his own. J. Lloyd Trump raises the issue of better community coordination; he questions,

> . .. why do we waste time and money on separate schools and libraries? Separately trained personnel? Separate boards and taxing bodies? Where does one stop, and the other begin? Who owns 4:30 P.M.? Who owns Saturday? Sunday? Who owns July?19

Trump answers his own questions by recommending a new approach throughout the total community. He suggests a community director and a board of learning resources, and adds,

> Under this community director of learning resources should come schools, churches, educational institutions, museums, libraries, everything in the community that has an educational program or a collection of educational resources. All of these need to be coordinated, so that the

17*Computers and Teaching, and Interactive Newsletter*, Northwestern University Computer Aids to Teaching Project 7, October, 1973, A Computer-based Information Exchange, p. 5.

18*Ibid.*, p. 7.

19J. Lloyd Trump, "Trends in Learning and Education Affecting Community Library Services," Guy Garrison, ed., *Total Community Library Service* (Chicago: American Library Association, 1973), p. 15, (response to A. Harry Passow).

financial resources of the community can be justly and wisely allocated.

Unless this is done, we will never truly have a community program for continuing education, or a community program for learning resources.[20]

The public library has absorbed the impact of community educational thrusts for years, and generally the library is the last to know. Even today, with the new and innovative options to learning through newspapers and other media appearing in the community, few educators recognize a need to coordinate with the library.

Independent students have added their demands for education to those of the on-campus students' demands for relevancy in education, which has resulted in an interesting realignment of educational offerings. Educators have recognized that the on-campus student is moving out into the community for part of his educational experience; the adult unaffiliated student is moving on to the campus for part of his educational experience; and both are asking for relevancy in learning experiences. The independent student moves on to the campus to learn what the student on campus finds irrelevant, and the campus student moves out into the community to learn about the relevancy in which the independent student lives and works. When the balance is reached, it would appear that what now may appear only as faddism to some may be the beginning of a circular flow of learning from the community to the educational institution and back into the community. If the flow continues, learning should retain those disciplinary structures of knowledge essential to allowing for the changes necessary for relevancy to all students. The challenge to libraries and educators in the future is tremendous, and today both educators and librarians are moving toward meeting that challenge.

The 21st report of the Carnegie Commission on Higher Education has emphasized a need across the nation to develop better utilization of non-college institutions to aid people to pursue education "at a stop-and-go-pace throughout their lifetimes."[21] Among

[20]*Ibid.*, p. 19.

[21]Larry Van Dyne, "Carnegie Scans Alternatives to College," *Chronicle of Higher Education*, October 1, 1973.

recommendations listed by the commission are: "consideration of regular, paid 'educational leaves of absence' for all adult employees, coupled with a national 'educational endowment' " allowing two years of subsidized education for every adult to draw upon at his time convenience. Early library closings are mentioned as environmental barriers to adults' entering of colleges and universities. The commission is also suggesting the possibility of a dual system of accreditation with a government-run agency affording a branch of accreditation other than the single academic accrediting route. The commission also recommends the creation of counseling centers to provide information across the entire range of educational options at the post-secondary level.

What is happening is, perhaps, not innovation; it is directed action to meet needs and demands from society for change. Much of what is "new" today is already in the implementation stage somewhere else, and implementation can only serve as input to another stage further down the line. Academic campuses and libraries are opening their doors to the community, and through them students are using the total community as a learning scene. Minnesota Metropolitan State College is operating with the community as campus, people in the community as educators, and the community libraries as resource centers for the students. Louis Shores and Janiece Fusaro believe that "what is now needed is a Gestalt that will produce more of a pattern among all these components,"[22] and their answer is the Library-College. If this influence toward pattern leaves the independent student free to choose, free to a mastery over his educational goals, then, perhaps, Shores and Fusaro's following statement is true:

> As the Library-College reaches out to influence more persons at various levels of the educational system, the idea of Open Education will move with increasing speed from realism to reality.[23]

[22]Louis Shores and Janiece Fusaro, "Innovations," *Learning Today*, No. 88, (Summer, 1973), p. 5.

[23]*Ibid.*

THE FUTURE

The use of the public library as a center for independent study is appropriate, and for some students the library, without change, can be used effectively. In 1968, Mrs. Lillian Bradshaw, Director of the Dallas Public Library, said,

> A public library represents the most acceptable and accessible instrument for self education in a community. While this role can be aided by other organizations in the community, opportunities open to the public library for planning, cooperative leadership and the utilization of talents from all walks of life and all interest groups are countless. With clear educational goals based on understanding of the community's needs, group planning can truly forward group learning.[24]

The Dallas Public Library, perhaps, through the vehicle of ISP engaged in a dialogue with the community to better understand the learning needs.

---

[24]Lillian Bradshaw, "Cultural Programs — The Dallas Public Library," Grace T. Stevenson, ed., "Group Services in Public Libraries," *Library Trends*, XVII, (July, 1968), p. 67.

BIBLIOGRAPHY

Bradshaw, Lillian. "Cultural Programs — The Dallas Public Library." *Library Trends*, XVII (July, 1968)

Computers and Teaching, and Interactive Newsletter. Northwestern University Computer Aids to Teaching Project 7, October, 1973, A Computer-based Information Exchange.

Doebler, Paul. "Profile of an Information Buyer." *Publishers Weekly.* August 20, 1973.

Illich, Ivan. *Tools for Conviviality.* World Perspectives, Vol. 47, New York: Harper and Row, 1973.

McLuhan, Marshall. *Take Today: The Executive as Dropout.* New York: Harcourt Brace, 1972.

Morris, Roger. "Keep the Independent Student Independent." *American Libraries*, (July-August, 1973).

Morris, Roger. Commentary, "Libraries in the Education Game." *American Libraries*, IV (October, 1973).

National Association of Education Broadcasters; National Educational Radio Division, "Radio's Role in Instruction: Report and Recommendations of the Instructional Radio Task Force." Washington, D.C., September, 1972 [Special pre-publication copy.]

Shores, Louis and Janiece Fusaro. "Innovations." *Learning Today,* No. 88, (Summer, 1973).

Snow, Richard E. and Gavriel Salomon. *Aptitudes and Instructional Media.* Stanford, California: Stanford University School of Education, 1968.

The Council's Grants: May 1 - June 30, 1973. *CLR Recent Developments,* I.

Trump, J. Lloyd. "Trends in Learning and Education Affecting Community Library Services." *Total Community Library Service.* Chicago: American Library Association, 1973. [response to A. Harry Passow].

Van Dyne, Larry. "Carnegie Scans Alternatives to College." *Chronicle of Higher Education.* October 1, 1973.

Addendum

The examples from ISP presented in this Addendum
may serve as suggestions
for other approaches to independent study in libraries.

A PROPOSAL
DESIGNED TO
INVESTIGATE THE EFFECTIVENESS
OF THE PUBLIC LIBRARY
AS A CENTER FOR INDEPENDENT STUDY
TOWARD ACHIEVING
A TWO-YEARS COLLEGE EDUCATION

TOTAL AMOUNT OF REQUEST $100,000

Submitted by
THE DALLAS PUBLIC LIBRARY
CITY OF DALLAS, TEXAS 75201

Initialed by
MRS. LILLIAN M. BRADSHAW
DIRECTOR OF LIBRARIES
DALLAS PUBLIC LIBRARY

Submitted to
COUNCIL ON LIBRARY RESOURCES
ONE DUPONT CIRCLE
WASHINGTON, D.C. 20036

Revised April 27, 1971

PROBLEM:
Many adults are currently involved in independent study designed to enrich their personal lives, to improve their economic conditions, and to further their formal educations. Because these adults are unaffiliated with degree-granting institutions, little recognition is given to their activity. Within these self-motivated adults lies the potential for better educated citizens and a more profitable work force. At the present time, a large number of these adults read and/or study without proper assistance toward a planned course of study. If this independent study could be directed into approved channels which would provide academic credit for these efforts, such efforts would be much more meaningful in terms

of personal and professional benefits. The current existence of the College Board's College-Level Examination Program provides a potential source for such an educational opportunity.

It would seem that, to most successfully utilize this Examination Program, appropriate information and advice about the Program and appropriate study guides, reading lists, and tutorial services should be provided in a setting conducive to independent study. Since many persons directed to independent study use public libraries and since public libraries have traditionally worked in the areas of self-education and continuing education, often in cooperation with other educational institutions, it follows that a public library, with an institution of higher education cooperating and participating, could be an effective agent in providing informational and advisory services to these adults, said services designed to encourage independent study toward achieving a two-years college education.

In addition to information about assistance in self-education and the examinations program to encourage independent study toward achieving a two-years college education, the public library can provide service to those interested in college education in another way. Information about colleges and universities, including entrance requirements, participation in the College-Level Examination Program, tuition and fees, etc. can be made available in traditional formats of catalogs, bulletins, and brochures. A recent experiment in one Branch Library of the Dallas Public Library has suggested that a more successful and effective means of making college information available to inquirers is a multi-media approach; a Videosonic Audiovisual unit, which makes available tape listening and slide viewing presentations of colleges and universities in connection with printed materials from the schools, is utilized. The advantages of such a "College Information Center" is that it is available at the convenience of the individual inquirer, the information is repetitive, the message is multiplied in its impact through the different media used, and the information is coordinated at one point. The public library, which is a recognized source for information in the form of college catalogs, is an ideal place for such "College Information Centers," and such centers would support and supplement information being made available at the public library about the College-Level Examination Program.

This proposal seeks to investigate the role and the effectiveness of one public library system, the Dallas Public Library, with the cooperation and participation of one institution of higher education, Southern Methodist University, in assisting adults pursuing self-education directed to academic recognition in area colleges and universities and information about those and other colleges and universities.

PROPOSAL OBJECTIVES:

1. To serve as an information center for the examinations program of the College-Level Examination Program (CLEP) and of the participation of area colleges and universities.

2. To serve as a distribution center for materials relative to the College-Level Examination Program (CLEP).

3. To serve as a College Information Center by providing, for individual inquiry, multi-media presentations of information about area colleges and universities.

4. To serve as an advisory center to the adult interested in self-education by providing professional assistance in the selection of materials designed to further his goals in seeking academic recognition, by providing professionally prepared study guides and reading lists, and by making available tutorial services.

5. To serve as an educational resource in the motivation of business and industry to encourage employees toward independent study.

6. To determine, through ongoing evaluation of the project, the appropriateness and the effectiveness of the public library in this educational arena.

7. To provide information on and guidance to the entire public library field in this new area of educational involvement.

PROJECT DEVELOPMENT:

1. This project will be directed exclusively to the adult reader.

2. The Dallas Public Library system consisting of the Central Library and fourteen branches will serve as the base for the study.

3. Five branch libraries will be selected to participate as model public libraries serving different socioeconomic communities including lower middle, middle middle, upper middle, and higher stratifications, and one inner-city library serving a socioeconomically-culturally-ethnically mixed population.

4. A College Information Center will be established at each of the five branch libraries. An audiovisual unit will be installed in each location, and area colleges and universities will be provided audio tapes and slides or filmstrips for the production of sound-visual presentations of information about their entrance requirements, tuition and fees, curricula, examination programs, etc. Printed materials about the colleges and universities will be obtained to supplement the audio-visual presentations.

5. Southern Methodist University will hire appropriate members of the faculty to prepare study guides for the subject areas included in the CLEP examination program, such study guides to be made available at the five branch libraries to the adult seeking self-education and academic recognition through the Program.

6. Southern Methodist University will hire appropriate members of the faculty to prepare annotated reading lists of non-textbook materials available at the Dallas Public Library for the subject areas included in the CLEP examination program, such reading lists to be approved by the Project Director and to be made available at the five branch libraries to the adult in the Program.

7. Southern Methodist University will hire and make available appropriate resource persons from the academic community to act as tutors and seminar/workshop planners and leaders. These resource persons will provide aid, guidance, and seminars/workshops for the adults in the Program, such tutorial and seminar/workshop services to be provided on a scheduled basis at the five branch libraries. Seminars/workshops will include instruction in methods of effective independent study; the study of specific subjects; reading effectively; and the gatherin and presenting of information as a basis for understanding study and learning.

8. Professional librarians of the Dallas Public Library will provide information services for the College-Level Examination Program (CLEP) and the participation of area colleges and universities, readers advisory service for the adult in the Program, and workshops on using the library. The distribution of CLEP materials and information on participating colleges and universities will be handled by professional librarians in the five branch libraries.

9. The College Entrance Examination Board will provide training for the Project Director; workshops on the examinations and the philosophy of the CLEP for the librarians, resource persons, and faculty; printing of reading lists and study guides; and publicity materials for use by and in the Dallas Public Libraries and for the news media.

10. Southern Methodist University will provide an ongoing evaluation of the appropriateness and effectiveness of the two-years project by, in part, translating the objectives into measurable quantities, and including descriptions of the communities defined by the five branch libraries selected as model public libraries. The evaluation will be presented periodically in four (semiannual) reports and one final report.

11. Professional public relations services will be utilized to produce and provide continual publicity and promotional attention to the Program.

12. An Advisory Committee will provide direction, advice, and assistance in setting objectives within the philosophy of public library service and professionally oriented continuing education goals and in planning procedures and programs designed to implement the project. The Committee will consist of the Dallas Public Library Community Education Coordinator, Chairman; the Dallas Public Library Adult Coordinator; the Dallas Public Library Associate Director for Public Services; the Dean of Continuing Education, Southern Methodist University; and the Dean, School of Humanities and Sciences, Southern Methodist University.

13. A National Interest Council will be formed to review the project and to consider the possible implications of this project for other public libraries and the expansion of the concept and procedures for the project on a national basis. The Council will be appointed by the Advisory Committee and will consist of not more than eight members, including the following:

> One representative each from:
>> American Library Association
>> Council on Library Resources
>> College Entrance Examination Board
>> National Endowment For The Humanities
>> American Association of Junior Colleges
>
> Representatives from public library systems providing geographical representation

The Council will meet four times (semiannually) during the period of the project and will assemble to hear and consider the evaluation reports and the semiannual reports submitted by the Project Director.

PERSONNEL REQUIRED:

1. Project Director who will, with the direction, advice and assistance of the Advisory Committee, formulate procedures and programs for the implementation of the project; instruct Dallas Public Library staff in methods of assisting in the program; direct workshops; consult Dallas Public Library staff and Southern Methodist University faculty and resource persons concerning reading materials; coordinate scheduling and activities of tutors and workshop/seminar planning; initiate and maintain contact with appropriate community agencies, organizations, and institutions; initiate and maintain contact with business and industry in the community to encourage employee participation in the program; prepare and disseminate publicity and information about the project; prepare reports as required by this proposal and/or as requested by the funding agency.

2. Secretary who will, under the supervision of the Project Director, provide secretarial and clerical assistance to the project.

3. Consultant (part-time) for public relations and promotional services for the project.

4. Professional librarians and supportive staffs of the five branch libraries of the Dallas Public Library selected to participate in this project who will, under the guidance of the Project Director, provide direct informational and assistance services to the adults.

5. Existing staff of the College Entrance Examination Board's Council on College-Level Examinations who will provide training for the Project Director and orientation for the professional librarians, resource persons, and faculty involved in the project.

CALENDAR:

The period for the project will be two years beginning August 1, 1971, and concluding September 30, 1973. The first month, August, 1971, will be directed to the training and orientation of the Project Director, professional librarians, resource persons, and faculty in the form of training sessions, workshops, etc. Progress reports prepared by the Project Director and reports of evaluation prepared by the contracted evaluation services of Southern Methodist University will be furnished the Advisory Committee and the funding agency every six months according to the following calendar or as required by the funding agency:

March 1, 1972
September 1, 1972
March 1, 1973
September 1, 1973

Final reports will be due in October 1973 or as required by the funding agency.

FIRST YEAR BUDGET (12 MONTHS)

Refer To: Project Development Item No.	Personnel Required Item No.	Budget Item	Item Cost	Sub Total	Item Total
		I. Salaries ^A			
	1	A. Project Director (Full-time, Grade 16)	$12,024.00	$12,024.00	
		B. Secretary (Full-time, Grade 8)	6,528.00	6,528.00	
					$18,552.00
		II. Fringe Benefits (as required by City of Dallas)			
		A. Pensions (8½% of total salary including merit increases)			
	1	1. Project Director	1,048.07		
	2	2. Secretary	568.14	1,616.21	
		B. Employees Health Insurance ($6.55 per month per employee)			
	1	1. Project Director	78.60		
	2	2. Secretary	78.60	157.20	
		C. Employees Life Insurance ($1.425 per month per employee)			
	1	1. Project Director	17.10		
	2	2. Secretary	17.10	34.20	

^ACity of Dallas requires positions to fit established City positions.

175

Refer To:						
Project Development Item No.	Personnel Required Item No.	Budget Item	Item Cost	Sub Total	Item Total	
		II. Fringe Benefits (Continued)				
		D. Merit Increases (ca. 5% at the end of each six months period for first year of City employment)				
	1	1. Project Director	$ 1,272.00			
	2	2. Secretary	672.00			
				$ 1,944.00		
					$ 3,751.61	
		III. Supplies and Materials				
		A. Standard office supplies	271.00	271.00		
		B. Letterhead stationery	250.00	250.00		
		C. Printing and printing supplies for publicity and announcements and for duplication services	1,000.00	1,000.00		
		D. Postage	500.00	500.00		
		E. Telephone: Two direct lines, two instruments @ $51.75/mo. plus installation $36.00	657.00	657.00		
					2,678.00	
		IV. Travel Expenses				
	1	A. Car allowance @ $25/mo. for Project Director[a]	300.00	300.00		

[a] Rate paid by City of Dallas to Public Library employees.

176

Refer To: Project Development Item No.	Personnel Required Item No.	Budget Item	Item Cost	Sub Total	Item Total
	1	IV. Travel Expenses (Continued)			
		B. Travel for Project Director[c]			
		1. To New York, New York, for 1 week (5 days) orientation and training with CEEB and Educational Testing Services ($188.00 air fare; $25 per diem)			
		Transportation $188.00			
		Subsistence 125.00	$ 313.00		
		2. ALA Midwinter Meeting, Chicago, Jan. 23-29, 1972 ($122 air fare; $25.00 per diem)			
		Transportation $122.00			
		Subsistence 175.00	297.00		
		3. ALA Conference, Chicago, June 25-July 1, 1972 ($122 air fare; $25 per diem)			
		Transportation $122.00			
		Subsistence 175.00	297.00		
		4. Texas Library Association Conference, Galveston, April 5-8, 1972 ($60 air fare; $25 per diem)			
		Transportation $ 60.00			
		Subsistence 100.00	160.00		
		5. Seminars/Institutes of national significance pertinent to this Project (estimate 1 with duration of 3 days; estimate $200 air fare; $25 per diem)			
		Transportation $200.00			
		Subsistence 75.00	275.00	1,342.00	

[c]City of Dallas has no per diem rate; full expenses are paid for approved travel. Rate of $25 per diem is that suggested for normal travel by the American Library Association.

177

Refer To: Project Development Item No.	Personnel Required Item No.	Budget Item	Item Cost	Sub Total	Item Total
13		IV. Travel Expenses (Continued) C. Travel for Members of the Project's National Interest Council: 7 members assemble in Dallas, Texas, two times during first year of Project, each meeting's duration 2 days. (Estimate $200 air fare each, $25 per diem each)[c] Transportation $2,800.00 Subsistence 700.00	$ 3,500.00	$ 3,500.00	$ 5,142.00
	1	V. Special (All equipment to become property of the Dallas Public Library at conclusion of Project) A. Office Equipment[D] 1. Project Director Desk (double pedestal) $250 Executive chair 102 Side chair (2 @ $75) 150 Dictating equipment 283 Wastebasket 6		$ 791.00	

[c]City of Dallas has no per diem rate; full expenses are paid for approved travel. Rate of $25 per diem is that suggested for normal travel by the American Library Association.

[D]City of Dallas purchases office furniture and equipment only per authorized position; therefore, no such equipment exists in the Dallas Public Library's inventory. Office space will be made available.

Refer To: Project Development Item No.	Personnel Required Item No.	Budget Item	Item Cost	Sub Total	Item Total
		V. Special (Continued)[p]			
		A. Office Equipment (Continued)			
	2	2. Secretary			
		Desk (secretarial) $210			
		Posture chair 75			
		Side chair 60			
		File cabinet 127			
		Typewriter (electric) 500			
		Wastebasket 6	$ 978.00		
				$ 1,769.00	$ 1,769.00
		VI. Other: Contracted Services			
6		A. Public Relations Consultant: Part-time services	1,000.00	1,000.00	
		B. Southern Methodist University			
		1. Reading lists (producing 20 reading lists @ $125 each)	2,500.00		
5		2. Study guides (producing 20 study guides @ $250 each)	5,000.00		

[p]City of Dallas purchases office furniture and equipment only per authorized position; therefore, no such equipment exists in the Dallas Public Library's inventory. Office space will be made available.

179

Refer To: Project Development Item No.	Personnel Required Item No.	Budget Item	Item Cost	Sub Total	Item Total
		VI. Other: Contracted Services (Continued)			
		B. Southern Methodist University (Continued)			
7		3. Tutorial services: resource persons to provide tutorial and workshop/seminar services at the five branch libraries, number of tutors to be determined by need and advice of Advisory Committee	$ 5,000.00		
10		4. Ongoing evaluation: an ongoing evaluation of the Project including 2 semiannual reports during the first year of the Project ($2,000 per year)	2,000.00	$14,500.00	
		TOTAL DIRECT COSTS			$15,500.00 $47,392.61
		VIII. Indirect Costs (5½% of direct costs)[E]			2,606.59
		GRAND TOTAL			$49,999.20

[E]The City of Dallas is currently negotiating for an established rate. Rate of 5½% suggested for this Project by the Dallas Public Library.

SECOND YEAR BUDGET (12 MONTHS)

Refer To: Project Development Item No.	Personnel Required Item No.	Budget Item	Item Cost	Sub Total	Item Total
		I. Salaries[A]			
	1	A. Projector Director (Full-time, Grade 16)	$13,296.00	$13,296.00	
	2	B. Secretary (Full-time, Grade 8)	7,200.00	7,200.00	$20,496.00
		II. Fringe Benefits (as required by City of Dallas)			
		A. Pensions (8½% of total salary including merit increases)			
	1	1. Project Director	1,156.17		
	2	2. Secretary	627.81	1,783.98	
		B. Employees Health Insurance ($6.55 per month per employee)			
	1	1. Project Director	78.60		
	2	2. Secretary	78.60	157.20	
		C. Employees Life Insurance ($1.425 per month per employee)			
	1	1. Project Director	17.10		
	2	2. Secretary	17.10	34.20	

[A]City of Dallas requires positions to fit established City positions.

181

Refer To: Project Development Item No.	Personnel Required Item No.	Budget Item	Item Cost	Sub Total	Item Total
		II. Fringe Benefits (Continued)			
		D. Merit Increases (ca. 5% at end of first six months period in second year of City employment)			
	1	1. Project Director	$ 612.00		
	2	2. Secretary	372.00		
				$ 984.00	$ 2,959.39
		III. Supplies and Materials			
		A. Standard office supplies	200.00	200.00	
		B. Letterhead stationery	250.00	250.00	
		C. Printing and printing supplies for publicity and announcements and for duplication services	1,000.00	1,000.00	
		D. Printing of Final Report	1,500.00	1,500.00	
		E. Postage	500.00	500.00	
		F. Telephone: Two direct lines, two instruments @ $51.75/mo.	621.00	621.00	

Refer To: Project Development Item No.	Personnel Required Item No.	Budget Item	Item Cost	Sub Total	Item Total
		III. Supplies and Materials (Continued)			
		G. Audiovisual materials[B]			
4		1. Films	$ 500.00	$ 500.00	
		2. Tapes	500.00	500.00	
		3. Production	500.00	500.00	$ 5,571.00
		IV. Travel Expenses			
	1	A. Car allowance @ $25/mo. for Project Director[C]	300.00	300.00	
	1	B. Travel for Project Director [D]			
		1. ALA Midwinter Meeting, Washington, D.C., Jan. 28-Feb. 3, 1973. ($166 aid fare; $25 per diem) Transportation $166.00 Subsistence 175.00	341.00		
		2. ALA Conference, Las Vegas, New., June 24-29, 1973. ($152 air fare; $25 per diem) Transportation $152.00 Subsistence 175.00	327.00		

[B] Audiovisual materials required for College Information Centers described in Project Development, Item 4.
[C] Rate paid by the City of Dallas to Public Library employees.
[D] City of Dallas has no per diem rate; full expenses are paid for approved travel. Rate of $25 per diem is that suggested for normal travel by the American Library Association.

Refer To: Project Development Item No.	Personnel Required Item No.	Budget Item	Item Cost	Sub Total	Item Total

	1	IV. Travel Expenses (Continued
		
		B. Travel for Project Director (Continued)[p]
		
		  3. Texas Library Association Conference, Fort Worth, Texas, April, 1973, 4 days ($25 per diem)
		    Transportation None
		    Subsistence $100.00
			$ 100.00		

		4. Southwestern Library Association, New Orleans, La., Nov. 1-4, 1972 ($76 air fare; $25 per diem)
		    Transportation $ 76.00
		    Subsistence 100.00
			176.00		

		5. Seminars/Institutes of national significance to the Project (estimate 1 with duration of 4 days; Estimate $200 air fare; $25 per diem)
		    Transportation $200.00
		    Subsistence 100.00
			300.00	$ 1,244.00	

13		C. Travel for Members of the Project's National Interest Council: 7 members assemble in Dallas, Texas, two times during second year of Project, each meeting's duration 2 days. (Estimate $200 air fare each; $25 per diem each)[p]
		    Transportation $2,800.00
		    Subsistence 700.00
			3,500.00	3,500.00	

					$ 5,044.00

[p]City of Dallas has no per diem rate; full expenses are paid for approved travel. Rate of $25 per diem is that suggested for normal travel by the American Library Association.

Refer To: Project Development Item No.	Personnel Required Item No.	Budget Item	Item Cost	Sub Total	Item Total
4		V. Special (All equipment to become property of Dallas Public Library at conclusion of Project)			
		Equipment for College Information Centers: 5 Automatic Sound-Visual Projectors @ $265 each (Recommend DuKane Cassette Micromatic Sound Filmstrip Projectors)	$ 1,325.00	$ 1,325.00	$ 1,325.00
		VI. Other: Contracted Services			
11		A. Public Relations Consultant: Part-time services	1,000.00	1,00.00	
		B. Southern Methodist University			
6		1. Reading lists: Produce 10 reading lists not produced first year @ $125 each	1,250.00		
5		2. Study guides: Produce 10 study guides not produced first year @ $250 each	2,500.00		
7		3. Tutorial services: Continued tutorial services during second year	5,000.00		

Refer To:						
Project Development Item No.	Personnel Required Item No.	Budget Item	Item Cost	Sub Total	Item Total	
		VI. Other: Contracted Services (Continued)				
		B. Southern Methodist University (Continued)				
10		4. Ongoing evaluation: Second year of ongoing evaluation of the Project including 1 semiannual report and the final report	$ 2,250.00	$11,000.00	$12,000.00	
		TOTAL DIRECT COSTS			$47,395.38	
		VII. Indirect Costs (5½% of direct costs)[E]			2,606.75	
		GRAND TOTAL			$50,002.13	

[E]The City of Dallas is currently negotiating for an established rate. Rate of 5½% suggested for this Project by the Dallas Public Library.

186

ISP FLOWCHART SHOWING INTERRELATEDNESS OF PROCESSES
IN EVALUATION TO FUNCTIONS

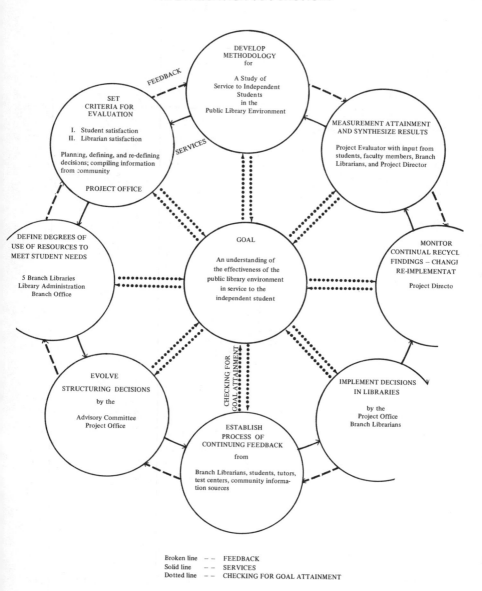

Broken line – – FEEDBACK
Solid line – – SERVICES
Dotted line – – CHECKING FOR GOAL ATTAINMENT

Library Patron:

   Would you give us your:

Name:_____

Address:_____

_____

Telephone Number:_____

so that we may ask your opinion of our
Independent Study Project at a later date.
Thank you!

Please leave this card with a librarian.

_____

The enclosed brochure will introduce the Dallas Public Library
Independent Study Project. If you have any further questions or feel
that it would be of value to members of your organization to have
one of the librarians participating in the Project come and speak to
them, please contact Mrs. Jean Brooks, Project Director (Area Code
241) 748-5256.

_____

When mailed to businesses and industries or community
organizations, the above postcard accompanied the *ISP Brochure.*

ISP is a program of self-education for purposes of self-enrichment and/or preparation for College-Level Examinations for credit.

There are no classes, no teachers in classrooms, no time limits, no pressures of competing in a group, and no homework assignments.

Independent study services and materials are available at no cost.

Dallas Public Library

1954 Commerce

HOW TO BEGIN

Go to any one of the following five participating branch libraries in the Dallas Public Library System to enter the program:

Audelia Road Branch
10045 Audelia Road
348-6160

Preston Royal Branch
5626 Royal Lane
363-5479

Hampton-Illinois Branch
2210 West Illinois Ave.
337-4796

Oak Lawn Branch
3721 Lemmon Avenue
528-6269

Crossroads Learning Center
2610 Forest Avenue
421-4171

Please call any of these branches or the ISP Office, 748-5256, for information.

Available at the branch libraries are:

CLEP brochures: CLEP May Be For You; Description of the General Examination; and Description of the Subject Examinations; and Bulletin of Information for Candidates.

Study Guides and Reading Lists: each guide corresponds with a subject examination to help you prepare for that test.

Workshops are held at the participating branches on a regular basis.

Special tutoring is available for independent students upon request.

Guidance and help from librarians at the branches are available during the hours the branches are open.

STUDY MATERIALS AVAILABLE

The following subject guides, prepared by members of the Southern Methodist University faculty, are available:

American Government	Dr. Ruth Morgan
American History	Dr. James O. Breeden
Analysis & Interpretation	Dr. Steven D. Daniels
of Literature	and Dr. Thomas R. Arp
Biological Sciences	Dr. Claude Nations
College Algebra and	Dr. Raymond V. Morgan
Trigonometry	
Computers and Data	Mr. James C. Collins
Processing	
Educational Psychology	Dr. Fred W. Bryson
English Composition	Mrs. Doris M. Johnson
	and Miss Kay Bethune
English Literature	Dr. Kenneth D. Shields
General Psychology	Dr. Charles Crumbaugh
Geological Sciences	Mr. David D. Gillette
Human Growth and	Mrs. Virginia Chancey
Development	
Introductory Accounting	Mr. James P. Barber
Introductory Business	Dr. Robert McGlashan
Management	
Introductory Chemistry	Dr. John A. Maguire
Introductory Economics	Miss Jo Anne Lowery
Introductory Marketing	Dr. Frank I. Millar
Introductory Sociology	Dr. Alex McKeigney
Statistics and	Dr. Wanzer Drane
Probability	
Western Civilization	Dr. John A. Mears

Pick up the study guides and reading lists you need and use the Library as your information and resource center. You can be notified of workshops if you wish; individual help in finding materials is available.

New subject guides are being prepared for the fall, 1972, and spring, 1973.

C L E P
COLLEGE-LEVEL
EXAMINATION PROGRAM

A program whereby one may take a test, have the score sent to a university of his choice and, if his score is acceptable, receive credit toward a college degree:

There are two types of tests offered:

The General Examination measures achievement in English Composition, Humanities, Mathematics, Natural Sciences, and Social Science-History.

29 Subject Examinations cover all the subjects listed below, so one can test himself in whatever areas he feels competent:

Business:
 Computers & Data
   Processing
 Elementary Computer
   Programming--
   FORTRAN IV
 Introductory Accounting
 Introductory Business
   Law
 Introduction to
   Business Management
 Introductory Marketing
 Money and Banking

Social Sciences:
 American Government
 American History
 General Psychology
 Introductory Economics
 Introductory Sociology
 Western Civilization

Sciences:
 Biology
 General Chemistry
 Geology

Humanities:
 American Literature
 Analysis & Interpre-
   tation of Literature
 English Composition
 English Literature

Mathematics:
 College Algebra
 Algebra & Trigonometry
 Introductory Calculus
 Statistics
 Trigonometry

Education:
 Educational Psychology
 History of American
   Education
 Human Growth and
   Development
 Tests and Measurements

PARTICIPATING INSTITUTIONS

Many colleges and universities in the Southwest accept credit by examination; however, each school may set its own policy as to how much credit it will accept and what score is required. For instance, The University of Texas at Arlington offers credit for the following examinations effective with the fall semester, 1972:

American Government
American History
American Literature
Analysis & Interpre-
  tation of Lit.
Biology
College Algebra
Algebra-Trigonometry
Computers & Data
  Processing
English Composition
English Literature

General Chemistry
General Psychology
Geology
Intro. Accounting
Intro. Calculus
Intro. Economics
Trigonometry
Western Civilization

A maximum of 21 hours of credit may be earned through the General Examination.

The amount of credit awarded varies with the score achieved. It is best to talk with a counselor-evaluator at the college.

If one is using this program for purposes of preparing for CLEP tests, it is advisable to contact the Dean of Admissions at the college of his choice to find out precisely what examinations and scores are accepted for credit.

A booklet is available which lists many of the colleges and universities in the United States which honor CLEP. Listed below are the schools in Texas which accept CLEP credits:

Abilene Christian College
Alvin Junior College

Angelo State University
Austin College
* Baylor University
* Brazosport College
Central Texas College
* Christian College of
   the Southwest
* College of the Mainland
* Cooke County Junior College
Dominican College
East Texas State University
Houston Baptist College
* Howard County Junior College
Howard Payne College
* Incarnate Word College
Kilgore College
* Lubbock Christian College
* Mary Hardin-Baylor College
* McMurry College
* Midwestern University
North Texas State University
Northwood Institute
Our Lady of the Lake College
Pan American University
* Paul Quinn College
St. Edward's University
* St. Mary's University
Sam Houston State University
San Jacinto College
* South Plains College
* Southern Methodist University
* Southwestern Union College
* Southwestern University
Tarrant County Junior College:
   Northeast & South Campuses
Texas College
Texas A & M University
* Texas Christian University
* Texas Wesleyan College
* Trinity University
University of Corpus Christi
* University of Houston

The University of Texas
at Arlington
The University of Texas at
Austin
* The University of Texas at
El Paso
The University of Texas
Southwestern Medical
School at Dallas
* Wharton County Junior College

* CLEP Test Centers

Test fees are $15 for each Subject Examination, $15 for one part of the General Examination, and $25 for two or more parts.

Southern Methodist University's Test Center gives the tests once each month (12 times a year) and you may apply to take a test when you feel you are prepared.

Tests are optional. If one wishes to study for personal enrichment, he never has to take a test. CLEP provides a flexible means for certifying knowledge, a way to progress at one's own speed toward postsecondary degrees or simply to satisfy his curiosity about the extent and quality of his learning. It has opened up new possibilities for those who have been unable to participate in full-time postsecondary education.

Many independent students use CLEP for job up-grading. Companies within the Dallas area are considering the extension of present educational benefits to include payment of fees for examinations taken by an employee. The CLEP tests are used as a basis for determining college equivalency and for providing non-college men and women the opportunity to advance to professional positions.

TO THE EMPLOYER

CLEP can help a company to:

Tap a source of talent that may have been previously ignored.

Develop a potential pool of well-educated employees within the company's ranks to meet future needs.

Utilize its best human resources in communities where local shortages of professional personnel exist.

Secure greater benefits and lower costs from company-subsidized tuition payments.

Improve and establish good company-employee relations.

CLEP's basic philosophy rests on the observation that there are well-qualified and mature adults without college degrees whose equivalent college-level achievements have not been properly recognized. Within any company there may be such individuals working in low-level positions, demonstrating responsibility and loyalty to their employers, who have more to contribute. By virtue of their experience and past training, they might be as well qualified for a better position and for further educational development as a new college graduate brought into the company by outside recruitment.

Employers have an opportunity to tap this source of talent by utilizing the Independent Study Project's materials and by recognizing CLEP credits.

A brochure published by the College Entrance Examination Board which explains the uses of CLEP in business is available for employers from the ISP Office. Ask for <u>College Credit by Examination</u>.

The CLEP concept is new enough to the Dallas area that educational institution accrediting policies may be undergoing rapid change. The ISP Office will have the latest information available. Call 748-5256.

PROJECT DIRECTOR
Mrs. Jean Brooks

ADVISORY COMMITTEE
Community Education Coordinator
Dallas Public Library
Mrs. Margaret M. Warren
Chairman

Dean, School of
  Continuing Education
Southern Methodist Univ.
  Dr. Fred W. Bryson

Associate Director,
  Public Services
Dallas Public Library
  Mr. David L. Reich

Adult Coordinator
Dallas Public Library
  Mr. Ervin Eatenson

Associate Dean of Faculties
  School of Humanities and
  the Sciences
Southern Methodist Univ.
  Dr. James Early

NATIONAL INTEREST COUNCIL

National Endowment for
  the Humanities
Mr. Robert J. Kingston

Council on Library Resources
Dr. Fred C. Cole

College Entrance
  Examination Board
Mr. Jose A. Toro

American Association of
  Junior Colleges
Mr. Roger Yarrington

American Library Association
  Mr. Gerald M. Born

Miami-Dade Public Library
  Mr. Edward F. Sintz

St. Louis Public Library
  Mr. James J. Michael

San Diego Public Library
  [Representing the Serra
  Regional Library System]
  Miss Margaret E. Queen

Funded ,1971-1973, by:
National Endowment for the Humanities
Council on Library Resources
College Entrance Examination Board

INDEPENDENT STUDY NEWSLETTER DALLAS PUBLIC LIBRARY

INDEPENDENT STUDY

Study Guides/Reading Lists, a guide on How to Study Independently, and one on Reading Improvement, in addition to the CLEP materials, are now available at ALL Branch Libraries and at the Central Library.

The College-Level Examination Program (CLEP) is national and will always continue. The examinations are administered the third week of every month in testing centers at most colleges and universities in the Dallas area. Information on registration is available at the testing centers.

The Dallas Public Library and the Dallas Independent School District are jointly setting up tutoring sessions within the Branch Libraries to help people prepare for the GED exam. There is no charge to attend the sessions and those interested in tutoring the GED groups will be paid a small honorarium by the Dallas Independent School District. The sessions will begin in October at the Crossroads Community Learning Center, the Hampton-Illinois, Lancaster-Kiest, Pleasant Grove, and West Branch Libraries. You may call the Branch Library for additional information.

The Librarian at your nearest Branch Library will be pleased to give you assistance in locating books for your study.

EDUCATIONAL OPTIONS FOR THE INDEPENDENT STUDENT

You may not choose to take the courses listed below for college credit, but you should consider them as options available to enhance your independent learning experience.

*America and the Future of Man

This is a series of 20 articles by world-famous scholars to be published Sundays in the Dallas Morning News beginning September 30. You may take advantage of the series in one of three ways: you may read it for enjoyment; explore the subject further with the aid of supplemental materials; or earn college credit through Southern Methodist University. SMU is among 155 colleges and universities participating in this educational adventure called Courses by Newspaper. The Project was set up by the University of California at San Diego and is supported by a grant from National Endowment for the Humanities (also a funding agency of ISP). The articles will deal with a broad spectrum of studies--history, psychology, sociology, social ethics and political science--and their relationship to such scientific fields as genetics and biology. They will deal with issues such as: Do the achievements and costs of modern, materialistic society need reassessing? What is the good life and how can it be won for now and for the future? What are the ethical and scientific problems posed by overpopulation?

Students who want to take the course for college credit may choose either of 2 SMU study plans. They may enroll for 2 semester credits or for 3. A minimum of 2 evening classroom sessions will be required under the 2 credit option. Additional classroom sessions and assignments will be required for 3 credits. The SMU fee is $75 for 2 credit hours, $100 for 3. To order the supplemental kit of information you may send $10, your name and address to America and the Future of Man, PO Box F, Wayne, N.Y., 07470. For additional information you may call Southern Methodist University, 692-2333.

*Dallas Morning News, September 16, 1973.

Man and His Environment

"Man and His Environment" (Biology 290) is a general education course offered by the Dallas County Community College District in cooperation with KERA, Channel 13 television. This is a 15-week survey course designed to explore environmental problems which man must solve in order to have a quality existence. The course will examine all types of pollution, population dynamics, and conservation of resources. Stress is placed on the concept of environmental interdependence with man as a part of, rather than separate from, the eco-system.

The cost for this 3-credit-hour course is $25 with 4 classroom sessions held on campus during any given semester. A student may register for the course (and purchase his textbook and 2 study guides) at any of the Dallas County Community Colleges.

A new unit which is divided into 2 parts (A and B) is presented each week on Channel 13. Each program is 30 minutes, and the student must watch both parts A and B (1 hour total TV watching time). Each program is presented many times during the week--check your TV listing for times. Part A of each unit is a nationally produced documentary film of environmental problems while Part B is produced locally showing environmental problems in the Dallas-Ft. Worth area. Two examinations are given during the semester--a mid-term and a final.

A Hotline, 746-4588, is open 5 days a week from 10:00 a.m. to 4:00 p.m. to answer questions from enrolled or prospective students regarding the course. In addition there is a monthly newsletter mailed to each enrolled student as another means of direct communication between the instructor and the student.

Keep in mind that other options to enrich your learning experience are non-credit courses offered through the DCCCD's Community Services Div., SMU's Continuing Education Div., Channel 13, plus local musical productions and Dallas-Ft. Worth area museums.

10/73

200

DALLAS PUBLIC LIBRARY

ISP TELEPHONE QUESTIONNAIRE
(REVISED)

NAME: _____ DATE: _____

I'm Mrs. _____ a volunteer working for the Independent Study Project of the Dallas Public Library. We're calling a number of the persons who have been interested in the Independent Study Project to ask them a few questions. Do you have time to talk with me for a few minutes?

1. Have you been receiving the Independent Study Project's newsletter?

2. What kind of information do you get from the newsletter that you wouldn't otherwise know about?

3. Have you picked up any of the Study Guides and Reading Lists the Independent Study Project has available at the library?

   If yes, could you tell me which ones you chose?

4. Have you had time to pursue your interest in any of these (or this) Study Guide(s)?

   If yes, how do you feel the Study Guide has been helpful in your study?

   If no, drop to question number 7.

5. Have you used books from the Reading List?

   If yes, how did you choose the books you wanted to study from all the books on the Reading List?

   If not stated in the above answer, ask, Did the librarian help you choose books from the Reading List?

   If not stated in the above answer, ask, Did the librarian help you locate the books you wanted?

   If no, how have you obtained reading material for your study?

6. Have you asked for any help from librarians on questions you may have about college courses, degree plans, or what courses are needed for certain careers or occupations?

   If yes, has this information been helpful to you?

   If yes, how?

   If no, why not?

7. Have you attended any of the help sessions at the Library Branches?

   If yes, which one was most helpful to you?

   If no, is there some topic you would like to have a help session on?

8. Have you taken a CLEP exam?

9. Do you plan to take (an) (another) CLEP exam?

10. Did you use the Library before you became involved in the Independent Study Project?

11. Are there any other comments you would like to make about the Independent Study Project or CLEP?

ONE HALF HOUR TELEVISION SCRIPT

1. *What is CLEP?*

   CLEP is the College-Level Examination Program through which any adult may take tests for college credit. At some colleges he can earn up to 2 years of college credit without ever attending a formal classroom lecture.

2. *If I don't go to any classes, how am I supposed to know enough to take a college-level test?*

   It is pretty certain you know more than you think you do — things you have learned from on-the-job experience, reading books and newspapers, military experience, and watching television. To help you organize this material the Dallas Public Library conducts an Independent Study Project at 5 branch libraries which will assist you in planning a course of study. Reading lists and study guides and resource persons to conduct workshops are supplied by SMU professors.

3. *How much does all this cost?*

   Materials and assistance provided by the Independent Study Project at the branch libraries are free. The CLEP tests are $15 for subject exams; $15 for 1 general exam and $25 for 2-5 of the general exams.

4. *Are the tests given at the library?*

   No. The tests may be taken at SMU's Testing Center on every 3rd Friday of each month. When you take the test, you may ask that your score be sent to a university of your choice if you wish to get credit.

5. *How much credit can I get?*

   This varies with the institution; so, early in the program you should get to the university or college you wish to attend and find out what subjects they credit and the amount of credit they will give.

6. *Do all universities and colleges accept these scores?*

No. The Independent Study Project has a list of those participating schools in Texas.

7. *This all sound great, but I'm not sure I want to go on to college. Do I have to take the tests if I enter the ISP?*

Not at all. What you learn now can always be used later. Personal enrichment can be just as important to you as college credit.

8. *Do I have to attend the workshops?*

Not unless you want to. The workshops are merely to help those who want to learn more about how to use the library study independently, familiarize themselves with CLEP test formats, and use subject guides.

9. *How long do I have to study before I can take the tests?*

There is no time limit. You can spend as long or as short a time in study as you feel you need to prepare. When you feel confident you know your subject, go ahead and take the test.

10. *What if I fail the test?*

There is no passing or failing grade. You just get a score — if it is good enough you will get college credit when you enter a participating school. The acceptable score for credit varies with each college, so this is something else to ask about when you visit or write the institution you want to attend. If you score falls below the acceptable level, study the weak spots and, after a while, take the test again.

11. *How do I get started?*

There are 5 branch libraries which can supply the study materials and CLEP information. Those branches are Audelia Road, Crossroads Learning Center, Hampton-Illinois, Oak Lawn, and Preston Royal. Go to the one nearest you and ask a librarian for study guides and reading lists, CLEP brochures, workshop information, and descriptions of the examinations. All this is free of charge.

ADULTS GAIN COLLEGE CREDITS
THROUGH EXAMINATION PROGRAM

Adults in the Dallas area now have a chance to gain up to two years of college credit without ever attending a formal classroom lecture under a new program of non-traditional education. With the aid of study guides, book lists, workshops and tutorials, an individual can be assisted toward a planned course of study on his own time in preparation for the tests available through the College-Level Examination Program (CLEP) or for personal enrichment to up-grade organize, and enlarge the information he has gleaned through daily experiences, at work, watching television, or reading books and newspapers.

For those who choose CLEP tests as a goal, college level examinations are given at South Methodist University. SMU has been instrumental in the development of study guides and reading lists, and supplies resource persons to conduct workshops.

Two types of examinations are offered under the CLEP program. General examinations are designed to measure undergraduate achievement in basic areas of liberal arts — English composition, mathematics, natural sciences, humanities, social sciences and history. Subject examinations cover 20 different subject areas.

Area institutions that have agreed to recognize scores made by CLEP students on the exams include the Northeast and South Campuses of Tarrant County Junior College, Texas Christian University, and Texas Wesleyan College in Fort Worth; SMU, Christian College of the Southwest, and the University of Texas Southwestern Medical School, all in Dallas; North Texas State University, Denton; and East Texas State University in Commerce.

All of this is made available to Dallas adults through the Independent Study Project (ISP) of the Dallas Public Library. Mrs. Jean Brooks, project director, noted that "there are thousands of persons in the Dallas area who have learned through on-the-job training or private study the equivalent of many hours of college instruction. This program is designed to determine how much these persons have learned, by means of tests. If their scores are accepted, they receive college credit when they enroll in participating colleges and universities."

Mrs. Brooks stresses that "taking the CLEP tests is not a requirement of the Independent Study Project; many people are enjoying study for personal enrichment."

Five branches of the Dallas Public Library system serve as information centers for the study. They are audelia Road, Crossroads Learning Center on Forest Avenue, Hampton-Illinois, Oak Lawn, and Preston Royal Branches. Study materials and special library assistance are available to participating adults at no charge from these locations.

The Dallas area program is a two year project funded by grants from the National Endowment for the Humanities, Council on Library Resources, and the College Entrance Examination Board.

The purpose of the funded project, the only one of its kind in the United States, is to investigate the effectiveness of public libraries as centers for independent study in conjunction with CLEP.

Due to the uniqueness of ISP, a National Interest Council meets with project leaders every six months to assess progress.

Further information can be obtained from the Independent Study Project office, 214-748-5256, or the five participating branch libraries.

Reprint from The Dallas Morning News - Sunday, March 26, 1972

FIRST STUDY PROJECT GRADUATE ENTHUSIASTIC

A vivacious North Dallas housewife was the focal point last week of the Dallas Public Library's campaign to sell the city the idea of ongoing, beyond-the-classroom education.

Mrs. Mary Lou McCormick of 5230 Del Roy is the first of some 1,200 Dallasites to wind up independent study work under the library's Independent Study Project.

"If you're capable of working on your own, it's excellent," said Mrs. McCormick, who picked up two desperately needed courses in American history under Independent Study Project tutelage.

Mrs. McCormick was already pretty much into independent study, having spent much of the past three years completing master's work in French at SMU.

Her on-campus work at SMU and subsequent trips to Northern Texas State University in Denton to complete teacher certification requirements left her ready for some quiet, at-home study at her own pace. That's exactly what the library program is all about.

Independence is the project's central theme. Some 20 freshman-sophomore level college courses, mostly of the survey type, are offered at the main library and five branch locations.

Study guides and reading lists outline the subject matter to be covered. The libraries furnish the materials for no charge. Tutoring is available. The rest is up to the student.

When he feels ready for examination in a particular subject, he pays $15 for the cost of a College Level Examination Program (CLEP) test and finds out what he knows.

"The only charge is $15 for the exam," Mrs. McCormick commented. "You can't take a course anywhere for that little."

"And if one studies the course outline, he can't help but do well on the test," she added, offering her 90th percentile test results as proof.

Mrs. McCormick needed the American history to meet Texas teaching requirements but didn't want the hassle of returning to a college campus to get classwork out of the way. Most participants in the library project enroll for similar reasons.

Project Director Mrs. Jean Brooks of the library reports interest in the project is widening across the city. More courses are planned. SMU is broadening its work in preparing study guides, and the University of Texas Southwestern Medical School is planning a series of medical technology courses.

The practical matter of equating independent study to campus study has been resolved by the College Entrance Examination Board, which administers the CLEP tests and recognize their equivalency to traditional final exams given at universities. The Dallas project is one of several across the nation.

Further information may be had by calling 748-5256.

Reprint from the Dallas Morning News - Sunday, July 16, 1972

EL DIPLOMA DE SECUNDARIA NO ES NECESARIO PARA GANAR CREDITO DE COLEGIO

El Dallas Public Library auspicia un proyecto de estudios independientes llamado Independent Study en conjuncion con el College Level Examination Program (CLEP) del College Entrance Examination Board.

Cinco sucursales de la Bilioteea Publica de Dallas participan en el programa ofreciendo listas de libros para diferentes materias, guias de estudio, cursillos y materiales de biblioteca. Estos le ayudan a prepararse para los dos tipos de examenes. Un tipo es general y cubre las cinco materias basicas de ingles, humanidades, matematicas, ciencias naturales y ciencias sociales. El otro tipo es especifico y mide sus conocimientos en mas de 20 cursos de colegio, desde gobierno americano hasta computadoras y procesos de datos. Todos los examenes y materiales estan en ingles.

Los servicios de las biliotecas son gratis. El unico gasto para usted es por cada examen. Si toma solamente uno de los examenes generales o especificos usted paga $15 por cada uno. Pero si toma 2 o mas de los examenes generales solo paga $25 por todos. Los examenes se administran en el Campus del Southern Methodist Unviversity (SMU) en la tercera semana de cada mes.

En el area de Dallas las siguientes entidades de educacion superior han accedido a reconocer los resultados de los examenes del CLEP: Northeast Campus del Tarrant County Junior Colleg, Texas Christian University, Texas College of the Southwest, University of Texas Southwestern Medical School, University of Texas en Arlington, North Texas State University en Denton, y East Texas State University en Commerce.

Usted no tiene que tener un diploma de High School o secundaria para participar, ni tiene que tomar los examenes para usar los servicios de las bibliotecas. El programa le da la oportunidad de mostrar lo que sabe, continuar su educacion despues en un colegio, recibir credito y reconocimiento por su trabajo y experiencia, calificar para posiciones mas altas o seguir un plan de estudio organizado para su propio regocijo.

Para mas informacion llame al Independent Study Project (748-5256) o a una de las bibliotecas participantes: AUDELIA

209

ROAD)348-6160) CROSSROADS LEARNING CENTER (421-4171), HAMPTON-ILLINOIS (337-4796), OAK LAWN (528-6269) o PRESTON ROYAL (363-5479). La que escribe esta a sus ordenes en la biblioteca de Hampton-Illinois (2210 W. Illinois).

Reprint from the El Sol De Texas - Viernes, 2 De Febrero Df, 1973

LIBRARY CONTINUES EXAM STUDY

Dallas' Public Library System is continuing its Independent Study Project through November, DPLS officials say.

The program helps area residents obtain up to two years of college credit through home study and on-the-job training.

Southern Methodist University faculty members teach two-hour tutorial sessions and direct workshops for ISP.

The program is part of the College Level Examination plan.

This month's schedule:

• Three tutorials on "Educational Psychology" will begin at 7 p.m. Nov. 6, Nov. 20 and Dec. 4 at Preston Royal Branch Library, 5626 Royal Lane;

• "Introductory Accounting" tutorials will begin at 7 p.m. Nov. 14 and 28 at Audelia Road Branch Library, 10045 Audelia Road.

• A "Computers and Data Processing" tutorial will begin at 7:30 p.m. Wednesday at HamptonpIllinois Branch Library, 2210 W. Illinois;

• A workshop on "General Psychology" will be held at 7:30 p.m. Tuesday, Nov. 14 at Preston Royal Branch;

• A workshop on "Effective Ways of Reading Books" will be held at 2 p.m. Saturday, Nov. 18, at Crossroads Learning Center, 2610 Forest Ave.;

• A workshop on "Psychology of Taking Tests" will be held at 7:30 p.m. Monday, Nov. 20, at the Oak Lawn Branch, 3721 Lemmon Ave.

Students' only charge is an examination fee.

Reprint from the Dallas Times Herald - Sunday, November 5, 1972

A GUIDE ON

HOW TO STUDY INDEPENDENTLY

OR

WHAT TO DO UNTIL THE PLUMBER COMES: A SELF-MODIFICATION

PROGRAM FOR INDEPENDENT STUDY PROJECTS

Prepared for Dallas Public Library

Independent Study Project

by

Charles M. Crumbaugh
Psychology Department
Southern Methodist University

WHAT TO DO UNTIL THE PLUMBER COMES: A SELF-MODIFICATION PROGRAM FOR INDEPENDENT STUDY PROJECTS

This paper is not intended for everyone who starts an independent study project. Some people have the ability to begin a project and continue non-stop until they have accomplished their goals. If you are like I am, you envy them their fortitude and their ability to study. This paper is intended for all those who feel that envy and for those who have ever found themselves saying any one of:

1. "My problem is that I just can't get started."

2. "Not me. My problem is I just fizzle out."

3. "This just doesn't interest me anymore."

4. "I can't study on my own. I need direction."

5. "This is not what I wanted. I thought it would be, but it isn't."

6. "My family needs my attention. I have too many other things to do."

7. "I don't see the value in it. What good will this do me?"

8. "I'm too changeable. Before I finish_____, I'm more interested in_____."

9. "I know all I wanted to about_____."

This paper is intended to help you avoid having to make one of these or similar statements and to help you be successful with your independent study project.

DETERMINING THE PROBLEM

Don't skip this section. All too often the student who has begun a project and encountered problems will say: "I know what my problem is. It's..." In order to modify an existing study pattern or to develop a successful pattern, it is necessary to know exactly what the starting point is and to know both the good and bad aspects of the existing pattern.

Finding Baseline

To determine the nature of our problem, we will begin by recording our study behavior. We can do this either by (1) counting the number of times the behavior occurs, (2) counting the amount of time spent studying; or (3) both. This is called finding baseline, and the only time it is not necessary to determine baseline is when the behavior never occurs. In this case, baseline would be zero. But if the behavior occurs at all, even if only infrequently, we should spend time collecting baseline, for this will (1) suggest to us the study characteristics that need change, and (2) give us a way of knowing when and how much change has occurred.

First, make a list of the characteristics of your study behavior you are dissatisfied with. These may be (1) "I don't spend enough time studying when I do study", or (2) "I spend sufficient time, I just don't study often enough", or (3) "I don't take notes. I just read and forget", or any other dissatisfaction you may have with your study habits. Keep this list for later use.

Second, begin recording your study behavior. Over the next week or so, record (1) when you start, (2) when you stop, and (3) the total time spent studying each time. Subtract from the total time, any interruptions, time spent getting a snack, etc. Also record what happened (1) immediately before you began, (2) where you studied, and (3) what happened immediately after you finished. We do this because a study pattern can break down because of any of a number of factors which might not be obvious to begin with. A recent student, for example, professed great trouble in studying and an inability to determine why, for he enjoyed the material and was really "motivated" to learn about it. Unfortunately, he scheduled his study time after a full day and just before bedtime. Each day he would terminate study a few minutes earlier to "get ready for bed." Bedtime crept earlier and earlier until he did not study at all.

Finding Rewards

While we are recording baseline, there is plenty to do. No matter how well intentioned the final study plan is, it will not be successful unless we have made study rewarding. Now study is supposed to be "intrinsically" rewarding and to some degree it is. Nevertheless, our plan will be more successful if we can make study a behavior that is rewarded in other ways also.

Begin by making a list of things that are rewarding to you. Include things you like to do and things you spend time doing that you don't have to do. Some examples gathered from lists supplied by students like yourselves are: reading science fiction, dancing, smoking, watching T.V., going to movies, listening to records, eating, drinking, camping out, visiting friends, etc. Your list should be fairly complete and include your major interest, hobbies, things you do every day, things you would hate to give up, etc. The list you develop will be individual to you and may not resemble anyone else's at all. It will include the things that are rewarding to you.

Now, examine the list of rewards. We want to choose one that is (1) accessible to you, (2) easily dispensed, (3) consumable, and (4) highly rewarding to you. The reward must be accessible to be effective. One thousand dollar bills would no doubt be highly rewarding. but not too many of us have $1000 to play with. The reward must also be easily dispensed. Camping out might be rewarding, but it would not be easy to reward yourself with a camp-out for studying in the library. The reward must be consumable, which in this case simply means that you would want more than one. A new car might be rewarding, but it lasts too long as a reward to be effective in rewarding studying. We want something that you want today and, if you got it, would want again tomorrow. And the reward must be rewarding to you, something you do not really want to do without.

Delivering Rewards

Immediacy. In rewarding our behavior, we want to deliver the reward as soon as possible after the behavior occurs. The longer the delay between the behavior and the reward, the less effective it will be. Not all rewards will fit this scheme, and we may want to achieve the same end by putting ourselves on a token system. To do this, we might say that certain behaviors, say 15 minutes of studying, earned, say, three tokens or checkmarks in our record book. When we get 25 checkmarks, we could trade them in for, say, an evening at the movies. One of the good things about a token system is that you can set it up to buy a number of different rewards. Thus, by studying, you would be earning tokens which you exchange for rewards of different sorts. This requires an exchange system in which a given reward is worth a given number of tokens. Thus, an hour of TV news might cost 3 tokens but your favorite one-half hour comedy program might cost 5 tokens. The most common mistake is to make the rewards cost too much. This is exactly what we want to avoid. For example, if the movies cost 25 tokens and you could earn 5 tokens an evening, you could go to the movies about once a week. This is probably about right if you really enjoy movies that much. But suppose TV, lunch, and your evening reading were also on your token system. Then, to go to the movies means you not only have to study, but you have to do without TV, lunches, and light reading.

This is much too harsh. Our whole point is to make study rewarding whereas this system would probably do the reverse. So,
in the beginning especially, make the exchange system more than
equitable. Whether we are using a token system or directly
delivering the reward, we can not deliver the reward the moment
after the study behavior occurs.

Contingency. In addition to being immediate, we want to
deliver our rewards on a contingent basis. This means that we
earn the reward only if we perform the behavior and if we perform the behavior we always receive the reward. Another related
point is that it is better to give than to take away. To increase a behavior, it is better to earn TV viewing time than to
assume if you don't study, you will take away viewing time. If
you make the exchange system equitable enough, you will earn all
the viewing time you really want anyway.

You can test your reward system while continuing to collect
baseline data. Assume that you were studying the way you eventually want to and were thus earning either the tokens or the
rewards. Do you earn enough tokens or rewards to get what you
want? If not, your reward system is too stringent. If you have
tokens or rewards left over, it is too lenient. In either case
you can make the adjustments necessary before beginning on your
self-modification program.

DETERMINING GOALS

Content Goals

We need to distinguish between two kinds of goals of an
independent study project.

First, there are the "content" goals, e.g. to learn enough
about child psychology to pass the CLEP exam in child psychology.
Most often our "content" goals are too broad and poorly defined.
We need to make them specific enough to know when we have accomplished them. Each of the broad content goals needs to be
sub-divided into its specific sub-goals. These might be (1) to
read a general text on child psychology, (2) to attend public
lectures on child psychology, (3) to examine the books on CLEP
exams, (4) to register for the exam, etc. Each one of these
will have its own steps required to accomplish it.

Procedure Goals

In addition to the "content" goals we will have "procedure" goals, that is goals which help us accomplish each separate content goal. Take, for example, the content goal of "To study a general text in child psychology." Procedure goals might be (1) to study an hour a day, (2) to outline each chapter (3) to discuss this particular chapter with a friend, etc. Goal setting is a very individual process, yet, if a goal is to help us, it should specify the behavior necessary to accomplish the goal. "To know something about child psychology", for example does not tell us what to do. How do we accomplish it? On the other hand, "To read a book in child psychology", tells us exactly what to do. If the goal does not specify the behavior necessary, the goal will be almost impossible to accomplish.

Setting Our Goals

Our baseline information on study habits will help us set our "procedure" goals, and it is now time to examine the data we have been keeping on our study behavior. Compare your baseline data with your list of dissatisfactions. If you said "I don't study often enough", see if this seems to be true of the baseline data. If you didn't study often, one of your goals may be "To increase my frequency of studying to three times a week." On the other hand, if the baseline data suggests that you did study frequently enough, you can stop being dissatisfied with how often you study.

Now make a separate list of those dissatisfactions from your original list that seem to be substantiated by the baseline data. Add to this list those that are suggested by the baseline that you didn't think of before. Look at the baseline to see if there are any obvious problems. What happened before study? Did anything in particular seem to frequently cause you to stop studying? Did you frequently interrupt your own studying to do something else? Did these interruptions occur early or late in your study period? How long was it from when you went into study until you actually began studying? The baseline record should provide the answer to many of these questions and should make obvious which ones need the most immediate attention.

DEVELOPING THE CONTRACT

We are now going to develop a contract for ourselves of what we are going to do to earn our reward or tokens. We will begin by picking from our list, one of the behaviors that seems to need most immediate attention. By way of example, we will use the fairly common finding that in a given study period, very little study occurs. Frequently the student will go in to study, spend several minutes arranging his materials, begin study but interrupt it to obtain something forgotten (pencil, cigarettes, etc.), return to study a few minutes, remember a letter that must be answered immediately, etc. As we develop our contract, we must remember two important things: (1) Start small, i.e. at the beginning, and (2) Take small steps. The easier it is to go from one step to the next the less we will fail, and the more likely we will reach our goal. Not only must the steps be small, but we must start at the beginning. Another student I know, had the ability to study for an hour when "he wanted to" but he did not do so often enough to pass his courses. In developing his contract, he started with "study for an hour", which he did the first time and earned his reward. Unfortunately, he had never been rewarded for "getting started" and rarely got started. To make his contract successful, he had to begin at the beginning, i.e. contracting to "study for two minutes". Once he was daily earning his reward, the two minutes was stretched to five minutes until he was daily succeeding at five minutes. Then the contract was set for ten, then fifteen, then twenty, then thirty, then forty-five, then forty-five with a five minute break at twenty minutes, and then sixty with a break at thirty. This "beginning at the beginning" with a very slow progression from one step to the next was successful in producing a very studious individual.

An Example Contract

For our typical individual who is frequently interrupted, the first step of the contract might look like this:

1. If I am at my desk between 7 and 8 p.m., I will study, but I do not have to be at my desk during that time to earn the reward. I do not earn the reward if I am at my desk but do not study.

Note that by this contract, if the student is studying and wants a coke, he need only leave his desk to drink it. The same with cigarettes and that important letter, and day dreaming. In fact, he does not even have to go to the study area to obtain the reward. Succeeding steps in the contract might be:

2. Same as number 1 except now I must study for two minutes.

3. Same as number 2 for five minutes.

4. Same as number 3 for ten minutes.

5. Same as number 4 for 15 minutes.

Note at this point, that nothing says that the 15 minutes must
be in one block. If the student now notices that he is being
distracted by other activities, the contract might now be amended
as follows:

6. Study for five minutes uninterrupted and 15 minute
   total.

7. Study for five minutes uninterrupted and 20 minute
   total.

8. Study for ten minutes uninterrupted and 20 minute
   total.

In this way, both the study time total and uninterrupted time
are being increased. These interruptions refer to self-inter-
ruptions since the individual has no control over the interruptions of others. Should these interruptions become a problem,
he may need to select another study place or include the others
in the contract, e.g. his children earn their rewards by not
interrupting. Most often, however, study interruptions are
ones we ourselves cause or allow to happen. In this case, we
can control them by making them part of our own contract. The
individual stays at each step long enough to assure that he is
consistently earning the reward. Should he notice that he is
failing, he needs only to make the size of the step smaller.
Although this procedure may seem slow in the beginning, remember
that we are building a study pattern to last a lifetime if we
want. It must be done well.

When you start your contract, continue to record the baseline information. This will allow you to see the changes take
place and allow you to demonstrate that you have accomplished
your procedural goal.

Some Problems

There are certain problems that may arise that the student
should know how to handle. Suppose he finds himself cheating,
e.g. he didn't earn his five tokens Thursday so he did not have
enough to "buy" a movie Saturday night, but he went anyway.
What can be done? One solution is to have someone else deliver
and exchange the reinforcements or tokens. Perhaps a husband, wife,
or roommate. Another solution is to require less, i.e. rewrite
the contract or exchange schedule and slowly build back up to
the original contract. Almost everyone will "cheat" once in
awhile, but if cheating is occurring more than 5-10% of the
time, the contract should be rewritten from an earlier and
successful point. In rare instances, it is also possible to

allow "debt financing" or borrowing. If this is done, however,
the debt should not exceed a week's earnings (preferably much
less) and must be paid back before further earnings or exchanges
are allowed.

Another problem is what to do when Christmas comes, i.e. when
there is an unavoidable interruption of the study schedule such as
when company comes. If these interruptions are infrequent and
involve only a couple of days, the schedule can just be suspended
for the short time required. If it is going to be for more than
a day or so, amend the contract for a short and specified time.
If, for example, you have been contracting for an hour a day,
reduce the contract to 20-30 minutes, or perhaps you can schedule
two 30 minute periods tomorrow. If the interruption lasts for a
week or more, slowly step back up to your previous contract.
Thus, rather than going from twenty minutes to an hour after two
weeks of only 20 minutes, go first to 30, then 40 , etc. This
will insure that the pattern does not break down.

EXTENDING THE CONTRACT

Once the basic study program has been established, it is
possible to extend the contract. If, as in our example, the
amount of time spent studying was the only major problem, you
could now ride off into the sunset wiser and happier. On the
other hand, time may not be the only problem and it may be
necessary to extend the program. Many people find that the
so-called SQRRT method is successful. The letters stand for
Survey, Question, Read, Review, and Test. This system may
have to be somewhat modified for independent study, but it is
a good starting point.

Survey. Preview the material to be covered. Read the topic
headings. Try to get an overall picture of what is to be
covered and the approach the author takes.

Question. Frame questions about this material. Often the
author will provide questions at the end of a chapter to allow
you to test your understanding. If so, these should be read
before you read the chapter. Whether or not the author provides questions, you should pose your own questions. What do
you want to know about this material?

Read. Read the material. Most often this should include note
taking or outlining. It is not necessary to copy the book,
just the major points and their importance.

Review. Look over the chapter again. Are there sections you
have already forgotten? Without your notes, can you summarize
this chapter? Re-read the necessary sections.

Test. In a conventional directed study program, the instructor
usually provides tests and examinations to allow you to guage
your progress and understanding. Sometimes the textbook itself
will offer such tests and if so, these should be taken. Even
if you have such tests provided, another excellent method of
measuring your understanding should not be overlooked and that
is explaining the material to someone else. For independent
study, we might well change the T from test to talk. If you
can explain the material to someone else so that he under-
stands, you very likely have a good grasp of that material.
If he does not understand, you probably need to do additional
reading.

If there are some of the above steps that you do not make,
you should extend your contract to include them. Remember,
however, start small, take small steps, and do one thing at a
time. These are the same principles that we used earlier to
get our study pattern started and they will be successful
here also.

Becoming a "Natural" Student

Your ultimate goal, of course, is to become a "natural"
student, someone who studies and is rewarded by learning.
This is not possible, of course, unless your study pattern is
such that learning takes place. Thus, we have used other rewards to develop such a study pattern. But now that our study
behavior is adequate, we don't want to continue to rely upon
these rewards. On the other hand, we don't want our study
pattern to extinguish--to revert to its older, less effective
form. We will therefore begin to thin our reward schedule very
slowly. We have been rewarding ourselves 100% of the time
that the appropriate behavior occurred. Our next step is to
reduce that to 90%. We continue to count how often the behavior
occurs (as we did with baseline on all the way through our
program). If our studying does not decrease even though we are
now rewarding it only 90% of the time, we can proceed to reduce
the 80%, etc. If, at any point, our studying decreases very
much, we need to return to the previous stage for awhile.
Going too fast can ruin all of our previous work. If thinning
the reward schedule seems to be difficult, alternating between
the thinning schedule and the 100% schedule is often effective.

Thus, if you had problems going from 70% to 60%, return to 70% for a week then alternate 60% and 100%, and slowly decrease the 60% to 55% to 50%, etc., continuing to alternate with 100%.

TERMINATING THE SELF-MODIFICATION PROGRAM

The thinning procedures just discussed are a way of terminating a particular portion of a self-modification program when the goals of that project have been accomplished. By thinning in the way described, the student assures that the behaviors will continue even though the modification project has been discontinued. An independent study project, however, is rarely discontinued. As one goal is achieved, another takes its place. For this reason, and others, it always pays to set specific goals that allow you to know when they have been achieved and which behaviors will and which will not assist you toward those goals.

SEEKING THE ASSISTANCE OF OTHERS

There are times in an independent study project that the assistance of someone else is required. This may happen at the beginning of a project when the student is not sufficiently knowledgeable about an area to set realistic goals, or it may happen anywhere along the line when the student may seem to keep hitting dead ends or keep being side-tracked from his ultimate goals. In these cases, the student should seek "professional" advice.

The Librarian. The first and most frequently successful resource is the librarian. The librarian is not just a person who compulsively checks books in and out and takes sadistic glee in fining you for an overdue book. Librarians are experts at using the library's facilities to satisfy an individual's needs, even when they themselves may not have even a precursory knowledge of the field of interest of the individual. With guidance from you, they can locate for you the resources that will lead you to the information you seek. Most libraries have cooperative arrangements with other libraries such that the librarians can provide you with resources not directly available in a particular library. By searching out a library that does have the material, they can "borrow" from one another for your benefit. And books are far from the only resource of a library. Many libraries have (and, again, if they do not, they can "borrow") record collections, tapes, special interest films, discussion groups, advisors, and "experts" all lined up and ready for your use. If you go to the library just to borrow books, you may be shortchanging yourself.

The "Experts". In addition to the library, you can often receive assistance from overlooked community resources. The "expert" you need may be found at the local college, junior college, or high school. Again, the librarians can usually put **you in contact with individuals knowledgeable in the appropriate area who are often more than willing to share their time with an interested student. Before consulting with the "expert", however, the student should carefully consider his problem, have specific questions, and be prepared to receive "I don't know, but I can help you find out" for an answer. This, after all, is what the student needed.**

Study Guide and Reading List

Afro-American History

Prepared for Dallas Public Library

Independent Study Project

by

Carole A. Buchanan
Department of History
Southern Methodist University

This study guide and reading list is part of the service
of the Dallas Public Library System for its Independent Study
Project. It would be especially helpful to readers who want
to continue their education at the college level by following
a program of independent study using the services and materials
of the Library. Many universities now recognize that adults
learn through independent study, and they will award credit
toward a college degree to those who can demonstrate their
knowledge on the tests of the College-Level Examination Program
(CLEP) of the College Entrance Examination Board. The reading
lists in various subject areas are not meant to guarantee that
the reader will pass the examinations. They should serve as a
starting point for readers who wish to begin studying in a
certain field or as an aid to others who are looking for some
reinforcement of learning that they may have acquired through
other means. For other reading materials and further information about the examinations, please see a librarian.

INTRODUCTION

The purpose of this Study Guide is to assist you in directing your own learning about Afro-American History. The Study Guide will focus specifically upon those Americans known to History as Colored, Negro, Afro-American or Black --which are some of the terms used at different stages of the Afro-Americans' historical experience. The main emphasis of the readings will be upon the Afro-American experience and as much as possible upon an "internal" view of this experience in the sense that Black historians, authors, and informants will dominate the choice of readings, although major studies by white specialists will not be excluded. This same bias will be evident in the central themes or chronological per-iodization of the Afro-American experience, although some chronological periods may be familiar as "traditional" categories of American History. There will also be a bias in favor of the readability of recommended books, distinc-tions being made where possible between the purely "scholarly history," "general introductory history," and "specialized studies." Using suggested readings with the Study Guide you can also be preparing yourself for the College-Level Exami-nation Program's Subject Examination in Afro-American History.

At times the distortions associated with the history of the Afro-American experience seem limitless, and there is a temptation to focus upon the distortions themselves (for example, on the racist mythology and the evolution of racist ideologies). Instead the central focus of this Study Guide will remain on the Afro-American himself. Since the second World War there has been an explosion of publications ex-ploring Afro-American History: many of these have "revised" what had been the "standard" treatment of American History, i.e. with whites in all the "starring" roles and Blacks and other minorities as the cast of nameless thousands--the backdrop against which "History" occurred. So different is this revised American History once the shift from the old view to the new is made that a student being introduced to Afro-American History may feel he is being taught "some other country's history!" (as a Jules Pfeiffer cartoon character once remarked). But Afro-American History is, of course, most definitely "American History": it reflects most poignantly the themes of struggle for justice and freedom, of uprootedness, of survival against odds, of creativity, and of self-betterment that is at the core of the American heritage.

The sections of this Study Guide are listed below: In addition to Pictorial Histories, General Works, and Source Materials and Documents, Afro-American History has been divided chronologically into nine general periods:

1. The African Heritage

2. The Uprooting: Era of the Slave Trade

3. The First Revolutionary Generation

4. Slavery: the System; Accomodaters and Resistors, Comparative Histories

5. Toward War: Freedmen, Abolitionists, the Underground Railroad, and the Years of Crisis

6. From Reconstruction to Jim Crow: Reconstruction; the Westward Movement, Jim Crow and Ostracism

7. From Plantation to Ghetto: the Rural/Urban Shift; the Harlem Renaissance, the "New Negro," and renewed Struggle

8. From Depression to War

9. From War to Protest: the Contemporary Era

This Study Guide is not geared to any single text; rather the student is encouraged to read widely, guided by the suggested readings, the availability of sources, and his own taste. Almost all of the books suggested are available in the Dallas Public Library or can be purchased in inexpensive paperback editions. The Library also has recordings of Black music and spoken words of Black authors and leaders. There are also films which are relevant to the periods listed above. As you read, you may want to enrich your learning through viewing some of these short films available from the Dallas Public Library Film Library.

One of the most painless ways for an individual to approach Afro-American History is through pictorial histories, which should be skimmed selectively for an overview whose images will enable the student to visualize and interpret readings encountered later:

Ebony. Pictorial History of Black America.

Franklin, John H. An Illustrated History of Black Americans. New York, Time-Life, 1970.

Fuller, T. O. Pictorial History of the American Negro.

Year. Year's Pictorial History of the American Negro. Maplewood, New Jersey, Hammond, 1965.

225

General History: John Hope Franklin's <u>From Slavery to Freedom</u> is the closest to a "standard" text as exists in the field. It is "solid" with an excellent bibliography that can lead the student to other works, but it is long and demanding. Two more readable general histories would be either Lerone Bennett's <u>Before the Mayflower: A History of the Negro in America, 1619-1962</u> (Chicago, Johnson Publishing Company, 1962, and Penguin), or August Meier and Elliot Rudwick's <u>From Plantation to Ghetto</u> (Rev. Edition, New York, Hill and Wang, 1970). Other general studies of broad subjects within the Afro-American experience would include:

<u>Music</u>: Jones, Le Roi. <u>Black Music</u>. New York, W. Morrow, 1967. Essays, reviews and analyses of contemporary jazz musicians and their work.

Southern, Eileen. <u>The Music of Black Americans: A History</u>. New York, W. W. Norton, 1971.

<u>Dance</u>: Emery, Lynn. <u>Black Dance in the United States</u>. Palo Alto, National Press Books, 1972.

<u>Art</u>: Porter, James. <u>Modern Negro Art</u>. New York, Arno Press, 1969.

<u>Social</u>: Brawley, Benjamin G. <u>A Social History of the American Negro</u>. New York, Collier Books, 1970. Reprint of the 1921 edition. Although it is now somewhat dated, it is a classic in the field written by a great Black social historian.

<u>Intellectual</u>: Cruse, Harold. <u>The Crisis of the Negro Intellectual from its Origins to the Present</u>. New York, Wm. Morrow and Company, 1968. This work is more difficult and should be read after the student is well into the material.

Thorpe, Earl E. <u>The Mind of the Negro: An Intellectual History of the Afro-American</u>. Baton Rouge, Ortlieb Press, 1961. Reprinted by Negro University Press. Argues that the quest for freedom and equality has been the central theme of Negro thought.

<u>Religious</u>: Frazier, E. Franklin. <u>The Negro Church in America</u>. New York, Schocken, 1963. This brief work by one of America's great Black sociologists should not be overlooked, but a more recent work might also be of interest: Hart M. Nelson, et al. <u>Black Church in America</u>. Basic Books, 1972.

Mays, Benjamin E. and J. W. Nicholson. <u>The Negro's Church</u>. New York, Arno Press, 1969. A thorough study of the Negro church and its role in the community.

Woodson, Carter G. <u>The History of the Negro Church</u>. Washington, Associated Publishers, 1921, 2nd edition, 1945. Still an important general study of the Negro church.

Hough, Joseph C. <u>Black Power and White Protestants: A Christian Response to the New Negro Pluralism</u>. New York, Oxford University Press, 1968.

<u>Constitutional</u>: Berry, Mary Frances. <u>Black Resistance, White Law: A History of Constitutional Racism in America</u>. New York, Appleton-Century Crofts, 1971.

Other general histories available in the Dallas Public Library include: Aptheker, Herbert. **Essays in the History of the American Negro** (New York, International Publishers, 1964, c. 1945); Bontemps, Arna W., **100 Years of Negro Freedom** (New York, Dodd, Mead and Company, 1961); and Logan, Rayford, **The Negro in the United States: A Brief History** (Princeton, D. Van Nostrand Company, 1957).

Documentary Materials: For some students there is no substitute for the immediacy of statements, speeches and documents drawn from a particular period. A student should sample at least one of the following collections of documents:

> Aptheker, Herbert. **A Documentary History of the Negro People in the United States**. New York, Citadel Press, 1951, 2 vols.

> Ducas, George. **Great Documents in Black American History**. New York, Praeger, 1970.

> Foner, Philip S. **The Voice of Black America: Major Speeches by Negroes in the United States, 1797-1891**. New York, Simon Schuster, 1972.

> Osofsky, Gilbert. **The Burden of Race**. New York, Harper and Row, 1967. Documents and description--a source book from slave trade to Black Power.

> Ruchames, Louis. **Racial Thought in America: A Documentary History**. Amherst, University of Massachusetts Press, 1969.

Teachers might be interested in using the following documentary:

> Play: Duberman, Martin B. **In White America: A Documentary Play**, Boston, Houghton Mifflin and Company, 1964.

1. The African Heritage

Two excellent illustrated histories of Africa are **The Horizon History of Africa** (American Heritage Publishing Company, 1971), and Basil Davidson's **African Kingdoms** (New York, Time-Life Books, 1966). Together these provide an impressive introduction to the African continent. A concise, one-volume general history is Roland Oliver and J. D. Fage's **A Short History of Africa** (revised edition, Penguin). For those interested in a more detailed regional history of sub-Saharan Africa consult:

> Webster, J. E. and A. A. Boahen. **History of West Africa: The Revolutionary Years-1815 to Independence**. New York, Praeger, 1970.

> Ogot, B. A. and J. A. Kieran. **Zamani: A Survey of East African History**. Longmans, 1968.

> Keppel-Jones, A. **South Africa: A Short History**. London, Hutchinson University Library, 4th edition, 1968.

Also, Melville J. Herskovits' The Myth of the Negro Past,
(Boston, Beacon Press, 1958), should be read since he
systematically tackles and disposes of some of the mythical
stereotypes concerning African society and culture. In
Ezekiel Mphalele's The African Image (New York, Praeger,
1962), this South African born writer explores how Africans
and American Blacks feel about each other. And Basil
Davidson's The African Genius: An Introduction to African
Cultural and Social History (Boston, Little Brown, 1970),
is both current and readable. An excellent twenty-six minute
film for this area of study is "Black Heritage, Black Struggle,
Black Hope" in which the building of ancient African kingdoms
is recalled.

2. The Uprooting: Era of the Slave Trade

A recent major study of the slave trade that focuses upon
its impact in the New World generally is Phillip Curtin's The
Atlantic Slave Trade: A Census (Madison, University of Wis-
consin Press). It is too specialized for the general reader,
but the introductory chapter and conclusions should be read.
Basil Davidson's Black Mother: The Years of the African Slave
Trade (Boston, Little Brown, 1961), is one of the more read-
able accounts of this period. Additional works include
W. E. B. DuBois' The Supression of the Slave Trade, 1638-1870
(New York, Schocken, 1969). Peter Duignan and Clarence
Clendenen, The United States and the African Slave Trade,
1619-1862 (Stanford, 1962), and Daniel P. Mannix and M. Cowley's
Black Cargoes: The Story of the Atlantic Slave Trade, 1518-1865
(New York, Viking, 1962). Within the United States, slave
trading is described in Frederic Bancroft's Slave Trading in
the Old South (New York, Ungar, 1959). Winthrop D. Jorden
has written the best study to date of the response to the
Negro during this period in his book White Over Black:
American Attitudes Toward the Negro, 1530-1812 (Chapel Hill,
University of North Carolina Press, 1968). Winner of the
1969 National Book Award, this work explores the ambivalence
of the white conscience even before the founding of the
Jamestown settlement. For racial attitudes in the 1815-1859
period, consult William R. Stanton's The Leopard's Spots:
Scientific Attitudes Toward Race in America, 1815-1859
(Chicago, University of Chicago Press, 1960).

3. The First Revolutionary Generation

For a general study of the role of the Black soldier in American History, consult Bill Adler's, The Black Soldier: From the American Revolution to Vietnam (New York, Morrow, 1971). The following works examine more specifically the American Revolution and can be consulted either by reading selected chapters of particular interest to the reader, or by selecting one of the following and reading it in its entirety:

Livermore, George. An Historical Research Respecting the Opinions of the Founders of the Republic on Negroes as Slaves, as Citizens and as Soldiers. New York, Arno Press, 1969. A reprint of the original 1863 edition with a new preface by Benjamin Quarles.

Mazyck, Walter H. George Washington and the Negro. Washington, D. C., Associated Publishers, 1932.

Nell, William Cooper, The Colored Patriots of the American Revolution. New York, Arno Press, 1968. A reprint of the 1855 edition.

Perhaps the best study by one of America's foremost Black historians is

Quarles, Benjamin. The Negro in the American Revolution. Chapel Hill, University of North Carolina Press, 1961.

The films "Slave Revolt" and "Beyond Abolition: The Black Radicals" trace slave history and the rise of the insurrection movement.

4. Slavery

There are a number of collections of slave narratives that provide the reader with a vivid account of what it meant to be a slave, including

Armstrong, Orland K. Old Massa's People: The Old Slaves Tell Their Story. Indianapolis, Bobbs-Merrill, 1931.

Bayliss, John F. Black Slave Narratives. London, Collier, 1970.

Bontemps, Arna W. Great Slave Narratives. Boston, Beacon, 1969.

Botkin, B. A., ed. Lay My Burden Down: A Folk History of Slavery. Chicago, University of Chicago Press, 1945.

Lester, Julius. To Be a Slave. New York, Dell, 1970.

Nichols, Charles H. Many Thousand Gone: The Ex-Slaves Account of the Bondage and Freedom. Leiden, Adler, 1963.

Osofsky, Gilbert, ed. Puttin 'on Ole Massa. New York, Brown and Northrup, 1969.

Both "accommodaters" who adjusted themselves to slavery and "resisters" are reflected in the above collections, any one of which would be useful to the student. However, works that focus more specifically upon resistance to slavery include the following:

Aptheker, Herbert. Nat Turner's Slave Rebellion. New York, Grove Press, 1968. The background and evidence of the rebellion.

Aptheker, Herbert. American Negro Slave Revolts. New York, International Publishers, 1969. A standard work in the field.

Bradford, Sarah. Harriet Tubman: the Moses of Her People. New York, Corinth, 1961.

Chapman, Abraham. Steal Away: Stories of the Runaway Slaves. New York, Praeger, 1971.

Cheek, William F. Black Resistance Before the Civil War. Beverly Hills, Glencoe Press, 1970.

Halasz, Nicholas. The Rattling of Chains: Slave Unrest and Revolt in the Ante-Bellum South. New York, McKay, 1966.

Henson, Josiah. Father Henson's Story of His Own Life. New York, Corinth, 1962. A reprint of a slave narrative written by a conductor for the underground railroad.

Lofton, John. Insurrection in South Carolina: The Turbulent World of Denmark Vesey. Yellow Springs, Ohio, Antioch Press, 1964.

For the non-specialist in the ante-bellum South one of the better one volume readers of the historiography of slavery is Allen Weinstein and Frank O. Gattell, eds., American Negro Slavery: A Modern Reader (New York, Oxford University Press, 1969). This work provides chapter length excerpts from the major interpretations of slavery. Having acquired an overview of the writing on slavery and having been introduced to the major writers on this subject, some students might wish to consult the complete work by the authors that interested them, such as

Elkins, Stanley M. Slavery: A Problem in American Institutional and Intellectual Life. Chicago, Chicago University Press, second edition, 1968.

Genovese, Eugene D. The Political Economy of Slavery: Studies in the Economy and Society of the Slave South. New York, Vintage Books, 1967.

Stampp, Kenneth M. The Peculiar Institution: Slavery in the Ante-Bellum South. New York, Vintage Books, 1956.

Wade, Richard C. Slavery in the Cities: The South, 1820-1860. New York, Oxford University Press, 1964.

More recently, some extremely interesting comparative studies have been written, which are also represented in Weinstein and Gattell:

Davis, David B. The Problems of Slavery in Western
Culture. Ithaca, Cornell University Press, 1966.

Degler, Carl N. Neither Black Nor White: Slavery and
Race Relations in Brazil and the United States.
New York, Macmillan, 1971.

Klein, Herbert S. Slavery in the Americas: A Comparative Study of Virginia and Cuba. Chicago, University Press, 1967.

5. Toward War: Freedmen, Abolitionists, the Underground Railroad, and the Years of Crisis

For information on the Freedman in the pre-Civil War
period, consult the following:

Franklin, John Hope. The Free Negro in North Carolina,
1790-1860. New York, Norton, 1971.

Jackson, Luther P. Free Negro Labor and Property Holding
in Virginia, 1830-1860. (Studies in American Negro
Life Ser.), 1942.

Litwack, Leon F. North of Slavery: The Negro in the
Free States, 1790-1860. Chicago, Chicago University
Press, 1961.

Malvin, John. North into Freedom: The Autobiography of
John Malvin, Free Negro, 1795-1880. Cleveland,
Press of Western Reserve University, 1966.

Russell, John. The Free Negro in Virginia, 1619-1865.
Baltimore, Black University Press, 1913.

For the student particularly interested in the underground
railroad, William Still's The Underground Railroad, (New York,
Arno Press, 1968), contains the only near-complete collection
of records of any underground railway station. A juvenile
version of the story of the railroad can be found in Henrietta
Buckmaster's Flight to Freedom: The Story of the Underground
Railroad.

Perhaps the best general work on the role of Afro-
Americans in the Abolition Movement is Benjamin Quarles,
Black Abolitionists (New York, Oxford University Press, 1969),
which examines the activities of preachers, writers and
agitators who worked to overthrow slavery. In addition, see

Bennett, Lerone. Pioneers in Protest. Chicago, Johnson
Publishing Company, 1968. A readable study of the
abolitionists.

Bernard, Jacqueline. Journey Toward Freedom. New York,
Norton, 1966. A biography of Sojourner Truth.

Coffin, Levi. Reminiscences. New York, Arno Press, 1968.
Of a man often referred to as the "President" of
the Underground Railroad.

Douglass, Frederick. Life and Times of Frederick Douglass.
New York, Grossett and Dunlap, 1970.

Douglass, Frederick. Narrative of the Life of Frederick
Douglass. New York, Dolphin Books, 1963. The story
of his slave life.

Gara, Larry. *The Liberty Line: The Legend of the Underground Railroad*. Lexington, University of Kentucky Press, 1961.

Gilbert, Olive. *Narrative of Sojourner Truth*. New York, Arno Press, 1968.

Quarles, Benjamin. *Frederick Douglass*. Englewood Cliffs, New Jersey, Prentice Hall, 1968. Excerpts from his speeches and writings, and evaluations by his contemporaries and modern historians.

Strother, Horatio T. *The Underground Railroad in Connecticut*. Wesleyan University Press, 1970.

The following miscellaneous works supplement the information provided in the general histories listed in the early pages of this Guide.

Bell, Howard H. *A Survey of the Negro Convention Movement, 1830-1861*, New York, Arno Press, 1969.

Cornish, D. T. *The Sable Arm: Negro Troops in the Union Army, 1861-1865*. New York, W.W. Norton, 1966.

Franklin, John Hope. *The Emancipation Proclamation*. Garden City, Doubleday, 1963. Places the Proclamation in its historical setting.

McPherson, James M. *The Struggle for Equality: Abolition and the Negro in the Civil War and Reconstruction*. Princeton, Princeton University Press, 1964.

McPherson, James., Ed. *The Negro's Civil War: How Negroes Felt and Acted During the War for Union*. New York, Pantheon, 1965. Text and eyewitness accounts of both the military and intellectual battlefield.

Quarles, Benjamin. *Lincoln and the Negro*. New York, Oxford University Press, 1962.

Woodson, Carter G. *The Mind of the Negro: As Reflected in Letters Written During the Crisis, 1800-1860*. Washington D.C., Association for the Study of Negro Life and History, 1926.

6. **From Reconstruction to Jim Crow: Reconstruction; the Westward Movement, Jim Crow and Ostracism**

Several solid but readable works on the era of Reconstruction are

Bennett, Lerone. *Black Power, U.S.A.: The Human Side of Reconstruction 1867-1877*. Chicago, Johnson Publishing Company, 1967. The Black struggle to attain political and economic power during Reconstruction.

DuBois, W. E. B. *Black Reconstruction*. New York, Harcourt-Brace, 1935. A Marxian point of view.

Franklin, John Hope. *Reconstruction After the Civil War*. Chicago, University of Chicago Press, 1961.

Stampp, Kenneth M. *The Era of Reconstruction, 1865-1877*. New York, Knopf, 1965. Exposes the falsehood of the Southern version of Reconstruction and the genuine concern of Radical Republicans for Negro rights and welfare.

A case study of the activities of the Freedman's Bureau in one state is

Abbott, Martin. **The Freedman's Bureau in South Carolina, 1865-1872.** Chapel Hill, University of North Carolina Press, 1967.

The following works examine the post-Reconstruction period. C. Vann Woodward's **The Strange Career of Jim Crow** (New York, Oxford University Press, Second Revised Edition, 1966), is both a brief and readable account of how "Jim Crow," although a relative latecomer to the South, flourished there by the end of the 19th Century. Woodward's **Origins of the New South, 1877-1917** (Baton Rouge, Louisiana State University Press, 1951), is a more solid, university level study on the period tracing the growth and impact of industrial and professional elements of the urban South. Two excellent works of the period are

Aptheker, Herbert. **Afro-American History: the Modern Period.** New York, International, 1970. From the end of the 19th Century to the present.

Logan, Rayford. **The Betrayal of the Negro.** New York, Collier, 1965. This is the revised and enlarged version of Logan's The Negro in American Life and Thought: The Nadir, 1877-1901. New York, Dial Press, 1954. Highly recommended, but detailed.

A more scholarly intellectual history of the period is

Meier, August. **Negro Thought in America, 1880-1915: Racial Ideologies** in the Age of Booker T. Washington. Ann Arbor, University of Michigan Press, 1963. Traces how Negro thought became dichotomized into an ideology of integration and an ideology of separation.

A social history which views conditions in the South just before World War I is

Weatherford, Willis Duke. **Negro Life in the South.** New York, U.M.C.A. Press, 1911.

Forrest G. Wood's **Black Scare: The Racist Response to Emancipation and Reconstruction** (Berkeley, University of California Press, 1968), focuses on the white response, while Edwin S. Redkey's **Black Exodus: Black Nationalist and Back to Africa Movements, 1890-1910** (New Haven, Yale University Press, 1969), is one of the most recent treatments of the response of some Black groups, and William Henry Heard's **From Slavery to the Bishopric of the A.M.E. Church** (New York, Arno Press, 1969), provides an autobiographical perspective of the period.

There are numerous studies of two of the major figures of the period--Booker T. Washington and W. E. B. DuBois--in addition to Meier's (mentioned above).

DuBois, W. E. B. **The Emerging Thought of W. E. B. DuBois: Essays and Editorials from the Crisis.** New York, Simon and Schuster, 1972.

DuBois, W. E. B. **The Souls of Black Folk.** New York, Dodd, Mead, 1970. Brief, readable, a classic.

Spencer, Samuel R. **Booker T. Washington and the Negro's Place in American Life.** Boston, Little, Brown, 1955.

Washington, Booker T. **Up From Slavery.** Garden City, Doubleday, 1963. Available in numerous editions, this autobiography has been Washington's most widely read work.

Washington, Booker T. **Working with the Hands.** New York, Arno Press, 1969. A reprint of the 1904 edition.

In addition to the above **The Negro Problem: A Series of Articles by Representative American Negroes of Today** (New York, Arno Press, 1969, a reprint of a 1903 publication) provides statements by other prominent Negroes of the day, and Charles F. Kellogg's **NAACP: A History of the NAACP, 1902-1920** (Baltimore, Johns Hopkins Press, 1967), examines the early history of one of the United States' most important civil rights organizations.

The role of Afro-Americans in the Westward Movement has enjoyed new interest on the part of historians in the 1960's. Some of these works are listed below:

Berwanger, Eugene H. **The Frontier Against Slavery.** Urbana, University of Illinois Press, 1967. A study of anti-Negro prejudice in the West.

Bonner, T. D. **The Life and Adventures of James P. Beckwourth.** New York, Arno Press, 1969. A reprint of this "autobiography" of a Black frontiersman.

Durham, Philip, and E. L. Jones. **The Negro Cowboys.** New York, Dodd, Mead, 1965.

Leckie, William H. **The Buffalo Soldiers.** Norman, University of Oklahoma Press, 1967. An account of the Negro calvarymen who helped tame the West.

Love, Nat. **The Life and Adventures of Nat Love.** New York, Arno Press, 1968. A reprint of an autobiography of a Negro cowboy.

The films "Freedom Movement in the Third World" and "Black Power in Dixie"--part one and part two cover the Reconstruction Period in the South.

7. From Plantation to Ghetto: the Rural/Urban Shift; the Harlem Renaissance; the "New Negro," and Renewed Struggle

One of the fundamental transformations in the history of any people occurs when they leave the farms for the city. Although this shift from the rural to the urban setting began with emancipation, the migration accelerated in the early years of the twentieth century. Some works that explore the implications of this change include:

Drake, St. Clair, and Horace Cayton. Black Metropolis: A Study of Negro Life in a Northern City. New York, Harper and Row, 1962. Chicago is the setting for this detailed sociological account.

Meltzer, Milton, and A. Meier. Time of Trial, Time of Hope: The Negro in America, 1919-1941. New York, Doubleday, 1966. This is a simpler (Junior high) work with illustrations.

Rose, Harold M. The Black Ghetto: A Spatial Behavioral Perspective. New York, McGraw-Hill, 1971. A current study.

Scott, E. J. Negro Migration During the War. New York, Oxford University Press, 1920. An account of the "Great Migration" of the First World War.

Spear, Allan H. Black Chicago: The Making of a Negro Ghetto, 1890-1920. An historical view of Chicago's Black ghetto.

The transition to urban life, while not without its bleakness, did not prevent a cultural explosion among the Black community which came to be known as the Harlem Renaissance. With this renewed cultural awareness came renewed activism and the first urban based movement led by Marcus Garvey.

Cronon, E. David. Black Moses: The Story of Marcus Garvey and the Universal Negro Improvement Association. Madison, University of Wisconsin Press, 1955.

Ferguson, Blanche E. Countee Cullen and the Negro Renaissance. New York, Dodd, Mead, 1966.

Garvey, Marcus. Philosophy and Opinions of Marcus Garvey. New York, Arno Press, 1968. Reprint of the 1923 edition.

Garvey, Amy Jacques. Garvey and Garveyism. New York, Collier, 1970.

Greene, Lorenzo J., and Carter J. Woodson. The Negro Wage Earner. Washington D.C., Association for the Study of Negro Life and History, 1930.

Hughes, Langston. The Big Sea. New York, Hill and Wang, 1940.

Johnson, James Weldon. Black Manhattan. New York, A.A. Knopf, 1930.

Johnson, James Weldon. American Negro Poetry. New York, Hill and Wang, 1963, edited by Arna Bontemps. One of the earliest such collections ever compiled.

Johnson, James Weldon. Along This Way. New York, Viking, 1933. An autobiography.

Locke, Alain. The New Negro: An Interpretation. New York, Atheneum, 1968. Analyzes and interprets almost every aspect of the Harlem Renaissance.

Meltzer, Milton. Langston Hughes: A Biography. New York, Crowell, 1968. Examines the life of one of the central figures of the Harlem Renaissance.

"The Problems of the 20s" is a film which pictures diverse occurences which eventually force the direction of the fabric of Afro-American cultural, economic, social, and political direction. "Black Renaissance" delineates the emergence of the popular Afro-American culture.

8. From Depression to War

For the Depression years, see

Frazier, E. Franklin. Black Bourgeoisie. New York, Collier, 1962. A more general work on business efforts since slavery days by a foremost Black sociologist.

Redding, J. Saunders. No Day of Triumph. New York, Harper and Brothers, 1942. With an introduction by Richard Wright.

Wolters, Raymond. Negroes and the Great Depression: The Problems of Economic Recovery. Westport, Connecticut, Greenwood Publishers, 1970.

Wright, Richard. Twelve Million Black Voices. New York, Arno Press, 1969. An informal folk history on Black Americans during the Depression, reprinted with illustrations.

For rather bizarre responses to the depression crisis, consult

Fauset, Arthur H. Black Gods of the Metropolis. Philadelphia, University of Pennsylvania Press, 1944. A most valuable study of Negro cults in the city.

Hosher, John. God in a Rolls Royce. New York, 1936. A description of Father Divine's movement.

For a recent study of Negro Labor Movement, read

Jacobson, Julius, ed. The Negro and the American Labor Movement. New York, Anchor, 1968.

The story of the growth of a powerful Negro labor union is told in

Brazeal, B. R. The Brotherhood of Sleeping Car Porters. New York, publisher unknown, 1946.

Two of the most powerful Black writers in the annals of American literature emerged in the 30's and 40's:

Ellison, Ralph. The Invisible Man. New York, Random House, 1952.

Webb, Constance. Richard Wright. New York, Putnam, 1968.

Wright, Richard. Native Son. New York, Harper and Row, 1969.

Wright, Richard. Uncle Tom's Children. New York, Harper and Row, 1969 (reproduction of 1936 edition). Set in the deep South during the Depression.

Wright, Richard. Black Boy. New York, Harper and Row, 1969 (reproduction of 1945 edition). Growing up in a Chicago ghetto.

A study of the relationship of the Communist Party to Negro organizations in the 1930's that demonstrates the

Communist line had no more appeal than the back-to-Africa
movement of the 1830's is

> Redkey, Edwin S. *Race and Radicalism: the NAACP and*
> *the Communist Party in Conflict.* Ithaca, Cornell
> Press, 1964.

For the War years:

> Lee, Alfred M. *Race Riot, Detroit, 1943.* New York,
> Octagon Books, 1967. For a description of some
> of the tensions on the home front.

> White, Walter. *A Rising Wind.* New York, Negro Univer-
> sity Press, 1945. An excellent account of the
> activities of Negroes on the fighting front.

9. <u>From War to Protest: the Contemporary Era</u>

The literature of the post-war years has grown beyond the
point of easy selection or listing. One of the most readable
accounts of this period is Charles Silberman's <u>Crisis in Black</u>
<u>and White</u> (New York, Vintage Books, 1964), as well as Louis
Lomax's <u>The Negro Revolt</u> (New York, Harper and Row, 1971);
and Benjamin Muse's <u>The American Negro Revolution: From Non-</u>
<u>Violence to Black Power, 1963-1967</u> (Bloomington, Indiana
Press, 1968).

More general studies of protest movements in the modern
though not exclusively post-World War II period include:

> Allen, Robert L. <u>Black Awakening in Capitalist America:</u>
> <u>An Analytic History.</u> Garden City, Doubleday, 1969.

> Bardolph, Richard. <u>The Civil Rights Record: Black</u>
> <u>Americans and the Law, 1849-1970.</u> New York, Crowell,
> 1970.

> Broderick, F. L., and August Meier, eds. <u>Negro Protest</u>
> <u>Thought in the Twentieth Century.</u> Indianapolis,
> Bobbs-Merrill, 1966. Source materials: 54 statements
> of Negro leaders from B. T. Washington to James
> Farmer.

> Chambers, Bradford. <u>Chronicles of Negro Protest: A Back-</u>
> <u>ground Book for Young People Documenting the History</u>
> <u>of Black Power.</u> New York, Parents Magazine Press,
> 1968.

> Foner, Eric, ed. <u>America's Black Past.</u> New York, Harper,
> 1970. A collection of readings that cover the full
> range of Afro-American History with greatest
> emphasis on the modern period to Stokeley Carmichael.

> Lincoln, C. Eric. <u>The Negro Pilgrimage in America: the</u>
> <u>Coming of Age of Black Americans.</u> Revised Edition,
> New York, Praeger, 1969.

> Sterling, Dorothy. <u>Tear Down the Walls! A History of the</u>
> <u>American Civil Rights Movement.</u> Garden City,
> Doubleday, 1968.

> Waskow, Arthur I. <u>From Race Riot to Sit-in: 1919 and the</u>
> <u>1960's, A Study in Connections Between Conflict and</u>
> <u>Violence.</u> Garden City, Doubleday, 1966.

More strictly contemporary histories include:

Bracey, J. H., A. Meier, and E. Rudwick. Black Nationalism in America. Indianapolis, Bobbs-Merrill, 1970.

Franklin, John Hope. The Negro in the Twentieth Century: A Reader on the Struggle for Civil Rights. New York, Vintage, 1967.

Goldman, P. L. Civil Rights: The Challenge of the 14th Amendment. Revised Edition, New York, Coward-McCann, 1970.

Hughes, Langston. Fight for Freedom. The Story of the NAACP. New York, Norton, 1962.

Keesing's Research Report No. 4. Race Relations in the U.S.A., 1954-1968. New York, Scribner, 1970.

Lewis, Anthony and the New York Times. Portrait of a Decade: The Second American Revolution. New York, Random, 1964.

Wolff, Miles. Lunch at the Five and Ten: The Greensboro Sit-Ins, A Contemporary History. New York, Stein and Day, 1970.

Wolk, Allan. The Presidency and Black Civil Rights: Eisenhower to Nixon. Rutherford, Fairleigh Dickinson University Press, 1971.

Zinn, Howard. SNCC: The New Abolitionists. Second Edition, Boston, Beacon. 1965.

The experiences of some of the participants in the protest movements are covered in the following works:

Baldwin, James. The Fire Next Time. New York, Dial Press, 1963.

Baldwin, James. Notes of a Native Son. Boston, Beacon Press, 1955. Essays.

Baldwin, James. No Name in the Street. New York, Dial Press, 1972.

Bennett, Lerone, Jr. What Manner of Man: A Biography of Martin Luther King, Jr. Chicago, Johnson, 1964.

Brietman, George. The Last Year of Malcolm X: The Evolution of a Revolutionary. New York, Schocken Books, 1967.

Brown, H. Rap. Die Nigger Die. New York, Dial Press, 1969. A political autobiography.

Carmichael, Stokely, and Charles V. Hamilton. Black Power: The Politics of Liberation in America. New York, Random House, 1967.

Clark, Kenneth B. The Negro Protest. Boston, Beacon Press, 1969. James Baldwin, Malcolm X, and Martin Luther King talk with Clark.

Cleaver, Eldridge. Soul on Ice. New York, Dell, 1968.

Essien-Udom E. Black Nationalism: A Search for Identity in America. Chicago, University of Chicago Press, 1962. A study of the Black Muslims.

Farmer, James. Freedom When?. New York, Random House, 1965.

Farmer, James. The Making of Black Revolutionaries: A Personal Account. New York, MacMillan, 1972.

Fox, Stephen R. The Guardian of Boston, William Monroe Trotter. New York, Atheneum, 1970.

Gregory, Dick, with Robert Lipsyte. Nigger: An Auto-biography. New York, Dutton, 1964.

Gregory, Dick. _The Shadow that Scares Me_. Garden City, Doubleday, 1968.

Hoskins, James. _Profiles in Black Power_. Garden City, Doubleday, 1972. Powell, Cleage, McKissick, Wright, Malcolm X, Forman, Cleaver, Newton, Carmichael, Everett-Karenga, Brown.

Hughes, Langston. _Famous American Negroes_. New York, Dodd, Mead, 1954. For young people.

King, Martin Luther. _Stride Toward Freedom_. New York, Harper and Row, 1958. The Montgomery bus boycott.

King, Martin Luther. _Why We Can't Wait_. New York, Harper and Row, 1964.

King, Martin Luther. _Where Do We Go From Here: Chaos or Community?_. New York, Harper and Row, 1967.

Lincoln, C. Eric. _Martin Luther King, Jr.: A Profile_. New York, Hill and Wang, 1970. 13 essays.

Lincoln, C. Eric. _The Black Muslims in America_. Boston, Beacon Press, 1961.

Little, Malcolm. _Malcolm X on Afro-American History_. New York, Pathfinder Press, 1970.

Little, Malcolm. _Autobiography of Malcolm X_. New York, Grove Press, 1965.

McKissick, Floyd. _Three-Fifths of a Man_. New York, Macmillan, 1969.

Metcalf, George R. _Black Profiles_. New York, McGraw-Hill, 1970. King, DuBois, Tubman, Evers, Young.

Metcalf, George R. _Up From Within: Today's New Black Leaders_. New York, McGraw-Hill, 1971. Bond, Chisolm, Mackey, Poussaint, Brimmer, Conyers, Gibson, Wharton.

Poole, Elijah. _Message to the Black Man in America_. Chicago, Muhammad Mosque of Islam, No. 2, 1965.

Reddick, L. D. _Crusader Without Violence: A Biography of Martin Luther King_. New York, Harper and Row, 1959.

Rowan, Carl. _Go South to Sorrow_. New York, Random House, 1957. Life of a Negro Journalist and Diplomat.

Rudwick, Elliot M. _W. E. B. DuBois_. New York, Atheneum, 1968.

Young, Whitney M. _To Be Equal_. New York, McGraw-Hill, 1964.

Special Topics: Racial Thought and Race Relations

Frazier, E. Franklin. _On Race Relations: Selected Writings_. Chicago, University of Chicago Press, 1968.

Herskovits, Melville J. _The American Negro: A Study in Racial Crossing_. Bloomington, Indiana University Press, 1964.

Lewinson, Paul. _Race, Class and Party: A History of Negro Suffrage and White Politics in the South_. London, Oxford University Press, 1932.

Mitchell, J. Paul. _Race Riots in Black and White_. Englewood, New Jersey, Prentice Hall, 1970.

Murray, Albert. _The Omni-Americans: New Perspectives on the Black Experience and American Culture_. New York, Outerbridge, 1970.

Myrdal, Gunnar. <u>An American Dilemma: The Negro Problem</u>
    <u>and Modern Democracy</u>. 2 vols. New York, McGraw-Hill,
    1964. Suggested that the average student consult
    the one volume condensed edition edited by Arnold
    M. Rose, 1964.

Richardson, Ken, ed. <u>Race and Intelligence: the Fal-</u>
    <u>lacies Behind the Race-IQ Controversy</u>. Baltimore,
    Penguin Books, 1972.

In the 1960's the Black family became a source of some
controversy after the publication of the Moynihan Report:

Moynihan, Daniel Patrick. U.S. Dept. of Labor. <u>The Negro</u>
    <u>Family: The Case for National Action</u>. Washington, D.C.,
    U.S. Government Printing Office, 1965.

For a study which challenges the Moynihan Report and its thesis
of the social disorganization of lower-class Negro families,
see

Billingsley, Andrew. <u>Black Families in White America</u>.
    Englewood Cliffs, New Jersey, Prentice-Hall, 1968.

"Three Black Writers," a film of Ralph Ellison, James
Baldwin, and Richard Wright might be a good one to round out
your study.

INDEPENDENT STUDY PROJECT MONTHLY STATISTICS

Distribution of CLEP Literature (By Title)   August, 1971 — August, 1973

	AR	CCLC	H – I	OL	PR	TOTAL
Bulletin of Info. for Candidates	912	136	627	263	448	2386
CLEP may be for You	1386	566	961	189	474	3576
Description of General Exam	254	46	145	156	282	883
Description of Subject Exam	284	34	145	155	286	904
What your Scores Mean	5	1	11		7	24
					Grand Total	7773

DISTRIBUTION OF READING LISTS AND STUDY GUIDES (By Subject)

	AR	CCLC	H – I	OL	PR	TOTAL
Accounting	65	46	66	47	54	278
Afro-American History	1	2		1	3	7
American Government	66	63	116	80	117	442
American History	123	75	134	81	120	533
American Literature	7		3	9	3	22
Analysis & Interpre. of Literature	22	13	70	55	57	217
Biology	32	24	70	53	49	228
Business Law				1	1	2
Business Management	46	63	54	42	50	255
Calculus	2		1	3	2	8
Chemistry	20	27	49	33	31	160
College Algebra	49	45	68	60	73	295
Computers	43	38	59	28	45	213
Economics	31	59	57	32	38	217
Ed. Psychology	29	12	51	34	41	167
English Composition	75	72	163	92	102	504
English Literature	119	74	157	92	117	559
Fortran	13		1	5	17	36
Gen. Psychology	67	29	106	63	87	352
Geology	24	36	42	18	38	158
History of American Education	2		3		5	10
Human Gr. & Develop.	53	56	80	55	71	315
Humanities			2		1	3
Marketing	38	34	63	30	38	203
Money & Banking	3		3	4	2	12
Sociology	70	72	73	44	60	319
Statistics	14	16	49	34	35	148
Tests & Measurements	3			1	5	9
Voluntary Action						
Western Civilization	60	34	89	67	78	328
					Grand Total	6000

241

Index

Academic calendar change, See Change, academic calendar

Accuracy of college and university information, 104

Adult use of CCLC Library, 75

Advisory Committee, 32, 35, 42, 116-117, 134

Attitudes, librarian, 63, 98-99, 106-107, 112

Audio-Visual materials. "See" Instructional media, "See also" College Information Center

Book acquisitions for ISP, 7, 70, 87

Book collections, participating branches, 69 (Table 4-1); Black literature, HI 78; Black Studies, CCLC, 75, 223-240; representing neighborhood needs 70; Spanish language 78, 209-210

Books, primary student resource: choosing independently, 87; renewals, 87; use by students, 57-59

Books, programmed: faculty recommended, 105; similarity to tutoring, 86; student request, 84

Bradshaw, Lillian, 15-16, 19, 25-26

Budgets, "See" ISP branch libraries

Business and industry, 28, 29

Change, academic calendar, 146-147

Changing neighborhood needs, 78

CLEP, 27; 168-172; Credit, 20, 56, 97; examinations, 8, 16, 21-22, 27, 33, 194; informational material, 23, 28, 202, 209; publicity, 24, 203-210; use by student, 40, 100

College Entrance Examination Board, 15, 20-21, 29, 31, 172

College information Center, ISP, 24, 28, 55-56; college catalogs, 87

Commitment, librarian, 12, 107-109, 151, 154

Community College/Public library coordination, 159-160

Community educational coordination, 162-163

Community resources, 5, 89

Conservative neighborhood, 79

Continuing learning, 80

Cooperative educational services, 18, 20-21, 135-139; cost, 147-148; school/library, 8-10

Cost, ISP. "See" ISP cost to library

Council on Library Resources, 15, 25, 29, 31

Counseling: academic, 22, 60, 104; by librarian, 10, 17-18, 154-155

Dependent student, 87, 100, 158-159. "See also" Independent student evaluation. "See" ISP Office, evaluation

Faculty. "See" Southern Methodist University faculty
Faculty training. "See" training
Fagin, Margaret, 33-34

GED information, 56, 92

Help sessions. "See" Workshops
Houle, Cyril O., 53, 83, 145
How to study independently: guide, 87, 211-222; with books, 86

Independent learners, 55-56
Independent learning, 13
Independent student, 5, 12, 39, 67; adult, 27, 39; anonymity, 12, 41, attitudes, 50, 85-86; complaints, 82, 84; continuing contact with ISP, 42, 43, 63-64; defined, 54; freedom of choice, 89, 100, 103; numbers, 40, 43, 64, 98-99
Independent student and the learning process, 52, 53, 55; motivation, 5, 12, 62-63, 155; readiness, 85; starting point, 103
Independent student and traditional education, 82; and value systems, 52
Independent student; identification by librarian, 40, 59, 80, 82-83
Independent student's goals, 6, 9, 27; credit and non-credit, 50-54; over-learned, 61; self-enhancement, 151-152; successes and failures, 66
Independent student's needs, 42, 54-55, 66, 67; aids to self-direction, 149-150; basic tools/GED, 76, 82-83; economic aid, 76-77; educational information, 100-101, 150; one to one help, 76; outreach, 78; weaknesses in meeting, 67
Independent student's use of ISP, 55, 74, 84-85, 105
Independent student vs. dependent student, 54-55
Independent study concept, 70, student direction of learning, 103; time-con-

suming information delivery, 82; tutoring, 140; wide reading choice; 84, 87
Information, 97; and referal, 56; coordination, 156-57; inputs, 115, materials, 55, 56, 193
Inquiries answered, 43, 74, 75, 80, 81, 82, 111
Instructional media: cable TV and radio 161; computer aids, 161-162; TV, 153; variety of media supports, 78; Video-taped courses 91-92
ISP branch libraries, 20, 29; neighbor-hoods, 71, 74, 75, 80, 82; potential ISP/CLEP users, 73, 76, 80, 81, 83; size and staff, 69 (Table 4-1)
ISP branch libraries independent student demographic profiles: OL, 70-75; CCLC, 75-78; HI, 78-80; PR, 80-81; AR, 81-82
ISP cost, 90, 92, 93, 158
ISP funding, 31, 175, 186
ISP impact on community, 150
ISP office, 22-23; and CLEP, 43; coordination, 88; evaluation, 23, 28, 134-135; purpose, 26
ISP as a Study vs. service, 36, 42, 95

Labor unions, 89
Learning, experiential, 1-3, 6
Learning needs, 4, 13, 40
Learning process, 1-5, 9
Learning vs. Study, 152-153
Librarian and CLEP, 102, 151
Librarian as: advocate, 104, 108; evalua-tor, 112; mentor, 95, 150
Librarian attitudes. "See" Attitudes, librarian
Librarian commitment. "See" Commit-ment, librarian
Librarian, relationship with student: concept, 9, 12; lack of, 40, 42; develop-ing, 63, 79; 96-97, 98; at workshops, 105-106
Librarian roles. "See" Roles, librarian
Librarian time available, 63, 100-101, 105, 110-112
Librarian training. "See" Training
Library change, 12-13, 16, 149
Library, college, 164
Library coordination with educational

institutions, 90, 131, 133
Library learning center, 4-5, 9, 13, 70, 79, 83, 90
Library learning environment, 2, 9, 10, 13, 69-70, 93-94, 95
Library publications, 43; College and university information booklet, 124; ISP Brochure, 122; ISP News, 124
Library resources, 54, 89
Library roles. "See" Roles, library
Library service priorities, 110-111; reallocation, 93

Mass media and non-traditional education, 145-146

National Endowment for the Humanities, 15, 25, 29-30, 31
National Interest Council, 24, 30, 31, 32, 42, 122, 199

Office of Library Independent Study and Guidance Projects, 160
Open learning community, 89

Programmed books. "See" Books, programmed
Public relations, 29, 35, 88-90, 203-205

Questionnaires: mailed, 44; by telephone, 57, 63

Reader's guidance, 5, 6-7, 9, 17, 28, 43, 95, 100, 103; at branches, 74, 75, 80, 81, 82
Reader's Guidance vs. counseling, 154-155
Reading guide, 87
Reading lists, 103, 104, 116-117
Recruiting, 89, 157, 205
Referral, 155
Regents External Degree, 144-145
Roles: Librarian, 10, 13, 16, 100, 103; counseling, 158; teaching, 158;

library, 12, 17, 24, 26-28, meeting place, 52, 90; possible new, 149

Southern Methodist University, 21, 41, 85, 133-134
Southern Methodist University faculty, 21, 23, 33, 61, 63, 115, 134; acceptance of CLEP, 141-142; recommending books, 86; relationship with independent student, 139-141; Study Guides/Reading Lists, 142-143; tutoring, 143
Study Guides/Reading Lists, 8, 10, 21-22, 32-33, 35; Afro-American History, 120; guidelines, 118-121; Medical technology, 121; SMU faculty, 142; top subject interests, 74, 75, 82; use, 41, 57, 82, 102-103, 117; voluntary action, 121-122
Study Unlimited, Chicago Public Library, 91

Telephone information and referral, 56-57
Test centers, 135
Test takers, (CLEP test takers), 65 (Table 3-5), 74, 78, 80, 123 (Table 6-2)
Time-lag between information input and study, 64
Toro, Jose A., 15-16, 17-18, 20, 23, 24, 35
Training: faculty, 23, 29; librarian, 23, 29, 97, 108-110
Tutoring, 11, 13-15, 21, 41, 87; GED, 77; by graduate assistant, 140; group and individual, 88, 130; sites, 88; vs. programmed materials, 86
University without walls, 12, 143, 145

Volunteers, RSVP, 60; students, 67

Workshop attendance, 128-129 (Table 6-3), 43-45; 223-240; format, 62, 63; workshop scheduling, 83-84, 87-88, 125-127
Workshops, GED, 77